BETWEEN THE SHEETS

Nine 20th-Century Women Writers and their Famous Literary Partnerships

Lesley McDowell

OVERLOOK DUCKWORTH

New York • London

This editon first published in paperback in the United States and the UK in 2012 by Overlook Duckworth, Peter Mayer Publishers, Inc.

NEW YORK
141 Wooster Street
New York, NY 10012
www.overlookpress.com
For bulk and special sales please contact sales@overlookny.com

London
90-93 Cowcross Street
London EC1M 6BF
inquiries@duckworth-publishers.co.uk
www.ducknet.co.uk

PHOTO CREDITS: 28: Courtesy of Alexander Turnbull Library, Wellington, New Zealand. 60, 94: Author's Collection. 128, top: Rue des Archives/Mary Evans. 128, bottom: CSU Archv/Everett / Rex Features. 160, top: Everett Collection / Rex Features. 160, bottom: SNAP / Rex Features.194: Sipa Press / Rex Features. 230: SNAP / Rex Features. 262, 297: Courtesy of Georgina Barker. 298: © James Coyne/ Black Star.

Cataloging-in-Publication Data is available from the Library of Congress

Book design and type formatting by Anthony Meisel

Printed in the United States of America

1 3 5 7 9 8 6 4 2

ISBN (US) 978-1-59020-438-2

ISBN (UK) 978-0-7156-4148-4

*To Irene McDowell,
Andrew McDowell,
and Lynda Mathieson.*

ACKNOWLEDGMENTS

I would like to thank my agent, Geraldine Cooke, for believing in this project and helping to get it into print; Juliet Grames, for being a patient, dogged, and meticulous editor with, bless her, a sense of humor; my Weegie Wednesday writer buddies, David Allan, Victoria Finnegan, Kirstie Wilson Love, Moira McPartlin, David Simons, and Liz Small, for letting me witter on about this book once a month and never telling me it was a bad idea; Suzi Feay, for commissioning an article for the *Independent on Sunday* from me, right at the start of my research, that made me realize I really could make it a book; and Laura Howell, Caroline McDaid, and Elisabeth Mahoney, for always essential encouragement—and cocktails.

Contents

INTRODUCTION

"Such violence, and I can see how women lie down for artists." So wrote Sylvia Plath on February 26, 1956. It was the night after she first met Ted Hughes at a college party. He had kissed her "bang smash on the mouth" and "ripped off" her red hairband. She responded by biting him on the cheek, drawing blood. Writing years later about Rebecca West, Fay Weldon endorsed Plath's view of women, willingly lying down for, not with, male artists, when she described West's acquiescence to her lover, H. G. Wells: "If young women lie down in the path of this energy, what do they expect? They will be steamrollered!"

Not only are these women victims of "energy" and "violence," but they have chosen to be. No one is forcing them to "lie down." They are chasing their own victimhood when they chase after their male literary partners, for isn't it true that Plath "chased" after Hughes ("whose name I had asked the minute I had come into the room")? They put up with their male partners' refusal to recognise them publicly, as West did with Wells, even after she bore him his son. They put up with the worst kinds of infidelity: Elizabeth Smart's partner, George Barker, betrayed her with other women, refused to help support their four children, took money from her, and pushed her into alcoholic dependency. Hughes abandoned Plath for another woman, Assia Wevill, an act many have since viewed as contributing to her suicide seven months later.

These victims endure lies and deceit and more: Martha Gellhorn was physically and mentally abused by Ernest Hemingway toward the end of their marriage; Jean Rhys was cast aside by Ford Madox Ford after their affair and succumbed to alcoholism; Anaïs Nin was financially bled dry by Henry Miller; H.D. (Hilda Doolittle) was betrayed by her fiancé, Ezra Pound. Katherine Mansfield allied herself to a weaker partner, John Middleton Murry, out of illness and fear of death, while Simone de Beauvoir pimped her female lovers out to Jean-Paul Sartre, who not only deceived her, but also left his papers in the care of another woman after he died. Such things are done to women who are victims, and that's what makes them victims.

When these women are as much artists as their male partners, the problem only appears to be compounded. Then, they feel compelled to act out the role of literary handmaiden as well as victim. They spend laborious hours typing up the words of their writing partners, as Plath did for Hughes, or they manufacture special books of their beloved's words, as Smart did for Barker. Sublimating their own literary desires in order to support the writing career of their male partners, they make victims of their art—and of themselves—in the process.

Or, at least, that's what we've been told, over and over again.

No one has ever been able to work out exactly why these women of genius, literary pioneers all of them, were attracted to men who only seemed to do them harm, or why, once the harm was proved, they stayed with them. The only answer has been: they were victims. They lay down. They were steamrollered. It was their own fault.

The aim of this book is to show that the opposite of this story is true. It sets out to demonstrate that none of the women artists mentioned here were victims at all, but that they chose their own fates knowingly and without the taint of victimization;

that they chose such relationships in order to benefit their art and poetic consciousness. These women artists may have made a Faustian pact when they fell in love with their writing partners, but it was a pact freely chosen and only occasionally regretted in the dark watches of the night many years later, when they were alone and momentarily doubting themselves.

The women featured here were all writers before they met their literary partners, and most of them had great ambitions for their writing from the very beginning. What is hard for us to understand now—in a time when women have the vote, can own property in their own right, be heads of corporations, and the like—is that so many of them believed they needed a writing partner. These women didn't believe they could do it alone—they really believed that they needed a partner in order to achieve their literary goals. "I must marry a poet, it's the only thing," wrote a young Elizabeth Smart, long before she met Barker. "One would dance with him for what he might say," wrote H.D. of Ezra Pound. And Pound was a terrible dancer. What we must try to understand is why they believed that such humiliation was worth it, that what they gained far outweighed what they lost—or surrendered.

• • • •

The idea for this book has its roots in two sources: one, appropriately enough, in personal experience. At the beginning of 2005, I began a relationship with a male writer. I had just had my first short story accepted for publication, after being short-listed in a national short story competition. I had written a poor historical novel that I couldn't get published, and I was wondering whether to start another book or try to make this one better.

I didn't chase my writer boyfriend: I had no plan, as Smart or Plath or Nin all had, from an early age, to marry a poet. We met at a publisher's dinner; he took my number. Then, a few days later, no longer able to wait, I called him and we arranged a date. On that first date, I learned that he had separated from his wife some months before and had two small children, and that both he and they lived very close to me. He was also dating about "five to six" other women. I made up my mind on that date not to see him again: too much emotional baggage, too little interest in committing himself to one person after the end of his marriage, too many other women in the picture. And it would have stayed that way, had we not, halfway through the date, begun to talk about writing.

What made me stay in a relationship with a man who dismissed monogamy, was seeing other women, had a soon-to-be ex-wife and very young children, and was emotionally shaky, relying on antidepressants and drinking heavily every day? What made me want to be with someone who didn't want anyone to know that we were seeing each other, as it would upset his ex? What made me put up with being denied in public, with being dropped at the last minute, then picked up again? What made me run round to his flat every time he called, with bags of wine and food, an extra expense that, on my freelancer's salary, I could barely afford?

A female friend told me at the time that it was simple: I loved him. Yes, I did love him. But it wasn't enough. What I was getting from this relationship was something I had never had before: a constant dialogue about writing, both his and mine. Someone who knew about writing, whose first book was about to be published, was talking to me about my work, reading it, encouraging me, making me take it more seriously than I had taken it before. Someone who knew about writing thought I was a good writer—no, he thought I was a really good writer. My self-esteem and my self-confidence—which should have been compromised and damaged by the secrecy of our relationship, by his refusal to be faithful, by the emotional demands from people in his life far more important to him than I was—were in fact being reinforced and enhanced by this remarkable exchange. I had met male writers before, and I had male writer friends. We talked about writing, sometimes. But it was a far inferior kind of dialogue to the one I was having with my writer boyfriend.

Our relationship came to an end in the summer of 2006, after he'd been abroad for a month. I found his sudden coldness and refusal to talk on his return the last straw, so I ended it. A week later, calling him from holiday in Italy to find out what had really happened between us, I found out he had met someone else while he was away. That was the reason for his coldness.

About a month after our relationship ended, I read a review by Andrew O'Hagan of Christopher Barker's remarkable memoir of his parents, Elizabeth Smart and George Barker, in the *London Review of Books*. His portrait of his father struck more than a few chords with me: charming, intellectual, a highly promising writer, dandyish, and mercurial, Barker was also an alcoholic, depressive, sexually flexible, and incapable of fidelity to any woman, or any man. He took what he needed when he needed it and didn't care what carnage he wreaked in the process. It seemed like a portrait of the man I'd just left, in every respect. But Elizabeth Smart didn't leave George Barker. I could understand, after my own experience, why she'd found him attractive in the first place (although without my own experience I doubt I would have understood that at all). But why did she stay with him? Why did she go on to have four children with a man who abandoned her just before the birth of their first child to go driving across America with a male friend (and with whom he also had sex)? What made her forgive him, time after time after time? That was something I couldn't understand. Yes, initially it smacked of victimhood. But if I didn't see myself as a victim, and I certainly didn't, why then should I see Elizabeth Smart as one?

. . . .

It may seem like a prurient exercise to focus on the private sexual relationships between writers instead of exploring the meaning of their public words, the art they produced. But desire and writing are so much entwined with each other here that to ignore the private side of these women's lives would be to ignore what made them writers, what produced their art, in the first place. Elizabeth Smart's greatest work, *By Grand Central Station I Sat Down and Wept*, is about her relationship with George Barker. Sylvia Plath produced her greatest poems, the collection known as *Ariel*, after Ted Hughes left her. Anaïs Nin's diaries are both personal and public at the same time, full of her version of her relationships with Henry Miller and his wife, June. Rebecca West and H.D. both wrote autobiographical novels about their relationships with their respective literary partners, H.G. Wells and Ezra Pound. Katherine Mansfield's letters to her husband John Middleton Murry were exposed to the public very soon after her death, when Murry published them. Simone de Beauvoir published letters to her from Jean-Paul Sartre. The personal finds its way into the public sphere very quickly when writers are involved, sometimes to help cauterize a wound, sometimes to settle a score, as Louise DeSalvo has shown. It's by no means exclusive to the women here—Hemingway caricatured Gellhorn in his novels both before and after she left him; Wells also put West into his novels, and gave permission for his son to produce a book about his thoughts on his many women partners, including West. Ford Madox Ford wrote about Rhys after she wrote about him.

Some have stayed silent; some have destroyed the words of their lover to stop the public ever seeing them. Ted Hughes destroyed some of Path's diary entries made shortly before she killed herself; H.D.'s father destroyed the letters Pound wrote his daughter, as Martha Gellhorn did Hemingway's and Wells did West's. Simone de Beauvoir declared her letters to Sartre had been lost, yet shortly after her death, her adopted daughter found them very easily. The urge to keep the public from viewing, and assessing, private words between two people with, albeit a very public profile, is an understandable one. But is it realistic?

Keeping silent about a relationship is also a way of consigning it to the margins. Some of these women writers were re-discovered long after they were first published, like Elizabeth Smart or Jean Rhys, thanks to the women's movement and feminist literary criticism, and the suggestion that these women owed some of their writing success to the men in their lives has been an unappealing one. Simone de Beauvoir was, after all, the mother of second wave feminism, the author of the epoch-making *The Second Sex*. Rebecca West and Martha Gellhorn were both pioneering journalists, proving that women could go to the same places in the world as men and report on them just as capably, if not more so. Elizabeth Smart virtually invented a whole new genre single-handedly with her novel-poem; Katherine Mansfield revolutionized the short story form, and Anaïs Nin wrenched female sexuality out of the hands of male psychiatrists and psychoanalysts. The nine women in this volume were all pioneers of a sort, helping to establish a women's literary history for generations to come. Good feminists as we are, we don't want to acknowledge the hand of a man in their stellar success.

And yet, the questions pop up with annoying frequency. Shari Benstock has dared to ask, "If H.D. had not met Pound, would she have become a poet?" and Rosemary Sullivan, the biographer of Elizabeth Smart, has suggested that women artists of a certain era attached themselves to artistic men as a way of validating themselves and their art. Certainly it is no accident—and yet it is astonishing to learn—that so many of the male literary partners in this book knew one another, but the women didn't. The connections are extraordinary: H.D. was friends with Violet Hunt, who had had an affair with Ford Madox Ford, who knew

H. G. Wells, who had also had an affair with Hunt. Ford also had a relationship with Brigit Patmore, who had an affair with Richard Aldington, H.D.'s husband. Both H.D. and Katherine Mansfield had very close friendships with D. H. Lawrence, who was the subject of Anaïs Nin's first published work. In Paris, Hemingway worked alongside Pound and Ford, Hemingway and Ford co-editing *transatlantic review*; Martha Gellhorn had a close relationship with H. G. Wells before she met Hemingway, and also wrote to Nelson Algren, who became Simone de Beauvoir's lover. Elizabeth Smart's lover, before George Barker, was the Greek artist Jean Varda, who was shown round London by Ford's onetime partner, Stella Bowen, many years before. Bowen was also introduced to Pound, long before she met Ford, and it was Rebecca West who introduced Pound to the editor of *The New Freewoman*.

Katherine Mansfield's cousin was the writer Elizabeth von Arnim, who, like almost every other woman around at the time, was a onetime lover of H. G. Wells, and George Barker had a fling with Anaïs Nin during the period he was writing experimental erotic fiction for her. Nin was one of the female writers Smart admired and longed to emulate, along with Katherine Mansfield; Simone de Beauvoir was also a fan of Mansfield's work, and Nin read Beauvoir's novels. That was about as far as the women knew each other—through each other's work. Both H.D. and Anaïs Nin met Rebecca West, but that was about the only contact these nine women writers had with one another—remarkable when we consider that H.D., Rebecca West, and Katherine Mansfield were all living in London at the same time, and that Anaïs Nin, Simone de Beauvoir, and Martha Gellhorn were all in Paris the same year. Rhys, Mansfield, and West even went to the same London stage school, all within months of one another.

There is no sense with Sylvia Plath in the 1950s, just as there is no sense of it with H.D. at the beginning of the century, or Elizabeth Smart nearer the middle of it, of any kind of special

kinship among literary women. They scarcely knew one another, and didn't seem to be interested in making female contacts.
The only woman in this volume who really tried to reach out to
other women writers, to befriend them and speak to them about
writing, was Anaïs Nin, and she was constantly rebuffed. Rebecca
West may have started out by reviewing for a women's magazine, but she didn't keep up those early contacts she made with
literary women. Women writers, it seems, didn't want to know
other women writers because other women writers didn't hold
the power male writers did. Shari Benstock has done an excellent
job of showing the "alternative" Modernist project that women
advanced in Paris, citing Natalie Barney's literary salons to which
women were invited, Sylvia Beach's publishing ventures, the work
of Gertrude Stein, Djuna Barnes and others while they lived in
the city. But as she shows, this kind of proto-feminist movement
was largely marginalized, as was the work they produced, result-
ing in a "female experience in the social and intellectual settings
of modern history...the modes of entrapment, betrayal and exclusion (which were) suffered by women in the first decades of the
twentieth century." Breaking into the male-dominated literary
world wasn't easy: as a result of women's exclusion, we see Smart
struggle to be taken seriously when she invites young male poets
round for literary evenings; we see Plath's work criticized by the
all-male editing team of the *St. Botolph's Review*. Not for nothing
was she encouraged to send her work to women's magazines.

The male literary partners knew each other because they
were public personae, which facilitated connections between
male writers and male editors. Even a working-class man from
the sticks could get taken seriously in literary London, as D.H.
Lawrence, the miner's son from Nottingham, found. Men in po-
sitions of power as editors at publishing houses tended to champion new male writers rather than female ones. T.S. Eliot, for
instance, would back both George Barker and Ted Hughes; where

was the equivalent female editor in a position of power to back either Elizabeth Smart or Sylvia Plath? Rebecca West was perhaps the only beneficiary of that brief flurry of first-wave feminism in the early part of the twentieth century, when feminist magazines like *The Freewoman* actively sought out new women writers. Most women in this volume, though, struggled to get their work into the public sphere at all, like Anaïs Nin, or lost the initial public notoriety that publication brought and were hidden from view for reasons of respectability, like Rebecca West once she had embarked on her affair with Wells. H.D. was shy of company, even literary company, as was Jean Rhys, and when Elizabeth Smart hosted literary evenings in the 1960s, she was expected to supply the drink, according to her son. No one asked her to read her work out loud, as the male poets who gathered there regularly did. Women writers kept to the private sphere so often because the public one was particularly difficult for them to negotiate on their own. Throughout the nineteenth century, the professional woman writer lacked respectability; the likes of the Brontë sisters and George Eliot had been forced to publish under male pseudonyms to preserve their reputations. The early twentieth century saw a struggle between a hangover from that Victorian mentality and the emergence of radical literary and political magazines edited by women like Harriet Monroe of *Poetry* or Margaret Anderson of *The Little Review*. But it shouldn't be underestimated how great that struggle was, how much it took to be an open pioneer of this kind. It is no accident that many emerging literary women from this time who were bold enough to enter a male-dominated public sphere, which ridiculed and marginalized their efforts, did so in exile, in cities like Paris. The literary establishments of their hometowns or countries rarely wanted them, and certainly did not encourage them.

Such women were usually brought into the public sphere, therefore, because the men did it for them: Ezra Pound sent H.D.'s poems off to literary magazines; Ford Madox Ford published Jean Rhys. It gives some credence to Benstock's question—if H.D. had not met Pound would she have become a poet? While the answer is undoubtedly yes, given that H.D. was writing poetry anyway, with or without Pound, the real question is, would she have become a published one? The male literary partners of most of these women actively encouraged them to publish, praising, editing, and polishing their work, at a time when being taken seriously as a woman writer was not easy. A bit of male valida-tion did them no harm, either in their own eyes or in the eyes of potential publishers. With the exception of Martha Gellhorn, who met Hemingway when her own career was well under way, the women in this volume met their male writing partners near the beginning of their careers. In many cases, as with Smart, Plath, Nin, and Mansfield, the men were already generating buzz in lit-erary circles, or, as in Rhys's case, they were well established.

· · · ·

This book is not, though, primarily about the men involved: it is about the women. In bringing their relationships with male writers to the fore, I mean to situate these liaisons at the cent-er of these women's emotional and literary lives, not to detract from their achievements, but to emphasize them, to show how important these relationships were to them, and why. These are not relationships that deserve to be consigned to the margins. A great deal was sacrificed by all of these women for their writing, and for their relationships. It is interesting to note, for instance, that the only unmarried women in this volume are Simone de Beauvoir and Elizabeth Smart. Beauvoir is also, quite remarkably, the only woman never to have experienced pregnancy. Of the other eight women, five of them bore children: H.D., Rebecca West, Jean Rhys, Elizabeth Smart and Sylvia Plath. H.D., Anais

Nin and Martha Gellhorn all had abortions (Katherine Mansfield also is reputed to have undergone an abortion, but there is too little evidence for this to stand as fact). Abortion was a dangerous procedure for all three women, and Nin and Gellhorn did it more than once. Only Plath and Smart ever really expressed any long-held desire to be mothers, and Plath would kill herself only eighteen months after the birth of her second child. Having children and being married were things expected of women; they were also remarkably tricky things to negotiate, and to maintain, especially when a literary career beckoned.

And yet, it's not either necessarily problems with either marriage as a state in itself, or being a mother to children, that explains why, in pretty much every case, the literary liaison in question did not last. The temporary nature of these literary partnerships is actually an important part of their dynamic and this book is also an attempt to explain why, in pretty much every case, that liaison did not last. Even though Beauvoir and Sartre remained close throughout their lives, they stopped having sex after the first months. Smart had four children with Barker and he remained in her life to the end, but she had given up on any more sexual or literary interaction between them long before then. Murry was part of Mansfield's life until she died, but, as biographers have suggested, that was only because she died so young. There was something about the intensity, the passion, the push-and-pull of these relationships that made them unlikely for the long term. I believe that the women involved in them knew that, too. Whether or not they were willing to acknowledge it, they knew, subconsciously, that they had only a limited time with their literary partners. It was important to make as much of that time as possible.

Their writing desires and their sexual desires have made them each extraordinary women, which is partly why I have given each chapter an ironic designation. Rebecca West was a reluctant "mother"; Anaïs Nin subverted the notion of a "mistress." Rhys was a thirty-four-year-old "ingénue" with a daughter; Plath's position as the "wife" of Ted Hughes has plagued the legacy of them both. These designations also play with the kinds of labels that are attached to women, labels that are only ever one-dimensional and caricaturing.

The first section, titled "New London Women," considers three women who were part of the London literary scene at the same time, and yet also *not* part of it, because illness, shyness, or respectability kept them behind closed doors so often. In Chapter 1, I attempt to show how the "companionship" between Katherine Mansfield and John Middleton Murry became essential to Mansfield's art, not just because she was diagnosed with tuberculosis early on in their relationship. Sexual desire between them became a childish thing partly because of their own child-like, unsatisfactory fumbles, and partly because after her younger brother's death Mansfield began to identify him with Murry. Murry's companionship was vital to Mansfield's survival, but it was also endemic to the work she produced, especially after the death of her sibling.

Chapter 2 focuses on H.D. and Ezra Pound's relationship, which began when they were adolescents and resulted in engagements and disappointments, publishing success and literary fame. As the "novice," H.D. was the one forever starting out, needing help and encouragement. But others' views of her, especially those of the women she competed with for Pound's love, like Frances Gregg, were different. H.D., I argue, was more comfortable in the ménage-a-trois setup, where she was the adored object of the other two. This situation allowed her to maintain her novice status and reduced the possibility of her being abandoned and left alone.

Chapter 3 is in many ways the trickiest chapter of this book, given that few of Rebecca West's letters to H. G. Wells exist, and that both seemed to feel the relationship had "harmed them both as writers," as Wells expressed it. How to argue the benefits of their ten-year literary liaison when both partners regretted it? I have posited West as the "mother" because she was such a reluctant one, and it was Anthony West's birth that kept his parents together for longer than they might have been. But the fact that it was while she was with Wells that West began writing novels cannot be dismissed: Wells encouraged her foray into fiction and kept after her to work.

In Section Two, "The Paris Set" explores three women who began their writing careers in the French capital. Jean Rhys, in Chapter 4, understood the necessity of a well-heeled friend, patron, or lover, and she found him in Ford Madox Ford. Her apparent innocence and vulnerability appealed to him, and he published her work, wrote introductions to her books, tried to get her to party with the influential up-and-coming expat literary community in Paris. Rhys was not the "ingénue" he thought she was, though, and when he discovered who she really was, it was impossible for them to continue together. Without his constant exhortations to work, she struggled between that burst of novels produced in the wake of her split from him and the book that would make her name so many years later, *Wide Sargasso Sea*.

Anxieties about work levels permeate this volume: several of the women writers here chide themselves regularly for their laziness, their lack of production. In Chapter 5, we see how Anaïs Nin credited Henry Miller with encouraging her, making her write, even though by the time she met him she was used to writing huge amounts in her diary every day anyway. She was the "mistress" who paid for her lover's upkeep, who published his work, bought him food, and kept a roof over his head. It was worth the money: Miller attended to her writing as scrupulously as he did his own, encouraging and supporting her in her attempts to get published.

In Chapter 6, Simone de Beauvoir appears as less financially needy than Rhys and less dependent on literary aid than Anïas Nin, but as the "long-termer" of this book, she was not prepared to relinquish her first literary partner for anyone, not even for Nelson Algren. Her relationship with Jean-Paul Sartre is the stuff of legend, partly because of the affairs they had with each other's students, and the way they described them in excruciating detail to each other. Their promise to "tell each other everything" was compromised many times, though, and their lack of sexual desire was masked by this voyeuristic description of their affairs. Nevertheless, it was Sartre whom Beauvoir needed above all, even if that need required keeping him at arm's length while tying him to her.

In the third section, "Transatlantic Chasers," I look at three women who were all accused of "chasing" after their literary partners. The eight years Martha Gellhorn spent with Ernest Hemingway were a survival test of sorts by the end, but the first woman to step on French soil with the liberating troops, beating her fellow journalist Hemingway to the push, was always destined to make it. This chapter explores the romance of their starry celebrity relationship and how the literary aid that Hemingway gave Gellhorn in the beginning was transformed into something else by the end.

In Chapter 8, I explore exactly why Elizabeth Smart felt compelled to stay with George Barker, after "chasing" him for four years, and the price she paid for her liaison with a man whose effect on her work was to help make it some of the most extraordinary prose ever written. Of all the women in this book, she is perhaps the most open about her need for a writing partner of the opposite sex, and is thus the most easily judged. Did she get some kind of a thrill out of a relationship that was "on" one minute and "off" the next? Why did she chase after a married man like Barker in the first place? Just how easy it is for us to understand and sympathise with the push-and-pull of her relationship with him?

And in my final chapter, I look at the relationship between Sylvia Plath and Ted Hughes. It seems impossible to imagine what more could be said about this pairing, but hardly ever has it been argued that Hughes actually might have been good for Plath, that in Hughes Plath found exactly what she wanted and needed, whatever it cost her in the end. As with so many of the women here, what became a deeply unhappy relationship nevertheless provided Plath the material that inspired her greatest work. And this was the kind of work that would speak to millions of readers.

• • • •

Many of these relationships were unequal: unequal in terms of how much one partner loved the other; unequal in terms of society, where one partner could vote and own property and betray a spouse without being vilified, while the other partner couldn't. Power was wielded and abused throughout these affairs; hearts were broken and spirits crushed, in one case with fatal consequences. But, at the same time, books were published and literary reputations made, and that was what each and every woman in this book wanted, as much as anything else.

"I need a big love," said Elizabeth Smart. She got one: a love that became a work of art. Love, or desire, is also unequal, for love, or desire, is always about power. These accounts of the relationships that Katherine Mansfield, H.D., Rebecca West, Jean Rhys, Anaïs Nin, Simone de Beauvoir, Martha Gellhorn, Elizabeth Smart, and Sylvia Plath had with their male partners are about many different things, but what they all have in common is sexual desire and the desire to write. Without the literary context for their liaisons, such liaisons would probably never have happened. And without those liaisons, the work of these extraordinary nine women writers, icons every one, would have been that much poorer. For art, too, is about power. Who wields the pen, who tells the story, is everything, and these women knew and understood this deep down in their souls. They paid a price; they relinquished many things. But what they got in the end was literary immortality. Power that once belonged to male gods alone, they took for themselves.

PART I

1910s–1920s: New London Women

Katherine Mansfield and John Middleton Murry, photographed during their time in France.

1. THE "COMPANION": KATHERINE MANSFIELD AND JOHN MIDDLETON MURRY

I have tried through my illness . . . to prevent him facing wholly what was happening. I ought to have tried to get him to face them. But I couldn't. The result is he doesn't know me. He only knows Wig-who-is-going-to-be-better-some-day. No. You do know that Bogey and you are only a kind of dream of what might be.

—Katherine Mansfield
14 October 1922

For you and I are not of the world, darling; we belong to our own kingdom, which truly is when we stand hand in hand, even when we are cross together like two little boys.

—John Middleton Murry
to Katherine Mansfield,
16 December 1915

The relationship between Katherine Mansfield and John Middleton Murry ought to be the least mysterious, the least difficult to understand of all the literary liaisons in this book, mainly because we have so much of their unqualified testimony to it. Mansfield's reputation as possibly the greatest short story writer in the English language rivals masters of the art like Chekhov. And it rests largely on the collections she published during her relationship with Murry, such as *Bliss and Other Stories* (1919) and *The Garden Party* (1920), as well as her posthumous work that

Murry continued to bring out, particularly *Something Childish and Other Stories* (1924). Murry himself is best known as an enthusiastic editor of Modernist writers such as T. S. Eliot and Virginia Woolf, whom he published in his magazine *The Adelphi*, although he also wrote fiction, now considered far inferior to the work of the other writers he published and read little. His contribution to literature lies in his editorial role, and as Mansfield's posthumous champion, it should not be underestimated. Their many letters to each other, as well as Mansfield's own journal entries and notebooks, were written during the ten years the couple were together. They make up a remarkably vivid testimony that explains their feelings about each other, about themselves, and about their work while living together and apart.

But that lack of mystery is partly a blind. It exists, insomuch as a "lack" can be said to exist at all, because Mansfield and Murry both insisted on it. The lack of mystery in their relationship may appear to have depended upon their being open and honest with each other about all things, even their feelings for other people. In reality, it relied on certain key strategies that were the very opposite of open and honest. It relied, instead, on their pretending and fantasizing and lying to each other repeatedly. They both used the strategies of delusion, and self-delusion, throughout their time together. These strategies, ironically intended to obfuscate, are what make both parties appear to be innocent and easy to understand.

Those scrupulously maintained letters and diary entries have provoked every biographer since to question their love for one another and their real motives for being together. Indeed, Murry's enthusiastic publication of his wife's private papers after her tragically early death at the age of thirty-four from tuberculosis has provoked even worse insinuations. Was he, the obvious lesser talent, merely cashing in on his wife's genius when he published her letters and journal entries? Did he merely hang on her coattails during their time together because she was so much the better writer? Or was it in fact Mansfield who was the dependent one, as the letters seem to show, the one who needed Murry's attention because she was ill and frightened of dying? Did she need him to help her with her writing, too, or is that another delusion?

I think it is quite clear that Mansfield and Murry's joint strategies of delusion and self-delusion were not intended to undermine their relationship, but to maintain it, as such delusion often is. Mansfield, for instance, as we will see with many of the women in this book, repeatedly emphasized the permanence of her sexual relationships (not just her relationship with Murry). It is almost as though she believed they would last forever as long as she reiterated it. The temporariness of a relationship—especially a literary and sexual one like this—frightened her.

It's therefore natural to conclude that, as dangerous as such willful self-delusion can be, it was the lifeblood of their (and many another) relationship. Without such self-delusion, Mansfield might have listened to stronger individuals who wanted her to to reside in various sanatoriums as soon as the first signs of tuberculosis appeared in 1918. And without such self-delusion, she might have proved Leonard Woolf's reading of her relationship with Murry correct, when he said that "in some abstruse way Murry corrupted and perverted and destroyed Katherine both as a person and as a writer. She was a very serious writer, but her gifts were those of an intense realist, with a superb sense of ironic humor and fundamental cynicism. She got enmeshed in the sticky sentimentalism of Murry and wrote against the grain of her own nature . . ."

Yes, without willful self-delusion she might have lived longer, and she might have written differently, too. But without deluding herself about him, and about her own feelings for him, perhaps the outcome for Katherine Mansfield would have been even worse. What is worse than death, some may ask? Well, death without leaving anything of value behind is one possible answer. Mansfield, after one miscarriage and possibly one abortion, and suffering from gonorrhea and tuberculosis, would never have been able to have children with Murry. But she could and did make her gift to posterity in the shape of her writing. Short story after short story, reviews and essays were all produced with Murry's constant exhortations and encouragement. After her death, he devoted himself to making sure the world didn't forget her. Had she left him after the first year or two, she might have lived longer, or written less, or just produced different kinds of books. But she wouldn't have become the Katherine Mansfield we celebrate today, the writer of such masterpieces as "Prelude," "Bliss," "Daughters of the Late Colonel," and "Je Ne Parle Pas Francais." And she might not have had the kind of champion after death that so many writers need in order to be remembered.

It is Leonard Woolf's notion of Mansfield, however, as the misdirected fly caught in Murry's web that has symbolized the conflict between Mansfield's and Murry's various biographers since her death in 1923. Some take the view of her recent biographer Claire Tomalin, who regards Murry as at best an "incubus" feeding off her talent, at worst little better than a killer for not pushing her into a sanatorium that might have saved her life, or at least prolonged it. According to Tomalin, Murry was "culpably stupid," a man who was "baffled" by his partner and who played "a crucial and largely unfortunate role in her life." She regards the Mansfield-Murry game of "encouraging one another into realms of high fantasy" as a destructive one that Murry could have stopped had he not been so weak and of such a "biddable nature."

There are other opinions, however. According to Murry's biographer, F. A. Lea, Mansfield was "controlling, dominant" and "in Murry, she found a child as much as a husband." Margaret Scott, the editor of Mansfield's notebooks and joint editor of five collections of her letters, also feels Murry has been harshly judged by too many. She expresses "no doubt whatever that Mansfield loved him for the ten years they were together," insisting that we read their exchange of letters "for what it was—a dialogue of troubled, intense and continuing affection." While acknowledging the "childlike" nature of their passion, she does not see it as lesser for avoiding sexual relations, as they seem to have done for most of their time together.

What, then, has inspired such divided reactions to Murry himself and to the part he played in their relationship? What has led to doubts even about Mansfield's own feelings for him? Was there indeed no real love between them, as Tomalin hints with her belief that Mansfield would have left Murry had she not been so sick? Or should we, as Scott says, take their often effusive correspondence, their repeated statements of true love, at face value, proof of a more innocent kind of love, as Mansfield and Murry constantly exhorted each other to do? Is it possible to read their many declarations of love simply, without cynicism, when we have evidence of lies on both sides, of heart-breaking weakness? And how are we to read what appears to be a sexual impotence in both partners, in the midst of passionate declarations of physical love?

Should we also believe that, undeniably deluding themselves about the extent of Mansfield's illness, they also deluded themselves about the extent and the true nature of their love for each other? Is Murry's support of Katherine Mansfield throughout their relationship and of her work after her death the only reason we still read her today? Or did her association with him do her reputation more harm than good, as Leonard Woolf believes? And, most crucially, were they really more companions than lovers? Did their writing absorb most of their passion?

• • • •

Any analysis of how passionate the Mansfield-Murry relationship really was must be mindful of two things: first, the nature of
their sexual life, and, second, how much of it was conducted in
the face of severe illness. Tuberculosis became the third "person"
in their marriage, directing how long and how often they could
spend time in each other's company. A jealous illness, isolating
the victim from contact with others, even from the most beloved,
tuberculosis hugs the host body possessively. When Mansfield was
first diagnosed with this dangerous infection, she and Murry had
been together for just over five years. It would dominate the next
five years of their relationship.

Virulent and damaging as it would b,e however, before that
diagnosis came, illness was not the controlling force behind their
sexual relationship. The question of their sex life may seem a prurient one, but, possibly more than for any other couple in this
volume, it is crucial to an understanding of the power dynamic
between the two of them. It raises precisely the kind of questions
about truth and lies that have troubled so many of their readers
ever since.

Katherine Mansfield and John Middleton Murry first met
in December 1911, through a mutual friend, Willy George, who
was also contributing to the same magazine as Mansfield, *The
New Age*. Mansfield was only a year older than Murry, but she
had much more life experience at this point than he did. She was
born into a rather typically bourgeois, late-Victorian family (her
Australian father was a banker) in 1888 in New Zealand, and was
the third of five daughters, one of whom died as a baby. The only
boy, Leslie, was the youngest of the siblings. Her relationship with
her cold, distant mother in some ways prefigures that of Elizabeth
Smart's with her mother, and, like Smart, Mansfield was to become the colonial writer who found her first artistic home away
from her native country, in London.

Fond of music at an early age, she had something in common

with the sons of the neighboring Trowells, an English family, who had settled in New Zealand. One son, Garnet, would reappear in her life a few years later. But that was all to come, after she had left New Zealand for good. Her first visit abroad in 1903 was a temporary one while still a schoolgirl, on a trip to England with her family. There she befriended Ida Baker, a girl who would become almost as constant and devoted a companion to Mansfield over the years as Murry. She then spent three years at Queen's College in London before returning to New Zealand in 1906. It was a difficult homecoming. She was homesick for the metropolis and chafed at her native country's narrower outlook and smaller cultural opportunities. Her musical talents were still much in evidence and she was already writing a great deal, jotting down outlines for stories in her notebooks, although, like Rebecca West and Jean Rhys, she also toyed with the idea of becoming an actress. Whatever kind of artist she chose to become, it was clear that she could not remain with her family in Wellington.

And so, in 1908, when she was twenty years old, she sailed alone back to the city she wanted to make her home. Mansfield had become physically close to other girls while she was growing up: Tomalin reports her kissing a school friend, Vere Bartrick-Baker, when she was fifteen, and four years later, she befriended the twenty-seven-year-old Edith Kathleen Bendall, who was an artist. Tomalin quotes the following passionate entry from Mansfield's 1907 journal about Bendall: "She enthrals me, enslaves me—and her personal self—her body absolute— is my worship. I feel that to lie with my head on her breast is to feel what life can hold . . . pillowed against her, clinging to her hands, her face against mine, I am a child, a woman, and more than half a man." This mixing of the sensual with the childlike—lying with her head on someone else's breast, "pillowed" and "clinging"—would also be a feature of her relationship with Murry. Tomalin claims that Bendall, recalling the relationship decades later, "said she thought Katherine had simply misinterpreted her motherly gestures," but throughout her life, Mansfield would confuse the maternal and the childlike in her relationships with both women and men.

Her most serious sexual affair to date, though, did not occur until one year later, and it took place while she was in London. She had fallen in love with the now grown-up Garnet Trowell, who was also in England, working as a professional musician. His job with a touring opera company meant a peripatetic lifestyle and inevitably long absences from Mansfield. She wrote him many letters which were physically passionate ("Lying in my bed at night—I feel your kisses burn my mouth—I long inexpressibly for you . . ."), and called him "husband" several times. He was, she told him, "the complement of me . . . ours will be the perfect Union." This anticipates the kind of love she will say she wants to share with Murry much later, where it will be just the two of them against the world ("I feel that we two, husband and wife, would be irresistible, would conquer the universe"). She and Trowell will be together "for ever"; she loves to think of "what the Future holds for us together"; she will love him "eternally." In another foreshadowing of her relationship with Murry, she emphasizes her need for Trowell, both physically and emotionally ("I could almost weep for longing for the shelter of your arms . . . I so *need* you"), and she reverts to the childlike here too, as she does so often with her lovers: "Last night I dreamed we were together in the country—happy, my dear, laughing like children," addressing her lover as "my darling little boy." Mansfield sent her letters only a day or two apart, testifying to the intensity of her feelings and the great need she had for him.

By the end of 1908, however, Trowell's parents had "put an end to their son's romance" with her, according to Scott (Tomalin speculates on a row over money between Mansfield and the hardup Trowell family, who were all now back in England), and on

March 2, 1909, Mansfield suddenly married George Bowden, a male admirer she barely knew. The reason for such a hurried marriage was, according to Tomalin, that Mansfield was pregnant by Trowell, who apparently had been unable to defy his parents and offer to marry her himself (not without his family's financial support, anyway). To save her reputation, she opted for Bowden, but she couldn't see the plan through: she left Bowden on their wedding night and went back to Trowell a week later.

In April, though, she wrote unhappily to Trowell on her way to Brussels. She was obviously planning to have her baby abroad and she was finding the situation, alone and pregnant abroad, a difficult one: "I am afraid I really am not at all myself—so here I am—I took a drug this afternoon and slept till after five . . ." She came back to London, then went off again, this time to Bavaria with her mother, who funded the trip. Tomalin doubts that Mrs. Beauchamp was ignorant of her daughter's physical state, especially as she subsequently cut her daughter out of her will. Did she want Mansfield to have an abortion abroad, or give the baby up, perhaps? She might not have got her way, because, in June, when Mrs. Beauchamp left her daughter alone in Germany, Mansfield wrote again to Trowell: "Some day when I am asked—'Mother, where was I born' and I answer—'In Bavaria, dear', I shall feel again I think this coldness—physical, mental—heart coldness—hand coldness—soul coldness . . ." This doesn't sound like a woman about to abort or give up her baby, and possibly she and her mother argued, hence her mother's departure and removal of her name from her will. Unfortunately for Mansfield, though, her fantasy of becoming a mother turned out only to be a fantasy, in the end. While she was staying at Pension Muller in Turkheimer Strasse in Bad Worishofen she suffered a miscarriage. There are no more letters to Trowell after this date.

It has been suggested that it was the loss of this baby that made her write to Ida Baker, asking her to send a motherless young child to her for looking after. Remarkably, Baker did this, and the young boy, Charlie Walter, stayed with Mansfield throughout the summer. What comfort looking after a young boy gave her is not known, but it seems that while she was still in Germany, she met her next lover, a Polish translator called Floryan Sobieniowski. There are few letters from this period, and her biographer Claire Tomalin admits that much of her own rendering of this affair is conjecture, but it seems that Mansfield, lonely and mourning the loss of her baby, was greatly attracted to Sobienioswki's slightly bohemian charm. Intellectual and literary, he must have attracted her enough to make her want to learn Polish, as in a letter she thanks her sister for her birthday gift of "a fat Polish dictionary with a green leather binding." Photographs of Sobieniowski do not show a particularly handsome man, but he was debonair and stylish, and Mansfield would have been vulnerable at this time.

It is interesting that, after suffering her miscarriage in June, she did not go rushing back to the arms of her "husband" Garnet Trowell, but stayed on in Germany until the end of the year. Trowell clearly knew about the pregnancy and the miscarriage: why did Mansfield not go back to him? Their relationship must have broken off for good at this time. Sobieniowski, another summer visitor to Bavaria, met Mansfield then, at the worst possible moment for her, when her relationship with Trowell was over and she had just lost their baby. Her affair with Sobieniowski, however, had tragic consequences for her. If Claire Tomalin is correct, it was Sobieniowski who infected Mansfield with gonorrhea. This disease, undetected and untreated for as long as Mansfield's was, would have resulted in infertility and seriously compromised her ability to fight off the later infection of tuberculosis.

Both this infection and her unplanned pregnancy suggest a sexually liberated woman, however, and surprisingly so, for one of her class and era. But Mansfield's letters to Trowell also show an expectation of marriage, and Tomalin claims that she and Sobieniowski also planned to marry, once she had divorced the unfortunate George Bowden. Mansfield was, I think, caught between the bohemian, sexually free world of the artist that appealed to her bisexual nature and to her literary aspirations, and the respectable world of the bourgeois in which she had been brought up and felt safest. Hence her need to pin down these artistic, roving, unreliable men in marriage. She needed to give herself a sense of intellectual freedom as well as a kind of domestic security.

But between the ending of one love affair, a disastrous encounter with another man, and her subsequent meeting with Murry, there was, of course, the writing. Mansfield's first publications in England were mainly short stories for the radical new literary magazine, *The New Age*, and almost immediately they brought her to the attention of important literary people. This incipient success may have given Mansfield the confidence to make the first approach to Murry in 1912, who was then co-editor of a magazine called *Rhythm*, when she encouraged him to rent a room in her flat. But, by many accounts, Mansfield could be very confident anyway, when the moment suited her. She was comfortable with both men and women, she had a sharp wit, and she seems to have enjoyed flirting and gossiping, although her tendency to draw favorites aside and whisper and snigger with them often caused others to find her intimidating, even snide. It certainly looks as though Murry initially found her intimidating too.

This was possibly also because he was not quite as much at ease as she was in this kind of company. As a young man from a lower-middle-class home, Murry felt awkward in such a middle-class milieu as literary London undoubtedly then was. He had nevertheless managed to get into Oxford to study classics, and made a little bit of a name for himself there. When Mansfield met him, he had dropped out of Oxford. He had previously spent some time in Paris, and gotten embroiled in an affair with a young Parisian woman whom he had left behind when he came to London. Now, having abandoned academia as well for his real love, the impecunious world of writing, he had, with the support of some friends and a few Oxford connections, launched the literary magazine *Rhythm*. He accepted Mansfield's offer of the room—her first recorded note to him is dated April 12, 1912: "This is your egg. You must boil it."

1912 was a momentous year. It was the year Mansfield and Murry really began to get to know each other; it was also the year Rebecca West met H. G. Wells, and the year Ezra Pound took tea with H.D. at the British Museum and gave her her poet's name, as well as the sobriquet, "Imagiste." There is no evidence that any of these remarkable women knew one another at all at the time, although West knew of Mansfield at least a year later. Given the parallel lines along which Mansfield's and West's relationships ran (they both ended in 1923, with Mansfield's death and West's final break with Wells), their on-off residences in London that the three women had over the years, as well as their mutual acquaintances (both Mansfield and H.D. would be immortalized by D. H. Lawrence in his novel, *Women in Love,* though they formed close friendships with him at different times), it is surprising that they didn't attempt to get to know one another. Perhaps they felt they didn't need to: they knew their literary partners and that was enough.

Katherine Mansfield, however, had to work hard to hook her literary partner. Murry was tentative and lacked confidence around her, it seems; Mansfield has been credited with making the first move on him, offering herself to him at some point, soon after he moved in (Tomalin quotes her saying to him, "make me your mistress"). He refused that offer, possibly because he was afraid of her (Mansfield had by now published *In a German Pension* and was getting well known), or because, as Tomalin suggests, he wasn't greatly attracted to her sexually. This latter suggestion is doubtful—Murry's second wife, whom he married shortly after Mansfield's death, bears a striking physical resemblance to her predecessor, which implies it wasn't Mansfield's looks that were the problem for Murry. The relationship he had had in Paris had not ended well, so he may have felt too close to Mansfield, living together in such close proximity, to want to get involved with another woman again so soon. He appears to have resisted her approaches three times. Finally, though, they did spend the night together, and one year later, in April 1913, their relationship now established, she was writing to him, "I'm very happy, darling. But when you come into my thoughts I refuse you, quickly, quickly. It would take me a long time away from you before I could bear to think of you. You see, when I am not with you every little bit of you puts out a flaming sword . . ."

Letters from Murry to Mansfield up to this date are cheerful and affectionate, often about work she has undertaken for *Rhythm*, or to arrange a date with her. After this particular letter, though, his reply to her is addressed "Tiger Darling" and its romantic thoughts ("You darling. I don't think I could have had a sweeter memory of you than I carried away last week.") strongly suggest that their relationship is no longer a casual, sexual one, but much deeper and more emotional. Several biographers though, including F. A. Lea, have suggested, that sex between Mansfield and Murry was fairly disastrous early on, in spite of the passion of these early letters (and references to "flaming swords"). They also maintain it continued that way throughout their relationship. Claire Tomalin writes that "by his [Murry's] account, their relations remained very childlike although both had had sexual experience . . . Murry adds that he found no real sexual fulfilment until his *fourth* marriage [Tomalin's italics]," and she argues that this sexual dissatisfaction led to what she calls the "sad, underlying inadequacy of their relationship."

Lea, meanwhile, quotes from Murry's own journal from April 1953, which contains the following reminiscence: "I was a terribly 'innocent' lover. It was only when we were settling in at Ructon, and I happened to read one or two passionate love-letters from S.V., an Austrian journalist . . . in which he spoke of kissing her breasts, that I plucked up the courage and dared to kiss them . . . Beyond that I never made love to her—right to the end." Lea's interpretation is that "in Murry she [Mansfield] found a child as much as a husband...in Katherine he found a mother as much as a wife."

Why should this be the case? As we have seen, neither Mansfield nor Murry were sexually inexperienced by the time they got together. Why should Murry have felt such apparent fear of sex with Mansfield, and why should Mansfield have been so reticent with him? Given her past experience, she might have been able to encourage him to do more than kiss her breasts. But it appears she didn't. Tomalin believes that Mansfield would have been scared to divulge fully her past to Murry for fear of shocking him and scaring him off, and that this made her too careful with him. But it's equally possible that, having suffered both a miscarriage and the removal of a fallopian tube infected with gonorrhea, she had good reason for a reticent attitude to more premarital, penetrative sex in the days before the pill. The declarations of passion that pepper their early correspondence, and which threaten to overwhelm their later letters, look a tad overwrought in the light of this evidence, a deluge of words to cover the lack of action. This contrast also explains the reluctance of some readers to give full credence to the passion that Mansfield and Murry always insisted underlined their relationship.

There is, however, another possible interpretation for all of this, one that says a great deal about the true sexual nature of their relationship and whether the passion it engendered was real or not. Certainly when he is expressing erotic thoughts in his letters to Mansfield, Murry never dares to go further than mentioning her breasts (supporting what he wrote in his journal forty years after their sexual relationship began, about not daring to touch them). The speedy introduction of childlike references to their early correspondence also implies that the sexual side of their relationship was quickly demoted to kissing and fondling. The pet names they gave each other have often been cited as further evidence of their mutual sexual impotence, although that alone seems unlikely to me to indicate anything necessarily in that direction (it was actually Murry's friend, the Scottish painter John Fergusson, who called them a pair of tigers, so they used the childlike names "Tig" and "Wig" for each other). Far more indicative is Murry's deliberate and direct first invocation, so soon after what was presumably their first experience of penetrative sex together, of the childlike: "And do you know I thought you were more lovely and lovable than ever this last weekend. O Tig, you were so sweet, and so like a little child that I feel like crying when I write it..."

Sexually active couples may continue to engage in baby talk and see their passion as childlike, of course. But what supports the conclusion that their particular passion stopped at this childlike stage of kissing and petting is the fact that Mansfield was infected with gonorrhea at this time. There is no evidence that Murry ever caught it from her, which he surely would have if they had been having regular sex throughout their long association. Although Murry had suffered from a bout of it in the past, it was before he met Mansfield and he was completely cured of it by the time they got together. His childlike encouragement of Mansfield's attentions (we have already seen how responsive she was to this tone with her lovers) suggests that he might well have known about her infection, that, in all possibility, they both did. Claire Tomalin believes that, in 1909, when her infected fallopian tube was removed, Mansfield "must have suspected something," even though many have assumed she was not told of her infection at the time. She may also have denied it to herself, of course, until now. In a serious relationship with Murry, she may have had to face the infection she carried and warn him. When both Mansfield and Murry were apart from each other, sometimes for months at a time, they both talked of longing to hold each other, touch or caress each other, kiss and stroke. Their letters never go further, which is strange. Letters written by couples who are apart for any length of time tend to be more erotic than the reality, not less so. Both Mansfield and Murry seem to have clutched at a kind of intimacy that satisfied them, without causing infection. But would this really have been enough to prevent any other, more serious, kind of sexual activity?

In 1915, Mansfield fell heavily for a friend of Murry's named Francis Carco. Carco, who would also crop up in Simone de Beauvoir's life, lived in Paris and would occasionally loan Mansfield and Murry the use of his flat there. The Mansfield-Murry letters through 1914, after their abortive attempt to live the life of writers based in Paris, a life they couldn't afford, had grown less personal and more concerned with practical matters: income, living accommodations, work. They had moved into Rose Tree Cottage in the Chilterns together, where they struck up a close friendship with their new neighbor, the writer D. H. Lawrence. Mansfield had previously written to Lawrence, asking him to contribute to *Rhythm*, and had begun a regular correspondence and friendship with him. Lawrence had suggested that Mansfield and Murry move in next to him and his lover, Frieda Weekley. The relationships among the four of them would fluctuate, but it seems that on the occasions Lawrence and Murry became especially close Mansfield would feel left out.

As she did at this time. For, in spite of the war that had broken out that year, Mansfield nevertheless persisted in leaving for Paris and her assignation with her prospective new lover, Carco.

This sexual adventure, though, failed to live up to expectations, as she wrote in her journal of the first night she spent with him: "We talked in whispers overcome by this discreet little lamp. In the most natural manner we slowly undressed by the stove. F. swung into the bed. Is it cold, I said. 'No, not at all, Viens ma bebe, dont [sic] be frightened. The waves are quite small.' His laughing face and his pretty hair, one hand with a bangle over the sheets, he looked like a girl. But seeing his puttees, his thin black tie & the feel of his flannelette shirt—& the sword, the big ugly sword, but not between us, lying in a chair.

"The act of love seemed somehow quite incidental, we talked so much. It was so warm and delicious lying curled in each others arms, by the light of the tiny lamp le fils de Maeterlinck, only the clock & the fire to be heard. A whole life passed in the night: other people other things, but we lay like 2 old people coughing faintly under the eiderdown, and laughing at each other and away we went to India....& then he was in my arms again & we were kissing."

This extract from her notebooks says quite a lot about Katherine Mansfield the woman, if not the writer. She is shivering, whether from anticipation or from cold isn't clear; she likes his femininity, his "laughing face" and "pretty hair," all of which appear to make him, his masculinity, and what they are about to do much less threatening; the sword, in a clearly phallic reference, lies not between them, but safely away from her, on a chair (and also brings to mind her reference to the "flaming sword" in her first love letter to Murry). What she does like are the cuddling and the closeness, the things that make him less masculine, more feminine.

Needless to say, this visit was not prolonged, the sex unsatisfactory here, too, perhaps, and the affair fizzled out before it barely began. She returned, with some misgivings, to Murry, of whom she subsequently wrote, "Perhaps the fact that Jack never says once that he longs for me, is desolate without me, never calls me..." It seems that she was cagey with him about the real reason for her trip to Paris. He appears to have suspected it, doubted anything would come of it, and forgiven her all the same.

Whatever the outcome for them both—and she was clearly in an unhappy state when she went to Paris to meet Carco, feeling left out by Murry's attentions to Lawrence—something from this extract reinforces the likelihood of Mansfield's bisexuality. She may well have felt dissatisfied, as so many have implied, with the limits of her sexual relationship with Murry, confined as it was to kissing and fondling. But neither was she entranced by actual penetrative sex with a man: "the big ugly sword, but not between us, lying in a chair." It is quite possible that in spite of some sexual dissatisfaction with Murry, the fairly innocent kind of interactions she had with men were, in the end, the only kind of heterosexual sex she could cope with.

Tomalin argues that lesbianism wasn't an option for her, that Mansfield had more or less dismissed it in adolescence, when she discovered that her strong feelings for other female friends like Edith Kathleen Bendall and Vere Bartrick-Baker made her uncomfortable, however willing, at one point in 1913, she might have been to visit lesbian nightclubs. Perhaps, in denying the bisexual element of herself, she could only manage a tentative sexual life with men.

So perhaps the innocent nature of her sexual life with Murry actually suited her. Although Murry blamed his own sexual innocence, and subsequent biographers cite Mansfield's illness, especially later on in the relationship, for their lack of sexual satisfaction, it would seem that she was only prepared to get so close and no closer. Part of that could be attributed to a fear of getting pregnant again. Or it could simply be that she didn't enjoy penetrative sex with men; that heterosexual imperative simply wasn't part of her sexual makeup, in spite, or perhaps even because, of her past experiences. Does that mean that we should distrust their declamations of passionate love for one another? Are words just a substitute for action that never takes place? Or is real desire still possible, even when physical intimacy is absent?

Part of the answer may have to do with something else that happened toward the end of that year, which I believe also significantly affected the nature of their sexual relationship, and which previous biographers have tended to play down. Up until this point, the letters of the previous two years are affectionate, sometimes romantic, sometimes businesslike, but they are always fairly short. By the end of the year, this has changed, and it's a change that will exist for the rest of their time together. Long, complex, intimate letters become the norm between them. Passion, the kind that so many refuse to believe is possible in a sexually impotent relationship, rarely leaves their correspondence. And one event is responsible for it.

• • • •

In October 1915 Katherine Mansfield learned that her younger and only brother, Leslie, who had just been staying with her before he left for the front, had been killed, blown up by his own hand grenade. This is what she wrote about that devastating event in her diary on October 29: "A misty, misty evening. I want to write down the fact that not only am I not afraid of death—I welcome the idea of death. I believe in immortality because he is not here, and I long to join him. First, my darling, I've got things to do for both of us, and then I will come as quickly as I can. Dearest heart, I know you are there, and I live with you, and I will write for you. Other people are near, but they are not close to me. To you only do I belong, just as *you* belong to me."

Both she and Murry subsequently left England for Bandol in the south of France, ostensibly to help her get over her grief. It is no surprise to us now to know, after we read that journal entry, that Murry couldn't cope with the intensity of her feelings for her dead brother. Mansfield speaks to him more like a lover than a brother ("my darling," "dearest heart," "you belong to me"), in phrases she soon would use to describe her relationship with Murry, descriptions she hadn't used before. To Murry, Mansfield's words for Leslie Beauchamp must have seemed horrifyingly close to the bone.

They are made even more explicit, and give another hint to sexual problems, when Murry joins her in France again and she writes in her journal, a few months later, in 1916, "the night before, when I lay in bed I felt suddenly passionate. I wanted J. to embrace me. But as I turned to speak to him or to kiss him I saw my brother lying fast asleep, and I got cold. That happens nearly always." And yet, in response to this mingling of her brother and her lover-companion, many readers have doubted the true nature of her feelings for both men, and have accused her of artifice, of making more of her brother's death than she really felt.

But it is undeniably true to me, at least, that Leslie's death marks a real change in her, because it's evident in how she thereafter writes to Murry. Her brother's death changes her as a person, and, I would argue, as a writer. Any "sticky sentimentality" that Woolf disliked in her writing (and which he blamed on Murry) would have come from this loss, I believe, insofar as I am prepared to accept Woolf's judgment of her work. It is apparent in the divergence between the early stories in *In a German Pension*—which are set in that Bavarian spa where she lost her baby, and which share some characteristics, like an interest in gender relations, with her later writing, but are very different in characterization—and "Je Ne Parle Pas Francais," which borrows from some of Murry's experiences in Paris, and which she wrote in this aftermath of her brother's death. These later stories show feelings of abandonment that are common after the death of a loved one, as well as a bitter view of the world, which are absent from that first collection, which was written in the aftermath of her miscarriage. Mansfield, ever the clever wit, distilled her bitter jibes into a more palatable mixture in these later stories, but they still make for uncomfortable reading.

It is when Murry rejoined her, once she realized she needed him and that he alone could respond to her need, that the passion in their subsequent letters became the passion of two people who have shared something profound. One moment that crystallized this came in December 1915, when, ironically enough, they were still apart. Taunted by Lawrence, who told him that Mansfield was not happy with him, Murry wrote to her on the December 20, 1915, with a new need for the truth about their relationship. He also offered reassurance that it was, in spite of everything, indeed an adult relationship: "Wig, do you just treat me as a child? Do you make your letters seem happy to deceive me? Do you just pretend to be happy in order to make me happy? And what has happened—is it that you were unhappy all the while & now do not care to conceal it any more?

"Perhaps I am just blind. Lawrence says to me that your superficial happiness never deceived him. I don't know what to answer, except that he never knew you. Was all our secret life together just a game you played to amuse me as a child…?"

There is no doubt that Mansfield could often appear "superficial," as Murry accuses her here, and manipulative, too. She would bitch about the literary hostess, Lady Ottoline Morrell, in letters to Lawrence, while accepting Morrell's hospitality time and time again, and professing her love for her. In company, too, she would often bait Murry, to show him up in front of their hosts, almost as if the confrontation made her look better. Murry is clearly worried here that he is being manipulated too ("just a game you played to amuse me"…).

If he hoped for reassurance back, he didn't get it. Mansfield carried on manipulating him. She didn't reply to Murry's desperate questions because she had anticipated them. In a previous letter to him, written the same day he wrote his own to her, which he would only have received after he had sent it, she told him: "By the way, I wrote to Lawrence the other day—a wild kind of letter, if I think of it and not fair to 'us.' You understand? It was just after I had been in bed and without letters and I had a fit of positive despair when life seemed to me to be absolutely over—& I wrote rather in that strain. I only tell you because when I have read your despairing letters to your friends I have always felt that you betrayed us and our love a little and I feel if you should see mine . . . you might feel a little the same. I am sorry I wrote it—To tell you the truth I am come to the conclusion that our happiness rests with us and with nobody else at all and that we ought to build for ourselves and by ourselves. We are very rich together for we are true lovers—and we are young and born in each other . . . How I love you—we are two little boys walking with our arms . . . round each others [sic] shoulders & telling each other secrets and stopping to look at things . . ."

This is a fascinatingly manipulative, even poisonous, letter from Mansfield for many reasons. It is only after her brother's death that these passionate references to her and Murry, alone together, really begin to surface in her letters with such force (earlier, too, in this letter, she echoes what she says about her brother in her journal when she writes, "I am *of* you as you write just as you are *of* me"). Everyone else must be shut out—they are in their own world; it's the only way they can survive. She does not answer Murry's central plea about treating him like a child— on the contrary, she reinforces the nature of their love as child-like, and crucially, boyish, when she says that they are "two little boys walking with our arms round each other." This is a clever, and, I think, pointed echo of the image of them that Murry had conjured in his letter to her a few days before, on December 16, and which she had received, where he describes them as: "cross together like two little boys." The childlike companionship that Murry imagines, though, is twisted now by Mansfield in her letter, where it becomes possessive ("our arms round each other") and all about power.

Mansfield further reinforced this troubling notion of power. In spite of the fact that she had manipulated Murry before (most notably in her letter to him of May 8–9, 1915, a couple of months after her assignation with Carco, when she lied to him that "F[rancis] C[arco] as you know simply doesn't exist for me . . ." She had, in fact, written to Carco that very same day), here, her manipulation of him reached a new level, which had nothing to do with her contracting TB—the illness was not diagnosed for another three years. Her manipulation here is about establishing power. In this letter to Murry, she not only reminds him of past hurts when he has spoken about their relationship to other people, in order to make him feel guilty. She also uses it to justify speaking to Lawrence about it, while appearing to apologize for doing so. She is the one who wants to isolate their relationship, and specifically to isolate her lover, but she, in fact, has "betrayed" them both by complaining of him to Lawrence ("not fair to us"). No one can understand him better than she can; no one can understand her like he can: that is part of her message to him. She is establishing control over their relationship, setting the boundaries and admonishing him for past misbehavior. It is a pivotal moment in their relationship: it is the moment when Mansfield finally takes absolute control and assumes power.

It is, of course, an easy fight for her to win, as Murry hasn't the kind of temperament to object too much. It's also a classically passive-aggressive kind of power and therefore the kind very well suited to an invalid, the person she would become after 1918. Murry would rush to respond to her injunctions about their being alone in the world together, having encouraged this kind of feeling in her ever since 1914, when he'd written to her, on February 11: "Don't think about the people who come and go. Shut the door fast and think of us both together." But a combination of the kind of relationship he fondly told her he always wanted and the death of her brother created a monster: this was an entirely new kind of isolation that Mansfield was suggesting, one that implied a special understanding between two people that excluded the rest of the world, and which was supported by her nasty, bad-tempered complaint about her literary partner to another man.

• • • •

Part of that exclusion came about not only to support a damaged Katherine Mansfield in the wake of her brother's death, but also to support her writing. At the beginning of 1916, they were both together in the south of France, a time even Tomalin refers to as "the most peaceful months of their life together," and where she says Mansfield and Murry "sat by the fire, writing together all day." This is the idyllic version of the writing partnership, which all of the women writers in this volume experienced at some time or another with their respective male lovers or husbands. Tomalin's description of Mansfield and Murry as "in many ways happy, he writing his Dostoevsky book on one side of the table, she for the first six weeks worrying about whether the impulse to write had died in her" conjures up the kind of happy literary concerns that such writing partnerships all too seldom enjoyed, but which were crucial to the work each woman produced.

Mansfield's writing at this time focuses once again on the brother she has lost ("Now—now I want to write recollections of my own country . . . Not only because it is 'a sacred debt' that I pay to my country because my brother and I were born there, but also because in my thoughts I range with him over all the remembered places"), but it also brings to light her ambition ("This year I have to make money and get known").

The story that emerges from this period is "The Aloe" (published as "Prelude"), which Mansfield ostensibly wrote for her dead brother, but with Murry's motivating presence beside her ("J.'s application is a perpetual reminder to me. Why am I not writing too?"), which kept her going with it. Over the next two years, as they moved from France to Cornwall and back to France again, she recorded her writing difficulties and obsessions. When she coughed up blood in February 1918, the first sign of tuberculosis, she said that "of course I am frightened," but for "two reasons," one of which was that the illness would keep her apart from Murry, and the second that she didn't want to find "that this is real consumption, perhaps it's going to gallop—who knows?—and I shan't have my work written. *That's what matters*. How unbearable it would be to die—leave 'scraps,' 'bits' . . . nothing real finished." In contrast to her welcoming death when her brother died, now she wanted to survive, to create.

Over the coming months, she lamented her lack of work, the "difficulty" of "delivery," her "timidity before closed doors." But while she was in France, she received the kind of support from Murry she needed for her writing. In February, for instance, after she sent him the manuscript for the story "Je Ne Parle Pas Francais," he wrote to her: "Your ms came this morning. It's not only first rate; it's overwhelming. The description, no, not description, creation of that cafe is extraordinary . . . It's all of such a different kind to any of your other work. Different, I mean, in scope and skeleton and structure, the exquisite exactness . . . of your vision in the detail is there just as before."

Mansfield didn't want criticism that would hurt her or damage her confidence. Murry's constant urging that they be geniuses together—when he read her story, "Bliss," in March 1918, he wrote to tell her: "I have now not the slightest doubt (seriously) that we are manifestations of the same being . . . I know this, too, that you and I are *geniuses*"—is exactly what she wanted from him in the midst of detailed analysis of her work. (Two and a half years later, she would pull him up for not giving her work the kind of attention she was used to getting from him, admonishing him, "You gave twice to your work . . . to what you gave my story. I don't want dismissing as a masterpiece.")

These fantasies of literary greatness are, I think, separate from the other fantasies they began to indulge in once her tuberculosis was diagnosed. For the next four years, they both fantasized about houses they would live in (houses they couldn't possibly afford), the number of children they would have, the long and happy life ahead of them. From this point on, it's easy to understand why Mansfield was so keen to keep referring to themselves as chil- dren—it was a warding-off of death. But the literary delusions of grandeur were also a kind of warding-off of death, an assurance of immortality that, I would argue, Murry knew Mansfield needed in order to keep going with both her work and her life. Entering a sanatorium, a residence specially designed for invalids suffering from incurable or difficult-to-treat diseases like tuberculosis, as she was urged by several doctors to do, would have curtailed her work because she would have been forbidden to write. Many of her doctors advocated complete rest from writing, even while she remained at home, but she always refused to take this advice. In a hospital, she would not have been allowed to disobey their orders. Instead, she and Murry behaved as though her writing could keep her alive.

From that diagnosis in 1918 onward, Mansfield and Murry would live apart for long stretches of time, even after they married. It was imperative that Mansfield spend the winters in a warmer climate; Murry, though, had to earn money, and he remained based in London. In the spring of 1918 we start to see the begin- ning of serious misunderstandings between them, and evidence of Mansfield's increasingly demanding nature. She was constantly on the lookout for letters from him and complaining loudly if she didn't get one. That Murry managed to write regularly (but not, Mansfield evidently felt, regularly enough) while holding down a job says a lot for his staying power, even if, as she pointed out to him on her first return from France after the diagnosis of TB, he turned away from her when she kissed him, and wiped his mouth with a handkerchief.

The biggest test of their relationship was to yet to come, however, in December 1919. Moving to Ospedaletti in Italy with Ida Baker in September, and expecting to remain there without Murry until May, Mansfield seems to have become completely unnerved. At the beginning of November she wrote to Murry, "Now listen. TRY to send me letters often or cards or papers from the office—anything. If I were there, you'd spend 10 minutes with me—give me those ten minutes here . . . HELP ME HELP ME!! . . . SILENCE is the ULTIMATE BLACKNESS." Was she entitled to be so upset? Certainly, at this point, Murry's letters had dropped in number and frequency, often leaving a full week between them. They had also become slightly more distant than before, more concerned with work and money and writing. Mansfield was always highly sensitive to changes in mood and tone, but now, isolated as she was in Italy and unwell, she was even more so. Murry wrote of having E. M. Forster to stay; of dinner with Virginia Woolf—his life was continuing, Mansfield clearly felt, without her. It all provoked the "New Husband" poems she sent him in December and which began:

> Someone came to me and said
> Forget, forget that you've been wed.
> Who's your man to leave you be
> Ill and cold in a far country?
> Who's the husband—who's the stone

Could leave a child like you alone?

Her journal from this time contains a bitter little story based on a dream about being pregnant and giving birth, and reflections on a landscape filled with "the noise of children crying." She writes, too, of her fear of death and, quite unconscious of her own attitude to the truth, that "Honesty (why?) is the only thing one seems to prize beyond life, love, death, everything. It alone remaineth. O you who come after me, will you believe it? At the end, *truth* is the only thing *worth having* . . . ."

Was her poem to Murry "the truth"? Was it the truth about their relationship? Or was it just a tactic to get him to write more often, to strengthen her hold on him? What had happened to their "being geniuses together"? Was the writing, the creative hold each had on the other, slipping away, when it should have bound them closer together?

There is some evidence that their moment of literary closeness was past. One of the crucial things about all of these literary partnerships is that when the passion wanes, so too does the literary investment, and vice versa. It suggests very powerfully that the intimacy engendered by a literary relationship that is also sexual in nature (however successful that sex is) is, ultimately, a temporary one. Certainly, Mansfield had her moments of clarity about that temporariness. At some point in 1922, she wrote in one notebook: "You hang on thinking to please him while he burns for you to be gone. How badly how stupidly you manage your life. Don't you realise that both of you have had enough contact to last you for years. That the only way for each of you to be renewed and refreshed is for you to go apart . . . You never will see that it all rests with you. If you do not take the initiative nothing will be done." This may have been the result of a liaison that Murry was having with Elizabeth Asquith this year, who now married and titled as Princess Bibesco and also writing short stories. Whatever the true nature of their relationship, Mansfield was thrown by it and when she accidentally read a letter sent by Asquith to Murry, which seemed to indicate a deep level of intimacy between them, she lost her temper. Her note to Asquith was icy, though: "Dear Princes Bibesco, I am afraid you must stop writing these little love letters to my husband while he and I live together. It is one of the things which is not done in our world. You are very young. Won't you ask your husband to explain to you the impossibility of such a situation. Please do not make me have to write to you again. I do not like scolding people and I simply hate having to teach them manners." As Claire Tomalin notes, the bohemian side to her character certainly lost out to the bourgeois side in this particular battle over Murry.

• • • •

Her great dependence on Murry was eventually transferred though by the end of her life, to a more maverick figure in the world of medicine: George Ivanovich Gurdjieff, who was the director of an institute based in Fontainebleau, called the Institute for the Harmonious Development of Man. It was a spartan existence where patients were required to do as much physical work as possible with few comforts, but Mansfield seems to have enjoyed it, preferring it to staying in bed attended by devoted helpers. Murry couldn't save her and neither could her writing: both of them failed her.

After her death on January 9, 1923, on the very day Murry had arrived at the institute to see her, he began publishing more of her stories and personal writing. He also quickly took up with another woman, Violet le Maistre, whom he made his second wife. Violet, pictures show, bore an uncanny resemblance to Mansfield, and, just like Mansfield, was also a writer. She even died tragically early from the very same illness, tuberculosis, as Mansfield had, just a few years later.

It's easy to see from the letters and notebooks that have come to light in the years since just how much Murry was in thrall to his genius writing partner, and how much he loved her. It's also easy to see that Mansfield needed his devotion, not just for the years she was seriously ill and dying, but to boost her often fragile ego, and to make sure she didn't feel alone in the world. Without him, Katherine Mansfield's work might have disappeared into oblivion. I think she loved him as much as she was capable of loving anyone, and that they both knew and understood the delusion at the heart of their relationship—not a delusion about how much, or even whether, each loved the other, but a delusion that they were literary and spiritual soul mates, "little boys cross together." They were not. They needed each other, but that is not the same thing. Far more likely as literary soul mates were Mansfield and D. H. Lawrence, with whom she shared a similar genius, even if she found his emphasis on sex in his novels excessive for her tastes. Even spiritually, she was perhaps better suited to her female friend, Ida Baker, than to Murry. And sexually, too—had she lived in different times, she might have found it easier to love women than men.

Given that they both had much to delude themselves and each other about, it is quite remarkable that the relationship between Mansfield and Murry survived for as long as it did. But perhaps we should not be so surprised. At its heart was a mutual need. Mansfield wrote in December 1920, "I am a writer first and a woman after." It was the needs of the writer that came first, and to those needs, she was ever faithful and true. There was never any deluding herself about that.

H.D. and Ezra Pound.

2. The "Novice": H.D. and Ezra Pound

He drags me out of the shadows.

—H.D., 1958

"How funny, I remember how he said to me in London . . . 'Let's be engaged—don't tell . . .' well, whoever it was, not just then Dorothy . . ." *"Then you were the third in line?"* *"No—I was the first."*

—H.D., 1958

It may seem willfully perverse to argue, as this chapter will, that Hilda Doolittle, or H.D., was a "novice," in either sexual or literary terms. This was, after all, a woman who had male and female lovers. She experienced marriage, childbirth, a miscarriage, and an abortion. She underwent psychoanalysis with Freud in the 1930s; and was lauded as a "goddess muse" right at the start of her literary career. Some of the most brilliant poetry of the twentieth century was produced by this "novice." How is it possible then to argue for H.D. as ever the inexperienced beginner? Especially when literary and sexual desire and experience lay at the heart of her work and her very being?

Yet the novice state was one that H.D. seemed to embrace, from her earliest days all the way through to her old age, and it was, ironically enough, thanks to a man she sexually desired and who read, advised, and helped to publish her poetry. He was the first of the men she called her "initiators," those "important men in her life"—including D. H. Lawrence and Freud, among others—and he gave her her identity, the identity by which we recognize her today.

It was Ezra Pound, Doolittle's friend and sometime fiancé from Philadelphia, who met with her in the tea room at the British Library in London one afternoon in September 1912, and changed her name, inscribing the now-famous signature at the bottom of her first poem, "Hermes of the Ways," as "H.D., Imagiste." Whether or not the newly initialized H.D. remained open to such inscribing by men throughout her life, never inscribing herself, always needing an "initiator" to help her begin again, is a question her first important sexual relationship poses. Later in life, H.D. would say that she should have become a nun, another kind of "novice" entirely, but one imbued with that sense of virgin newness. Did H.D.'s art, like her life, depend on her forever beginning again, forever being a "virgin"? And had that motivation been instilled in her by her earliest relationship with Ezra Pound, a man to whom she never lost her emotional or literary ties?

As a primary member of the Imagist movement and the author of complex, experimental volumes of poetry like *Trilogy* and *Helen in Egypt,* H.D.'s literary stature today is assured. She was always well regarded by her contemporaries, who included Lawrence, Ford Madox Ford, Marianne Moore, and Amy Lowell, but the growth of her reputation owes as much to the quality of her work as it does to her association with Pound. It also owes something to recent feminist scholarship, particularly from the 1980s and '90s, which has linked her sexual orientation, and especially her relationships with women, to her writing. That scholarship has launched an intellectual as well as a personal fascination with H.D.'s life and work, which led to the posthumous publications of semiautobiographical novels like *Asphodel,* and cemented her place in both a women's literary canon and a Modernist one.

But in 1912, Ezra Pound was the established figure, not H.D. A kind of enfant terrible of poetry on both sides of the Atlantic, he was far better equipped to launch an unknown novice into the London literary world than H.D. was to launch herself. Born in 1885 in Wyncote, Philadelphia, to a land assessor and a mother distantly related to Longfellow, Pound was brilliant even as a child. But he was miserable at school where his inadequate social skills attracted the wrong kind of attention and meant he was bullied. Even when he became a student at the University of Pennsylvania, he was picked on, according to H.D., though she wasn't there to witness it herself: "They would say, 'He is so eccentric.' 'What is it?' 'He is impossible; he told Professor Shelling that Bernard Shaw was more important than Shakespeare.' 'What is it?' 'He makes himself conspicuous; he wore lurid, bright socks that the older students ruled out for freshmen. The sophomores threw him in the lily pond. They called him 'Lily' Pound.'"

Pound's affected ways might have been exacerbated after his student years by the fact that he travelled back and forth between the United States and Europe from 1908 onward, neither fully at home in one place nor the other, no doubt coming across as ever more foreign to his contemporaries in Pennsylvania. 1908 was also the year he published his first work, *A Lume Spento*, which finally established him as a poet: he was only twenty-three. While in London that year, he also published poems in the *Evening Standard*. He might have been considered odd and bullied at school or university, but literary London, with its more bohemian ways, suited him. Here, he made important friends and good contacts. It was a more artistic and liberal world than his provincial hometown and narrow-minded university colleagues, and he used his new-found fame as a published poet to meet writers like May Sinclair and Ford Madox Ford (who would publish *The Good Soldier* in 1915). Pound also wooed the poets T. E. Hulme and F. S. Flint, who were then in the throes of starting up the new poetic movement,

Imagism, although its theories were not properly propounded in the early stages, not until Pound came on the scene.

In the four years between publishing his first work and initializing H.D. in the British Library tearoom, Pound would publish an astonishing amount of poetry. Work would appear in *The English Review.* Two collections, *Personae* and *Exultations* (1909) were produced. A volume of critical essays, *The Spirit of Romance,* was completed in 1910 and a collection of translations, *The Sonnets,* followed two years later in 1912. Another collection of poetry called *Ripostes* also came out that year. By this time, he could count figures like W. B. Yeats and Wyndham Lewis among his friends, and enjoy literary banter with the likes of D. H. Lawrence. He was greatly admired in London literary circles where he was viewed as something of a genius, if often also tactless, with bizarre manners and an odd way of dressing. But none of that held him back. On the contrary, his odd ways seemed to help him in his quest to know absolutely everybody worth knowing. In the process, he made sure he was one of the important people, too.

The growth of his reputation during those four years meant that people listened when Pound told them about new "finds.". He did so, conspiratorially and flatteringly, when he wrote to *Poetry* magazine's Harriet Monroe about H.D.'s work: "I've had luck and am sending you some *modern stuff* by an American . . . This is the sort of American stuff that I can show you here and in Paris without being ridiculed . . . it was only by persistence that I got to see it at all." Monroe knew to pay attention to his recommendations, and duly published "Hermes of the Ways," "Priapus: Keeper-of-Orchards," and "Epigram: After the Greek" in her magazine, attributing them not to Hilda Doolittle, but to H.D. These poems launched H.D.

More work would appear in the anthology *Des Imagistes* in

1914, and her first collection of poetry, *Sea Garden,* was published just two years later. Her passion for Greek myth would never leave her, and would inform subsequent collections like *Hymen* (1921) and *Heliodora* (1924), even though by then she and Pound were on different poetic wavelengths. He deplored her obsession with Greek myth and told her to "get out of the pigsty" (a reference to Circe, who traps men in her pigsty and turns them into pigs in *The Odyssey*). H.D. ignored his advice, which was the right instinct, as perhaps her most celebrated work turned out to be *Helen in Egypt,* about Helen of Troy, which appeared in 1961. The intervening years saw the completion of semi-autobiographical novels like *Her* and *Asphodel,* as well as the memoirs, *End to Torment* (written in 1958 but not published until 1979) and *Tribute to Freud* (published in 1956). These fictional and nonfictional prose works, added to her poetry, made for an almost continuous life of writing. Only in the 1930s, when she began analysis as a way of unblocking her mind and freeing up her poetic consciousness, did she not publish. Every other decade saw the publication of her work, up until her death in 1961 and beyond.

But when she arrived in London in 1911, H.D. was not the ambitious, go-getting writer that Pound was. London was a heady place to be before the advent of the First World War. The end of the nineteenth century had seen increasing interest in the Pre-Raphaelite painters, especially, according to one critic, "Dante Gabriel Rossetti's 'Bohemian Masculinity,'" which meant "the rejection of bourgeois monogamy and the celebration of desire and artistic freedom." Many artists of this new century, including H.D., found expression in a sudden desire for all things Greek—bohemian fashion favored draped fabrics, floating headscarves, a looser costume than the firmly corseted style favored at the start of the century. The somber, dutiful George V had recently come to the throne and would herald a more moralistic age;

but the era of his father, the Francophile playboy son of Queen Victoria, Edward VII, was not entirely over. It could still be felt in the loosening of manners, in the playfulness of the literary and artistic scenes, which encouraged all things "modern." It was the era of small magazines like *The English Review* and *Blast*, as well as feminist publications like *The New Freewoman*: suffragette activity was also on the increase, as was the growing Labour movement, the new party of the working class which had been formed in 1900. Writers like H. G. Wells were writing futuristic novels that warned against the new technologies; motorcars were beginning to change the face of city streets.

London's literary scene might be considered small compared to that of the present day, but the collection of names of those living and writing in the city at the time is extraordinary: Katherine Mansfield, Rebecca West, W. B. Yeats, May Sinclair, Dorothy Richardson, Ford Madox Ford, T. E. Hulme, D. H. Lawrence, John Middleton Murry, Wyndham Lewis, and Virginia Woolf were all passing through or making it their home. H.D., a shy, nervous, and unsure twenty-six-year-old, a novice in just about every conceivable way, was only too happy to be "chaperoned" by the more experienced, more confident Pound. She fell in love with the city, its history and culture, the leafy Bloomsbury squares and museums and galleries.

Born in 1886 to a professor of astronomy at the University of Pennsylvania and his wife, a member of the Moravian Brethren, a nonconformist Protestant sect, H.D.'s artistic and intellectual leanings had always been encouraged by her parents. By the time she arrived in London though, she was still the provincial young woman from Upper Darby, Pennsylvania, who had only recently left the safe environs of her hometown. With her first exposure to the British capital, she must have felt her provincialism keenly. She was also, quite literally at this time, still "a virgin . . . an untouched child." Inexperienced in the ways of the world as she apparently was, she needed a provider, a protector, someone to show her the way.

• • • •

There are many questions about H.D.'s relationship with Ezra Pound, a testament to how little we really know of its inner workings. This lack of information is partly thanks to three people. H.D.'s father apparently burned most of the letters Pound wrote to his daughter during their long early courtship. Pound burned all the letters from women he became involved with, apart from Dorothy, his wife. And H.D. herself did not keep a journal where she might have recorded her feelings about this strange, intense, dandyish young man to whom she was at one point engaged.

But what we do have is *End to Torment: A Memoir of Ezra Pound*, a single, slight, intensely moving and invaluable memoir about her early relationship with him. We also have, perhaps less reliable, two autobiographical novels. *Her* was written in 1927 but not published until 1981. It tracks the course of her engagement to Pound as well as her involvement with a young woman, Frances Gregg. A second novel, *Asphodel,* was completed during the 1920s but not published until 1992. It examines her relationship with Richard Aldington, whom she married, I believe, on the rebound from Pound. Autobiographical as they both are, they should reveal and clarify, but in many ways they do just the opposite.

What we do know of the Pound-Doolittle beginnings is that they met in 1901, at a Halloween party. It was held in an orphanage run by the minister father of one of her school friends in Philadelphia, Margaret Snively. She was fifteen years old and he was sixteen. Both of them lived in suburbs on the outskirts of the city, she in Upper Darby, he in Wyncote. She was introduced to Pound by Snively's brother. In her memoir, H.D. records what attracted her to Pound that very first time, and what comes across most strongly is her awareness of how unlike anyone else he is: "Immensely sophisticated, immensely superior, immensely rough-and-ready, a product not like any of the brothers and brothers' friends—and boys we danced with (and he danced badly). One would dance with him for what he might say." Not every girl there was so captivated, though. She recalls in later life that her female friends, also daughters of respectable academics and church ministers, viewed Pound, the first-year university student who adored the Troubadour poets and who saw himself as a Pre-Raphaelite figure even then, as "mad": "'O Ezra Pound's crazy" was the verdict of my schoolgirl contemporaries."

H.D. was captivated from the beginning, and not only by his words. She didn't know then that he was a poet, but she was as bewitched by his physical presence as she was by his highly articulate ways. Once they had begun to see each other, she found the force of his kisses "electric, magnetic, they do not so much warm, they magnetize." Theirs was a much more complex love affair than such a ready early intimacy would appear to suggest, though—in H.D.'s semi-autobiographical novel *Her*, Hermione, the character who represents H.D., has a far more ambivalent response to Pound's physical attractiveness than this memoir records.

We know little about the progress of their relationship during the intervening period, but four years later, she was a first-year student at Bryn Mawr, he was back at his alma mater, the University of Pennsylvania, for graduate work, and they were engaged. H.D. was by now the tall, graceful, classically handsome young woman later photographs would show. Pound was even more eccentric in his appearance, letting his mane of red hair grow wild, favoring spectacles and variously colored Byronic-style open-neck shirts, and swinging a cane. By all accounts he was, it would seem, deeply in love with her. They had a great deal in common besides writing poetry (H.D. was still making only very tenuous stabs, not overly encouraged by Pound, who was dismissive of these early efforts). Both preferred their father's company to their mother's, as they tended to take after that particular parent more; both were extremely bright and were encouraged in their academic endeavors by their families. Both also exhibited a ceratin sexual flexibility. Pound, who had been told he was considered bisexual, confided as much to H.D. when they were still teenagers and she barely knew what the term meant, but he almost certainly had no adult homosexual experiences. H.D., on the other hand, would go on to have relationships with women as well as men, and share her life with Bryher, or Winifred Ellerman, for more than forty years.

But it was Pound who encouraged H.D. to think beyond the world of Upper Darby, Pennsylvania. It was he who later pulled her away from the conventionality of respectable, middle-class East Coast America and into the more bohemian atmosphere in turn-of-the-century London. Her family were perhaps unsurprisingly concerned by her relationship with him. They were unnerved by Pound's unconventional behavior and dress, not to mention his bohemian ideas of living his life as a kind of vagabond poet, Troubadour-style. But they were also worried about his hold over their daughter. In *Her,* H.D. depicts her mother's concern that the Pound character is teaching her daughter what to say, and it's possible to read H.D.'s own unease at how overwhelming he could be.

Pound had written love poems to H.D., later published as *Hilda's Book*—containing one poem where he implores her "Be we well sworn / Ne'er to grow older"—over a two-year period that also covered his first trip to Europe in the summer of 1906. When he returned, he began teaching at Wabash College in western Indiana. During this time, though, he had become engaged to another young woman, Mary Moore, from New Jersey, as well as to H.D. This is something his love poems for the latter hardly give away. But the literary closeness between them remained intact, in spite of Pound's cheating. This small volume of early poetry has compelled one recent biographer to ask, "Did Pound learn from H.D.?" and to wonder if the focus on nature in these poems came from her, rather than from him. It seems likely that two poets of such ability, especially at this early stage in their writing careers, would have influenced each other, at least until they found their own paths. It also introduces a nice "novice" angle to the depiction of Pound as the more experienced, more manipulative, and more dissembling half of the partnership. Pound and H.D. were, clearly, learning from each other.

Pound soon lost his position at Wabash, though, and because of another woman altogether. He let a stranger stay in his rooms— he told H.D. that he'd met the unknown woman while out walking and that, as she was homeless, he'd simply taken pity on her and allowed her to sleep in his rooms, in his bed, while he slept on the floor. The authorities at conservative Wabash saw the matter very differently, however, and in 1908, Pound left for Europe once again, this time with disgrace hanging over his head.

In 1909, H.D. enrolled at Bryn Mawr College and dropped out the same year, returning to her family home in defeat. One can see a kind of mirroring here in her self-imposed exile from academic life, just as Pound headed for Europe to pursue poetry. Lonely without him, feeling like a failure, especially as the daughter of a university professor, H.D. seems to have suffered greatly from Pound's absence. She wasn't aware of his love for Mary Moore at this time, or of his involvements with other women, except the homeless woman who stayed in his rooms. She had his poems, but that was all, and the promise of an engagement to a man who was on the other side of the ocean. It wasn't enough, because it was while she was in this abandoned and hopeless state of mind that she met Frances Gregg.

Gregg was once described as a mix of male and female, "a beautiful girl in boy's clothes." In a short story she wrote about herself, H.D. and Pound, she hints at cross-dressing and taking the male role in their relationship. H.D. was to have an extremely intense physical relationship with Gregg, although it was interrupted by Pound's return to the States in 1910 (the novel *Her* records her greeting Pound's announcement of his return—"I am coming back to Gawd's own god-damn country"—with some trepidation) and his own sexual involvement with Gregg, which almost broke H.D., as she relates in *Her*. Yet, after this terrible hurt, she still went to New York, essentially to be with Pound. The vast, strange city didn't appeal to her. Left alone while Pound dazzled the literary community with his poems, she cut her visit short, and after she met up once again with Gregg, she accompanied her friend and her friend's mother on a trip to Europe. By this time, their relationship was very intimate; they kissed in secret on the boat over. On her way home, though, she once more cleaved to Pound, and decided to meet him, this time in London. It was a city where she immediately felt more at home.

• • • •

Throughout a period of five years, H.D. and Pound's long "engagement" was disturbed time and time again—possibly broken off on one occasion (after H.D. finally discovered he'd asked Mary Moore to marry him: "The engagement, such as it was, was shattered like a Venetian glass goblet, flung on the floor"), possibly reinstated, then possibly broken off again (after H.D. learned that Pound had asked Dorothy Shakespear to marry him while still engaged to her). This is all besides the betrayal she felt over his involvement with Frances Gregg. Pound's sexual infidelities simply seem to have proved far too much for her to handle. It's not overstating the case to say that his betrayals devastated her. In the first poem of hers that he sent off to be published, "Hermes of the Ways," there is possibly a hint of how she really felt about him, and of what he had done. The third stanza of the poem reads, "But more than the many-foamed ways / of the sea, I know him / of the triple path-ways / Hermes / who awaits." Hermes is the god of orators, wits, and poets, and the inventor of the lyre. He is also the god of liars and thieves. He is a mischief-maker who gets himself out of scrapes by telling wonderful stories and bewitching people with his words. How much of Pound did H.D. see in this mythical figure? The arch-poet, who declared his calling the moment he stepped into a room, he was also, she might have been saying, a liar. And who could blame her? H.D. trusted him, and there is a sense that she believed him, too ("one would dance with him for what he might say"). Time and again, no doubt, he won her round with his words, and time and again, he let her down.

Pound's treatment of her possibly reached its lowest point with his affair with Frances Gregg, but there were many other women, both before and after Gregg. It's little wonder his romance with Dorothy Shakespear proved a rejection too many for H.D., making this break the final one. I think it was Pound's infidelity and inability to be honest with her that did the real damage to H.D. The pain she experienced when he fell for Gregg made her, I believe, never want to be abandoned again, and to seek refuge in relationships that were not just made up of two people, but three. It seems like an odd response to being repeatedly cheated on by a fiancé: wouldn't she have shied away from the very format, the "love triangle," that had caused her so much pain? But I believe H.D. formulated a theory that made a third party seem like the solution to the problem of potential abandonment. As a result of Pound's treatment of her, his repeated lies and infidelities, she walked an emotional tightrope, courting that danger, in all her relationships for the rest of her life. It meant, tragically, that she was abandoned by a series of men in subsequent years. But it also meant that her insecurity about relationships, that need for a third party, kept her a novice, as this chapter will show. And it was staying a novice that helped her art.

The first man to betray her and teach her never to depend on just one other was her fiancé. The second was an extension of him, the man she ended up marrying. H.D. had already met another young poet, Richard Aldington, through Pound, when their engagement ended. It does seem likely though, given the haste with which she married Aldington in 1913, just a year or two after she had come to London to be with Pound, that she was on the rebound from her one-time fiancé. Helen Carr argues that "He [Aldington] and H.D. were very much in love," but she does admit that H.D. "did not feel so painfully intensely about Aldington as she had about Pound and Frances [Gregg]." She also states that it was Pound who suggested to H.D. that she and Aldington marry. Did that suggestion ease his conscience about going on to marry Dorothy Shakespear?

In any case, H.D. the novice became H.D. the wife, a move that was surely compelled by feelings of hurt and rejection at Pound's behavior, as much as interest in Aldington. And even more complex still: six months after H.D. and Aldington did marry, Pound took Shakespear as his wife and the happy couple moved into rooms right across the landing from H.D. and Aldington. Was Pound hurt and angered by H.D.'s marriage, even though he apparently suggested it? This kind of confused behavior, the mixed messages sent between them all, characterized much of H.D. and Pound's early involvement.

The exact details of their long, troubled, and erratic romantic relationship are still a little unclear today, and it's understandable that biographers have long disagreed over exactly who ended what, when, and why. In her memoir, H.D. records a conversation with her doctor, Erich Heydt, who questions her about the exact details of their engagement, and even he doesn't get straight answers:

> "You didn't say he gave you a ring. Did he give you a ring?"
>
> "Of course—how *German* you are—"
>
> "It was announced, everyone knew it?"
>
> "O, how you get hold of the unimportant details. Yes, no. I mean, it was understood but my parents were unhappy about it and I was shy and frightened. I didn't have the usual conventional party—lunch, dinner or announcement dance, if that is what you mean. But *what* does it matter?"
>
> "His parents came to see you?"
>
> "Of course."
>
> "They were pleased?"
>
> "Very—mine weren't, as I say. Mrs. Pound brought me an exquisite pearl pendant."
>
> "Then you *were* engaged. Did you give the ring back?"
>
> "Of course."

This exchange lets us hear H.D.'s voice, but also shows us her own uncertainty—"Yes, no. I mean . . ." If she can't be sure, it's almost impossible for her biographers to be. That she still sounds panicky and confused about it, forty years later, gives us some indication of how intense and tricky a situation it must have felt like at the time. There is little doubt about H.D.'s love for Pound, but she wasn't in control of their relationship, and that is reflected in her later obfuscation and nervousness.

What all H.D.'s biographers have tended to agree on, however, is that Pound was her mentor from the start, with some even speculating whether she would have become a poet at all without his influence. Shari Benstock argues, "The questions concerning Pound's role in her poetic development still nag, however. Had she not met Pound, would she have become a poet—if so, what kind?" Janice S. Robinson writes, "The fact that she became a published poet was a decision made by Pound over afternoon tea." Helen Carr also attributes H.D.'s realization of her own identity as a poet to Pound.

She was the novice, he the experienced instructor, or as H.D. herself would term it, her "initiator." And yet, in her memoir, she also writes, "Ezra would have destroyed me and the center they call 'Air and Crystal' of my poetry." What was he to her, exactly? What part did he truly play in her invention of herself as a poet? Creating her, could he indeed have destroyed her just as easily? H.D. appears to think so, even though, after claiming her for the Imagist movement and making her follow its poetic ideals, he then waltzed off in the direction of Vorticism instead, leaving her and her Imagist poems behind.

The sense of literary abandonment (never mind his sexual abandonments of her) lingered, even four decades later—when H.D. continued, in the same recollection from her memoir, to describe the experience of waiting for letters from Pound. At this point, Pound was being held in a psychiatric hospital in the States, from which he was about to be released. It is something of a cliché to portray artists as geniuses on their way to madness, but in Pound's case it seems to have been true. What began as anti-Semitic sentiments that Pound was voicing in the more politically dubious 1920s and '30s—when fascism was on the rise and respected poets like T. S. Eliot could publish their derogatory and racist attitudes to Jews in their poetry without fear of castigation—had become, by the time of the Second World War, almost incoherent rants and diatribes. Transcripts of these rants, which were broadcast over the radio from his home in Italy, almost fail to give offense today, so ridiculously paranoid, so clearly the product of a seriously disturbed mind, are they. Pound was arrested at the end of the war for these broadcasts, and it was while he was incarcerated in Italy, held for days on end in wire cages exposed to the full glare of the sun, that he had a complete nervous breakdown. Several friends, including Ernest Hemingway, while deploring the sentiments of his broadcasts, testified to the good he had done writers in the early days and stood by him, and it was only a medical diagnosis of insanity that saved Pound from execution. Some critics today still cast doubt on the diagnosis that saved his life and saw him transferred to a psychiatric institution in the States, where he remained for more than a decade.

H.D., however, had always been aware of Pound's "crazy" tendencies, as she recalled her school friends calling them (a notice in *Time* magazine from June 9, 1958, referred to him as "mad old poet Ezra Pound"), and she remained in contact with him throughout her life, even asking him later on for advice about her poetry. Her feelings toward him in her memoir are those of a young girl again, almost as though she never learned. She reflects how she was once in a similar state of "fever and excitement" when she used to wait to hear from him, "almost fifty years ago, when Ezra left for Europe." Yet this was a man who, she goes on to tell us, separated her from her family and her friends, "even from America." His power over her was such that it extended, it would seem, throughout her whole life.

Svengali figures often like to isolate their prodigies and their finds, and Pound certainly viewed H.D. as one of his "finds," if not *the* major find. As H.D. records, he was always "inexpressibly kind" to those whom he thought had talent, and his efforts in London were concentrated on finding a group of like-minded writers whose work he could nurture and advance. There is a hint at the kind of impression he must have made, not only on women but on men, too, in a photograph taken in London in 1914. It shows seven men, among them Yeats and Pound, as well as Richard Aldington.

Aldington was a promising young poet whom Pound took on, but he is described by Virginia Woolf in less-than-poetic terms as a "bluff, powerful, rather greasy-eyed, nice downright man, who will make his way in the world, which I don't much like people to do." And yet that description scarcely fits with the image of the man as evinced by the photograph—what is most startling to see is just how much Aldington, a year into his marriage to H.D., looks like Pound. Both have their hair swept up and back from their foreheads, both favor the same triangular mustache that reaches down to the edges of the mouth and beyond, and, while it could be shadow, it appears that Aldington also has a slight beard on his chin, similar to the one Pound has more obviously taken to cultivating. While eschewing Pound's favorite open-necked shirt, Aldington still looks like an acolyte, if an exceedingly handsome one; he is hardly the "bluff, powerful, rather greasy-eyed" man Woolf portrays. His bulk, which many others comment on, is disguised by his slightly dandyish style of dress.

Biographers have commented on Pound's sexual appeal to women, but it's clear he also had the power to attract young men who wanted to be like him, to emulate his lifestyle, his ideas, and, of course, his fame and his success. It wasn't just women who wanted to dance with him "for what he might say." Yet, H.D. was someone Pound had known since he was sixteen—she was his first: his first love and his first "find." So confident was he of his own genius, even in his teens, that he was sure he could recognize it in others and help to develop it. He had to remove her from provincial Pennsylvania, and if New York wasn't the place for either of them, then London would do the trick. And she knew absolutely no one there—she was entirely dependent on Pound for her introductions to people.

H.D.'s inability to find her own way around new places and make new friends herself, her natural shyness, might only have been made worse by an imposing figure like Pound, who took over and insisted he could show her the way. His natural authority took all the difficult, frightening aspects of being alone in a strange city and made them safe (in *Her*, the central character talks of feeling safe in the arms of her amour, George Lowndes, a stand-in for Pound), but it didn't help her get over her shyness or give her the confidence to strike out on her own. For the rest of her life, H.D. would need someone there to look after her, a protector of sorts. Pound was the first, but he wasn't the last. Aldington, Bryher, and Kenneth MacPherson would all be cast in this role in the years to come.

Was it the lure of safety and security that made H.D. run when Pound called? Surely not, given his propensity for a bohemian life-style, his lack of money, his unreliability. Was it sexual attraction, then, that made her flit to New York first, and then to London? Something made her succumb to a man whom she certainly seems to have found sexually attractive, but whose kisses she also found "pressurized," as one biographer puts it. H.D. may talk in her memoir of his "electric" first kisses that "magnetize, vitalize," but in her autobiographical novel, *Her,* they become "forcing" and "smudge her out."

Her ambivalent response to Pound as a lover may have arisen partly from her sexual feelings about women, at this time directed specifically at Frances Gregg. This ambivalence is more fully ex-plored in her novel, written almost twenty years after the events that inspired it. There are three main protagonists: Hermione Gart (H.D.), George Lowndes (Pound), and Fayne Rabb (Gregg). The novel begins with Her Gart's return from her academic failure at Bryn Mawr, just before George's return to the United States from a visit to Europe. Just like H.D., Her is still a novice: she has not even been able to complete her college degree, and no man has ever kissed her but George.

And it's the need to remain as a novice that creates a prob-lem in Her's relationship with her fiancé (as a novice, she will always need him; as a novice, he can never leave her, she can never be alone). As beautiful as she finds him, she doesn't seem to want him sexually, or at least not enough to commit to full sexual intercourse ("Why is it I can't *love* George Lowndes properly?"). George is the first person to kiss her, but she can't cope with it: "Kisses forced her on to soft moss . . . the kisses of George smudged out her clear geometric thought. . . Smudged out. I am smudged out." George's physicality, his maleness, is too much; it is animalistic ("The face of George looked like a wolf, was a wolf, it was wolf mask on a man's body . . . .") and she barely recognizes him. Nevertheless, she gets engaged to him—what they have between them is writing, as well as sexual desire, however ambivalent ("writing had somehow got connected up with George Lowndes"). That, and her hope that he can free her ("She wanted George to say, 'God, you must give up the sort of putrid megalomania, get out of this place'").

But Her's mother objects to Her marrying George because of his reputation (something disreputable has happened at the college where he is teaching—in this autobiographical novel, H.D. describes almost exactly what happened with Pound at Wabash), and because of his extraordinary influence over her, as she observes perceptively: "George Lowndes is teaching you, actually *teaching* you words, telling you what to say."

This sexual, but also creative, relationship produces a kind of attraction-repulsion dynamic, which keeps Her in her novice state, both as a virgin and as a virgin poet (she is using George's words, not her own). The contrast between Her's reaction to George's kisses and the feelings aroused when she is close to Fayne Rabb, another young woman aspiring to be a writer, couldn't be greater. "*Curled lips long since half kissed away* came right in the white face. The mouth was straight now, the mouth of a boy hunter. The mouth was a mouth that had hallooed across stones towards some escaping quarry . . . 'You might have been a huntress.'" Fayne's mouth is the ideal because it is both masculine, "boy hunter," and feminine, "huntress." This same-sex attraction is also, for Her, a new thing. She's a novice at this, as well. Backing off from consummating her relationship with George, she veers into the start of something else, an intimacy with Fayne Rabb.

As *Her* tells it, George and Fayne then embark on an affair, as Pound and Gregg did in real life. This pushes Her over the edge. At the end of the novel, though, Her manages to rebuild herself after her breakdown and become the artist she has always wanted to be. Similarly, H.D. managed, somehow, to survive the pain of Pound's sexual betrayals, just like the one he committed with Gregg, and with Mary Moore and Dorothy Shakespear. Perhaps that's partly because, in real life, H.D. didn't completely lose Pound to Gregg. It was Gregg who lost Pound, if she ever had him in the first place, as her own short story about the affair, "Male and Female," showed. In this story, there is a great degree of competitiveness between the two women for the one man, who is called Kiah, and who is based on Pound. Kiah exhibits an extraordinary arrogance and belief in himself, which leads him to be dismissive of others. Gregg's digs at Pound's vanity come after the fact, and her story has the bitter tone of thwarted love recalled much later: "She was in love with this youth, this beautiful youth, about whom she was not in the least deceived. He did not love her, would never love her, and she would never love anyone else. He was not worth it, but she could not help herself."

Gregg's publishers suggest that this story was "probably written in 1925." In 1912, Gregg had surprisingly married Louis Wilkinson, and asked H.D. to accompany them on their honeymoon. H.D. agreed, but Pound prevented her from going (as H.D. tells it in *End to Torment*, it was to stop her from messing up Gregg's marriage, and she describes Pound waiting "glowering and savage" until she had made her excuses to Gregg and the train had left the station.) But the jibes in this short story make one wonder if Gregg resented Pound's interference, and how much of a score is being settled here, especially as she and Wilkinson wrote a novel in 1916 satirizing H.D. and Pound (among others), called, somewhat tellingly (if unkindly), *The Buffoon.*

Pound comes out of Gregg's story badly, as a kind of sexed-up Svengali who thinks he can "train" women for sex ("sex is necessary to me as an artist," says his character), but H.D. fares just as badly, portrayed as a manipulative and dishonest woman. It's hardly the picture of the novice, the type who can't go far enough with a man, who relies on a man to tell her if her poems are any good, is it? And yet, in many ways, Pound was as much of a novice as H.D. There is something childlike in her portrayal of him in *Her,* and in *End to Torment* she describes him as "Ezra, at one time . . . an Idol, an Image of its adolescence, in its Ariel or Seraphitus stage." Always wanting to be in at the beginning of things, whether it was Imagism or Vorticism, finding new talents, launching new voices, he also liked newness, the as-yet uninitiated. It gave him a sense of power, to be new himself, and to launch the new.

And for H.D., who also liked being at the beginning of things, being mentored suited her down to the ground. The mentor keeps the mentee in the novice position, always learning, always beginning—why else would she have let him initialize her existence by signing her name that day in the British Museum tearoom, "H.D., Imagiste"? His literary ability and confidence were greater than hers then; there were things she knew she could learn from him. She'd known it, quite clearly, from the moment she met him. Like so many of the women in this volume, she was prepared to take the bad in her partner for the sake of the good—for what he could do for her art. H.D. may not always have appreciated Pound's "forceful, smudging" kisses, but there was undeniably still an appeal, both sexual and cerebral, to their literary intimacy.

Because literary closeness—being taken up in a literary way, being praised or critiqued for literary endeavors, working with another on a much-valued literary project—is extremely intimate.

It's possible H.D. actually preferred this kind of intimacy with Pound to sexual intimacy, and it's easy to see why, given the aspiring, ambitious poet she was. Pound may have been dismissive of her very early efforts, but later he not only encouraged her work and commented on it, but he also edited it and cut out what he didn't like: "'But Dryad (in the Museum tearoom), this is poetry.' He slashed with a pencil. 'Cut this out, shorten this line.' 'Hermes of the ways' is a good title. I'll send this to Harriet Monroe of *Poetry*. Have you a copy? Yes? Then we can send this, or I'll type it when I get back. Will this do?' And he scrawled 'H.D. Imagiste' at the bottom of the page."

His role here was, unusually for a male writer, both masculine and feminine: he took the masculine task of sending things out, being in control, editing and cutting. But he also adopted the feminine role of typing up H.D.'s poems for her. In the majority of the relationships explored in this volume, very few of the men offer to type out their lover's or partner's words: as with Sylvia Plath, for example, or Elizabeth Smart, it is nearly always the woman who does the typing for the man.

We know, too, that Pound liked to tell H.D. what to read and how to read it, very early on in their courtship. ("It was Ezra who really introduced me to William Morris. He literally shouted 'The Gillflower of Gold' in the orchard . . . And there was 'Two Red Roses across the Moon' and 'The Defence of Guinevere.' It was at this time that he bought me the *Seraphita* and a volume of Swedenborg—*Heaven and Hell*? Or is that Blake? He brought me volumes of Ibsen and of Bernard Shaw. He brought me Whistler's *Ten O'Clock* . . . He brought me the Portland, Maine, Thomas Mosher reprint of the Iseult and Tristram story . . .") Pound seemed to do this with every woman he subsequently met (and with men, too—he wasn't above advising Yeats on what his reading material should be). H.D. trusted his judgment, finding a lifelong love in the Greek myths in which Pound encouraged her (hence his nickname for her: "Dryad"). But sons must defeat their fathers; daughters reject their mothers; creations rebel against their creators. H.D. may have never exactly rebelled against Pound, but she did eventually turn away from him, both emotionally and artistically, in response to what she certainly perceived as his abandonment of her. When she did break away, she did so for good in some sense. Does this mean that the novice finally grew up?

· · · ·

At the beginning of her recollections of Ezra Pound in *End to Torment*, H.D. writes: "They used to say, 'Run around, children: it's all right as long as you don't stop running.' Had I stopped running? Stop running for a moment, if you dare call him back." The answer comes later—yes, she had stopped running—as she recalls her early childhood: "I was clothed with confusion. I had been forced into the wrong groove. Is every groove wrong? I resented the years preparing for college that might have been spent with music, drawing. Poetry? Well, I had read enough poetry. 'You are a poem though your poem's naught,' quoted Ezra . . ." and she goes on to describe herself and Pound climbing a maple tree in their garden, kissing and making him almost miss his train home. Later, when her father finds them "curled up together in an armchair" she describes herself as "gone." "I wasn't there. I disentangled myself. I stood up; Ezra stood beside me."

The essential childlike innocence of her relationship with Ezra Pound in those days (kissing in trees, missing trains, running around like a child) is crucial to understanding the nature of that relationship, and why it remained an unconsummated one (in spite of Pound's best efforts to consummate it). It also explains why H.D. would so often take up first the position of the child, then the Virgin Mother (in *Asphodel*, Hermione says that the George Lowndes character "said I was like the Madonna or something" and that he accuses her of being "too nun-ish"). She wanted to remain a woman "untouched" in her subsequent relationships (with D. H. Lawrence, for instance, with whom she had a close friendship but did not have sex, as well as with her female partner, Bryher—if biographers are to be believed, there was little sexual involvement in that relationship either).

Hence the reason she feels shame and embarrassment when her father finds her curled up in the chair with Pound. In *End to Torment*, she offers a defense of the sexually innocent aspect of their relationship: "I was hiding myself and Ezra, standing before my father, caught 'in the very act' you might say. For no 'act' afterwards, though biologically fulfilled, had had the significance of the first *demi-vierge* embraces. The significance of first love cannot be overestimated . . . By what miracle does the *mariage du ciel et de la terre* find consummation? It filled my fantasies and dreams, my prose and poetry for ten years . . ." In the same memoir, she says that she was not "equipped to understand the young poet," although she understands him better now that she is older. How does someone who values the childlike in a relationship advance to the adult part of it?

With Pound, it never really happened. H.D. is forever the young girl, nervously waiting for his appearance as he swings in from wherever he has been, worldly wise and all-knowing—except, of course, he doesn't really know her (as she wrote in *Her*, "George never understood me"). Yet there is a great deal of evidence that what she was attracted to in this relationship was a kind of "tripartite" structure. At first that doesn't seem to be the case: the Pound-H.D.-Gregg ménage à trois appears only to have done H.D. damage. But Gregg did operate as a kind of foil for H.D. She eased up the intensity of H.D.'s feelings for Pound, as well as Pound's feelings for her, by giving her someone else to focus on. Gregg helped H.D. cope, too, with the physical "repulsion-attraction" that she experienced with him. Perhaps

H.D.'s bisexuality demanded a threesome; perhaps her need to remain a child demanded it, too. (In *Asphodel*, H.D./Hermione says of Gregg's/Fayne Rabbe's impending marriage: "O Fay, you're grown up now in your bride things . . . a lovely mother. O Fay, let me be your first child.") Perhaps, too, it offered her a kind of security, having two lovers, not just one. Only when Gregg and Pound paired off, leaving H.D. not so much the adored child in the relationship but the discarded lover, did it all backfire.

It all suggests that H.D. was frightened by the demands of a truly intimate, one-on-one adult relationship, whether with a man like Pound, or with a woman like Gregg, even while she may have needed it. Was she frightened of what it would mean if that other one left her? Bringing in a third party might have eased the pressure she felt from any sexual demands of a lover or partner, while leaving her secure in the affections of a second partner, if the first failed her. In a section of a published volume of her letters written while she was seeing Freud for analysis in the 1930s, entitled "Ménage," her editor reflects on the "oddly configured family" of three she had set up by that time in 1933, and how it "clearly fascinated" Freud. H.D. herself is quoted, writing to Havelock Ellis in 1928 about her home setup with a female lover-companion, Winifred Ellerman, or Bryher, and a male lover, Kenneth MacPherson: "The MacPhersons are almost MYSELF. We seem to be a composite beast with three faces."

One of H.D.'s biographers argues that "it was characteristic of H.D. to place undue demands of affection upon those close to her, or those to whom she felt particularly drawn. As a consequence she suffered from imagined slights and disappointments. She also considered it a requisite to withdraw from a relationship when she chose, no matter how insistent her earlier demands had been upon the person involved." This type of push-pull behavior is entirely commensurate with a person who cannot cope with a twosome, possibly because she fears loss and abandonment, and needs the presence of another to lighten the load, as it were. The presence of a third party might also have allowed H.D. to divide her attention, to stop her focusing too much on one individual. Finally, a third party would have also allowed her to maintain the position of the child, the innocent, the novice, if she so wished it. She could be the one always beginning, always new: the "child" to the "parents," identifying with them ("the MacPhersons are almost MYSELF"), as long as the "parents" themselves didn't fall in love with each other the way Pound and Gregg had.

She took a long time to get it right. Her marriage to Richard Aldington, seemingly undertaken at the behest of a third party, Pound, would flounder when another third party intruded. H.D. became pregnant by Aldington during the First World War but lost the child, and she refused to have sex with him again (purportedly on the misadvice of a nurse, who told her not to try to conceive until the war was over). She told him he was "free" to find sexual satisfaction elsewhere while she recovered, but she was nevertheless hurt and dismayed when he fell in love with Dorothy Yorke, especially when they spent the night together under the same roof as her. Unable to manage this second threesome, which once again left her out in the cold instead of treating her like the child to loving parents, she left Aldington, and began a close, intense relationship with D. H. Lawrence. He had come to visit her while she was recuperating from the loss of her baby. They seemed to find something in one another, and H.D. would consult with him, too, just as she had with Aldington and Pound, over her work and her personal life.

There was a possibility that this threesome might just be the kind that would work for her, as Lawrence was then involved with Frieda Weekley, whom he would later marry. Perhaps here, as the second mistress of a writing man, she could find that comforting role where she would be neither the "mother" nor the "wife," but the child-lover, the one Lawrence and Frieda could take care of. It wasn't to be: it seems that Lawrence was not enamoured enough of H.D.'s physical attributes to consider an affair with her (she is caricatured as the rather sexless Hermione in *Women in Love*), and Frieda was far too dominating a presence in his life to acquiesce to another woman on the scene.

H.D. then took up with Cecil Gray, who was infatuated with her. She was frightened of his intense feelings for her, though, ever shy of that intimate one-on-one, and even though she fell pregnant with his child, she ended the relationship. Meanwhile, a wealthy young woman called Winifred Ellerman had begun courting her, and after the birth of H.D.'s daughter, Perdita, she and Ellerman, or Bryher as she was known, moved in together. The ménage à trois that had previously caused her so many problems suddenly seemed to be the answer: Bryher quickly married another ambitious young writer, Robert McAlmon, to keep her lesbianism a secret from her wealthy parents. Why did H.D. agree to her female lover marrying this man? Did she recognize that there was no sexual attraction between Bryher and McAlmon, and therefore felt secure about it, happy to have her own relationship with Bryher somehow "masked" from Aldington and any others who might have made mischief with it? This is not as likely as it seems, for H.D. felt left out when Bryher and McAlmon moved in together.

What seems more likely is that she felt comfortable with someone else absorbing some of Bryher's constant focus on her, while not presenting any danger to their relationship. H.D. played it all carefully, according to her desires and what she could cope with: she did live with Bryher and McAlmon eventually, and encouraged Bryher to adopt her daughter, Perdita. This adoption not only freed H.D. of her baby's need for its mother (yet another one-on-one relationship she doesn't appear to have been able to handle), but it also freed her up to travel, as Bryher could afford to board Perdita with the famous Norland Nannies. It took the pressure off her relationship with Bryher, too. A perfect situation, in other words. Or, almost.

Because it seems to have been a situation without a great deal of physical pleasure. H.D. may have been a mother, yet she also seems to have been a novice when it came to sexual satisfaction. Aldington was too physically similar to Pound, I think, for her to have felt truly eager for his embraces, and biographers have speculated that it was only when she met Kenneth MacPherson, with whom she fell in love, that she actually experienced sexual pleasure. Again, it has been suggested, that Bryher married him, after her divorce from McAlmon, to mask the relationship she and H.D. were sharing, but this seems unlikely, given that there was almost certainly nothing sexual between them at this point. But this extraordinarily odd setup was possibly, ironically enough, H.D.'s ideal: locked into a relationship with two people who loved only her, not each other, and who both actively protected and promoted her welfare, she was finally, I think, the child-lover she wanted to be. With Bryher and MacPherson as her "parents," she could still be the child, the novice. Yet, as she and MacPherson were the only sexually active partners in the triangle, she could also be the woman-lover that her feelings for MacPherson led her to be.

• • • •

The threesome was a lifelong pattern for H.D. that, I would argue, was set up by her early relationship with Pound, the man who was her lover (unfulfilled) and her mentor (fulfilled until she died). H.D.'s understanding that he was too much for her, that he could possibly damage her, but that she couldn't give him up either, made her turn to a third party. In her last memoir, *Tribute to Freud*, a work that records the period from 1933 to 1938, when she was a patient of Sigmund Freud's, first in Vienna and then in London, H.D. tries to answer the kind of contradiction she had set up for herself: how to be both an experienced woman and an innocent, a mother as well as a child? "A girl-child, a doll, an aloof and silent father form this triangle, this family romance, this trinity which follows the recognized religious pattern: *Father*, aloof, distant, the provider, the protector . . . *Mother*, a virgin, the Virgin, that is, an untouched child, adoring, with faith, building a dream and the dream is symbolized by the third member of the trinity, the *Child*, the doll in her arms."

Like Pound, Freud recalled her father for her, but both men were in some way figured as father-lovers in a relationship that would remain unconsummated because, of course, it must ("The Professor said, 'The trouble is—I am an old man—*you do not think it worth your while to love me*"). According to Freud, she was indeed the child, in Vienna "hoping to find my mother. Mother? Mamma. But my mother was dead." During her analysis with Freud, H.D. flagged up that child image, recalling her early family history of childhood games with her brothers and visits to her father's study, as well as her relationship with her mother.

So much of this book is taken up with H.D. as a child, or in the position of the child, that it seems to continue even when she recalls how she felt when she was first launched into London literary society: "My brain staggers now when I remember the deluge of brilliant talk I was inflicted with; what would happen if, and who would come to power when"—once again, in the position of the novice. Freud himself continually made her feel like a child with his manner, she says, imitating the behavior of those in authority: "I felt like a child, summoned to my father's study or my mother's sewing room or told by a teacher to wait in after school, after the others had left, for those 'few words' that were for myself alone. *Stop thief!* What had I done? What was I likely to do? 'I ask only one thing of you children'—my mother's very words."

H.D. struggled in many ways with being an adult, sexual woman, in spite of her engagement to Pound, her marriage to Aldington, her feelings for Lawrence, and her affairs with Gray and MacPherson. Her relationship with Bryher seems to have resembled more a close companionship without the trauma of passion. As a mother she miscarried one child and then gave the second away. After all, what mother can also indulge in being the child? As her quotation from *Tribute to Freud* at the beginning of this chapter indicates, only the Virgin Mother is allowed such status, to be the "untouched child" as well as the mother.

It tempts one to ask, who might be the father in this scenario? It can only be God, or god-like ("aloof, distant . . . a little too far away and giant-like"). In the "family romance," H.D. repeatedly wants to be that impossible combination of miraculous Virgin Mother, both woman and child—she plays the child to Pound's father figure but is devastated when he goes off with other women because she also wants to be the Virgin-Mother-lover. She plays the child to Bryher's dual adoptive mother and protective father roles (which is configured first by Bryher's marriage to McAlmon, then again when she marries MacPherson), while also playing the role of lover (again, possibly more platonic than sexual; an innocent role).

The father can be a man or a woman; H.D. herself wants to be both mother and child in the eternal family triangle. But in *Tribute*, another insight is given. Here, she recounts an incident from childhood when she and her brother were on a shopping trip with her mother: her brother defies their mother, refusing to go home, and sits on the curb in a sulk. Their mother laughs, walks away. H.D., the sister, is torn: should she follow her brother or her mother? She chooses the former, sitting on the curb beside him. She allies herself with the boy in this triangle. I would argue that, throughout her life, in spite of her alliances with and passions for women, H.D. always did choose to ally herself with the boy. It was Pound who launched her, after all, not Frances Gregg, and it was Pound's literary advice she sought, even though Gregg was a writer, too.

Yet it was the boy who also threatened the novice, virginal, untouched state that she maintained for herself. It was the boy who made her a mother (in the guise of Aldington and Gray), as well as a published poet (in the guise of Pound). It was the boy who made it all real. Which is what frightened her. This may have been psychologically divisive, as H.D. was aware. In a letter to Bryher on December 7, 1934, trying to figure herself out, she writes: "I have a sort of split-infinitive, or split dual personality. One of them is writing, and one of them is NOT writing. I am trying my best to get these two together . . . I know the whole catch. I date it back to pre-primal scene. And I made up a sort of 'ideal' brother or father who did not match the original, so the 'ideal' and the real go on, on quite separate rails, all the time. Rummel-Rodeck were 'ideal,' plus Frances Gregg and you (that is, I have father-mother together), the whole tribe, Ezra, RA [Richard Aldington], Cissie [Cecil Gray] etc were all 'real' . . . the problem is how to get the two rails together . . ."

The boys are "real"; the girls are "ideal." Boys threaten her novice state unless they can be sort of "brothers" to her. Pound, the brother who was there right at the beginning, presented H.D. with a choice. It's interesting that in this letter to Bryher, she links her writing with the split between the real and the ideal, too. It is the real that helps her produce the work, but she needs the ideal, too, hence her need to "get the two rails together." It seems that for H.D. the most conducive psychological state for her was one which carried two contradictory thoughts at the same time.

The state of the eternal novice suited H.D. In spite of the mixed relationships, the bisexuality, the births and the abortions, there is something nun-like that speaks to the untouched, the set-apart, in H.D.'s personal life—possibly the result of her fear of abandonment. Poetically, she remained a novice, too, in spite of the huge body of publications that stretch over six decades: even in old age, she was still asking her former mentor, Ezra Pound, for advice about her writing. Part of the reason H.D. became the great poet she did was that she recognized the importance of learning, of beginning. She wanted to remain in that place. She wanted, ultimately, to remain a novice.

Rebecca West and H.G. Wells.

3. The "Mother": Rebecca West and H. G. Wells

"You set out in life to be a free woman."
"But is it my fault," she asked, "that I have to be a free mother?
That wasn't in the bargain."

—*H. G. Wells in Love,*
1942

There is no life for us separately. Just a few nice hours over our
books and articles and then when we can't write any longer an
empty feeling.

—Rebecca West to
H. G. Wells, 1916

Unlike H.D. (or Jean Rhys later), Rebecca West needed no male lover to name her, or to give her her author's identity. She was the highly able author of her own public persona, claiming her name and her identity before any male mentor or poet could do it for her. More than that, she gave her only son her pseudonymous surname of West, too, calling him Anthony Panther West. There was no hint of who his father was in any of his names; the nick-name, "Panther," was another invention of his mother's, initially for herself. In some remarkable interplay between fantasy and reality, public and private, West manufactured most of her son's real name from her two invented ones.

Her son was the result of her affair with a married man, the writer H. G. Wells, whom she first met in 1912, so perhaps this strange interplay was necessary. Yet in her private reality of being an unmarried mother in the early twentieth century, West was far less confident or defiant than her public fantasy of assuming a fake name would suggest. Born Cicily ("Cissie") Fairfield on 21st December 1892, West took up her pseudonym apparently at the behest of her mother, who seems to have been worried about her reputation when she began writing. But the choice of name was Cissie's own: in Ibsen's 1886 play, *Rosmersholm*, Rebecca West is the name of the mistress of a married man who joins him in a double suicide. It was a connection some say West (the author) came later to regret, perhaps because instead of maintaining a distance between her private self and her public persona, as the name was meant to, it actually began to collapse that distance. Especially once H. G. Wells came into the picture and West really did, like Ibsen's heroine, become the mistress of a married man.

But when she chose this name in the spring of 1912, West was only nineteen years old, and perhaps she thought that an Ibsen heroine would be an appropriate role model for a young woman with feminist interests. West had just begun writing reviews for Dora Marsden's radical feminist weekly, *The Freewoman*, and she was catching important people's attention with the directness and lack of fear she displayed in those articles. The young woman who had initially thought she could make a career on the stage (another arena where public and private boundaries are blurred) was becoming a celebrated writer—and remarkably quickly.

West was more than the author of her own identity, though, and more even than the author of her son's. She named her lover, too: West is credited with inventing her own and H. G. Wells's nicknames for each other, "Jaguar" and "Panther," which they used throughout their ten-year relationship. Private names were not just a sign of special affection, though. They were used in this instance to shore up the reality of what was essentially a fantasy relationship: West and Wells would often refer to each other as husband and wife, while he was married to someone else. As he had no intention of ever leaving his wife, Jane Wells, for West or for any other woman, this could only have been a fantasy on both sides. How much more one of them may have invested in this fantasy than the other, however, is part of the perennial problem of West's relationship with Wells.

And it *is* a problem, for many readers, biographers, and critics of West's life and work. Maintaining a public fantasy against a private reality is one thing, but when that private reality is almost a fantasy, too, dangerous compromises are inevitable. It's remarkable that West and Wells didn't drive each other, and those around them, insane with their pretense. Sometimes even they themselves weren't sure which was reality and which was fantasy. (Wells wrote to West on one occasion, "I thought, 'I'm just going on with this business. Do I love this woman at all?' I thought, 'I've made up a story about her and it isn't the true one. What is the true one?'" He might well ask.)

But a messy confusion of fantasy and reality may be the nearest we get to explaining the true story, or in this case, the highly contradictory actions of Rebecca West. One-time suffragette, celebrated journalist, bestselling novelist, travel writer, Dame of the British Empire, West was also the mistress of a married man for ten years, and an unmarried mother at the age of twenty-one. She covered all the bases, both the powerless ones as well as the powerful. Hers is a story of success and strength, of celebrity and fortune, of influence and impact. And of the misery of a secret, destructive love affair; of an often dishonest, occasionally even cowardly, relationship with her only child.

How do we reconcile all these different, clashing aspects of Rebecca West's life? And those aspects of her affair with Wells, too, a man who said of her in later years, "In all my life I think I have really loved only three women steadfastly; my first wife, my second wife and Moura Broudberg . . . I do not know if I loved Rebecca West, though I was certainly in love with her towards the latter part of our liaison." Should we even try to reconcile those apparent contradictions?

• • • •

Rebecca West had a difficult upbringing. Her parents, Charles and Isabella Fairfield, had not had a happy marriage. Three girls were born in total: the eldest, Laetitia, or "Letty," became a doctor; next came Winifred, the gentle but nervous beauty of the family; followed finally by Cicily, or "Cissie," as she was known. All three were academic and interested in women's suffrage, perhaps all the more so because they had witnessed their errant father gambling away much of the family's income and experienced his constant absences from the home. West's 1957 autobiographical novel of her childhood, *The Fountain Overflows*, is an example perhaps of an attempt to turn reality into fantasy, what her first biographer Victoria Glendinning called "her need to handle this first crisis by turning it into writing." In *The Fountain Overflows*, West shows a younger version of herself, aware that the wife of a mayor from another town who has turned up on the family doorstep is actually one more of her father's abandoned loves. This was based, needless to say, on a real event.

In this novel, too, West shows the constant difficulties her mother had with money, her furniture being sold behind her back by her husband, as well as the daughters' skirmishes with fellow schoolgirls who looked down on them for being less well off. In real life, the couple had moved from Melbourne, where they had first met, back to England and then briefly to Scotland. But still they struggled, and soon they relocated to London, where West herself was born. By the time she was eight years old, the marriage had almost irretrievably broken down and her father left for

Africa. Isabella promptly moved her family back to Edinburgh, where they stayed until West was seventeen. West's father had returned from Africa some time before, but had chosen to continue living apart from his family, in Liverpool. Eventually, with her mother and sisters, West moved back to London to begin her stage career.

By 1911, when she was eighteen, she had already become disillusioned with the prospect of life on the stage, and she decided to try writing. Her first published reviews were for the newly established magazine *The Freewoman*, which focused on women's issues and included arts reviews as well as political pieces. West's precociously critical, amusing, and well-informed articles about some of the most famous writers of the day, literary figures like Mrs. Humphrey Ward and Arnold Bennett, caused a stir, as did her championing of that daring new writer of sexually provocative novels, D. H. Lawrence, and this all brought her to the attention of important people. Ford Madox Ford, together with his mistress Violet Hunt, invited her to the literary soirees they regularly held. West took all this newfound fame in stride, and it's interesting that her status as the youngest daughter of a single mother never appeared to affect her confidence.

Her father, by this time, had been dead for five years. West never really resolved her feelings about her father, adoring the charm of his personality while loathing the way he had treated his family. Fond of his daughters, he seems to have been an easy father to get along with. But West, like most children, missed the stability a more conservative and reliable father might have provided, and it meant that she formed a close bond with her mother, a bond Wells would come to loathe. West commented later in life that Wells had tried to part her from her family and friends, and Wells acknowledges as much in his memoir, *H. G. Wells in Love*, the "postscript" to his two-volume autobiography, *An Experiment in Autobiography*, where he complains that "we were never left to ourselves." Certainly it seems that her childhood experiences had impressed on West a need for independence, coupled with anger at her father's abandonment of them. But can that explain the fantasy/reality of the next ten years of her life, after her initial meeting with Wells?

Things moved fairly swiftly between them from the first moment. Explanations for West's interest in Wells have ranged from her being attracted to Wells's experience (she was almost twenty years old, to his forty-six) to her falling in love with an unattainable married man, or being dazzled by the celebrity of this literary star—Wells was, by this time, the extremely successful author of turn-of-the-century novels like *The Time Machine* (1895), *The War of the Worlds* (1898), and *The Invisible Man* (1897), as well as more recent social-realist fiction like *The History of Mr. Polly* (1910) and *Ann Veronica* (1909). One biographer, Carl Rollyson, cites sex as the reason, claiming West just "wanted to meet men" (possibly "to escape a home life that had become stifling"). He also presents West as man-hungry and gushing ("she wanted a lover"), and Wells as a highly satisfactory object of her affections, given that he had "'exceptionally smooth skin,' a honeyed scent and a rather large penis." The sex reason—that Wells might have been very good in bed and that he and West were very sexually compatible—can only be given in support of the *continuation* of their relationship, however. Presumably West didn't know about Wells's "qualities" when she first met him, fully dressed as they both were. And given her apparent desperation for a man, as Rollyson presents it, perhaps size wouldn't have mattered one way or the other.

Wells himself, in later life, rather nastily put West's interest in him down to her being "saturated with literary ambition," claiming that his "flagrant successfulness must have had a particular glamour for her." In the midst of myriad reasons for her initial feelings for this man, surprisingly, the obvious, simpler attraction of one writer for another is often ignored. West didn't need Wells to make her name, or to introduce her to powerful people, in spite of his certainty that the "glamour" of his fame must have won her over. Why isn't the writing itself considered to have been enough of an attraction?

After one early visit of Wells to the home West shared with her mother, West excitedly wrote to her sister in a letter: "Our drawing room was hallowed yesterday by the presence of Wells, who dropped in suddenly and stayed 2 ½ hours. Wasn't it glorious?" She loved his talk; he was "the most interesting man she had ever met," full of "immense vitality" and "a kind of hunger for ideas." One month later, after she'd been to lunch with him, she wrote to Dora Marsden, "I must say I like Wells. He hasn't made love to me and it is fun watching his quick mind splashing about in the infinite."

The fact she even felt the need to mention that he had not made love to her is revealing, especially coming as it does just after she describes her mother's disapproval of him, but it is not quite revealing enough. Was she disappointed by this lack of indiscretion on his part, or was she intrigued by it? Was she even, perhaps, relieved, given the difference in their ages? There's no sense here that she finds him physically attractive, in spite of his "vitality." It's hard to be sure what she was really feeling, just as it is hard to be sure what she felt about so much else in their relationship. And so, to understand this moment, and the subsequent moments between them, we must begin where anyone with an interest in the West-Wells affair must begin: with the writing.

Certainly, there is little evidence that West was the kind of woman who would see herself as the lesser half of the relationship, not at the beginning, anyway. And especially when we consider what she actually wrote about Wells in the first place. It was West's coruscating review of Wells's latest novel, *Marriage*, that first caught his attention: "Of course he [Wells] is the old maid among novelists; even the sex obsession that lay clotted on *Ann Veronica* and *The New Machiavelli* like cold white sauce was merely old maids' mania, the reaction towards the flesh of a mind too long absorbed in airships and colloids. The Cranford-like charm of his slow, spinsterish gossip made *Kipps* [Wells's 1905 novel] the delightful book it was; but it palls when, page after page and chapter after chapter, one is told how to furnish a house."

Fired straight at her target, undermining Wells's longstanding sexual reputation with her repeated "old maid" jibe as well as accusations about the focus of his new work, these are hardly words inclined to make a male writer fall in love with the woman writing them, and that was not, in any case, West's intention. But at this point in his life, Wells was a middle-aged man who was well into his comfortable but unexciting second marriage. He had married his cousin, Isabel, but it didn't last long, and after his divorce he settled with Amy Catherine Robbins, whom he had renamed "Jane." He and Jane now had two young sons, Gip and Frank, aged eleven and nine, and they were all living together at Easton Glebe, in Essex, in a new house specially designed for them.

Wells could afford such an extravagant residence after a decade or so of succeeding commercial hits. Credited with inventing a whole new literary genre, never mind writing superlative novels, Wells had indulged his fascination with the future as well as his social conscience in his works of science fiction. But it was his more personal, social-realist novels, like *The History of Mr. Polly* and the *Mr. Britling Sees It Through*, that he imagined would stand the real test of time.

As Wells later acknowledged, at the time he met West he had a sexual reputation to rival Don Juan's, and was regarded as a "promiscuous lover" (something which, he later maintained, "did me no harm with her"). He had shocked many in his political circle when he had an affair in 1909 with Amber Reeves, the daughter of two friends of his. The affair resulted in pregnancy and the birth of a baby daughter, Anna Jane. Two years previously he had also impregnated another former mistress, the novelist Dorothy Richardson, with whom he'd had an affair that lasted about two and a half years, but she miscarried. He subsequently had a relationship with Violet Hunt, who was now living with Ford Madox Ford, and just before he met West, he had become entangled with the writer Elizabeth von Arnim (whom he called "little e" and who was the cousin of Katherine Mansfield). But Arnim annoyed him with her mimicry of his wife, Jane, and her demands that he treat their relationship more seriously, and it seems he was looking for a way out of the affair.

Wells's wife, Jane, apparently consented to these affairs, provided they did not impact her family life with her boys, and did not reduce her to public ridicule. The question of her complicity in her husband's betrayals, though, at a time when divorce was still considered shocking, when she had two young boys to consider and when she had no income of her own, must be the subject of some dispute. Perhaps she, too, preferred to indulge in a fantasy of her own about her husband and her family life. It certainly made life easier, although the calm way she purportedly took Wells's announcement at dinner that West was about to have a baby, and the way she expressed her concern for West's welfare, surely stretches the happy family fantasy to its limits.

But it's true that West and Wells's relationship could be said to have begun on an antagonistic note, with this review by a daring young nobody of a girl, journalistically bear-baiting the famous, acclaimed older male author. It could also be argued that this moment set the pattern for their subsequent relationship, and more—that it was precisely this antagonism that excited Wells. It's quite something for a man of promiscuous sexual behavior to be called an "old maid" in print, and especially by a young woman. When West arrived for lunch at Wells's home at his own invitation, that September day, not long after he had read her review, she was unchaperoned and not exactly the epitome of "maidenly reserve," as Rollyson notes, implying by this description that she perhaps had the intention of seducing him. She might, at the very least, have expected him to try to seduce her (again, it's not clear in the letter she wrote after this lunch took place whether she is disappointed on this score or not). She would certainly have known of his reputation at this time, but, as Rollyson also points out, Wells was old enough to be her father. I don't believe West saw beyond the excitement of one of the most famous writers in the country inviting her to lunch with him, but she was certainly taken with him during this encounter. Also, she might have been alone, but he wasn't—his wife, Jane, was present, although whether she remained by his side for the entire five hours that West spent in his company that day is unclear.

Wells might have had other motives in inviting her to his home, however, although he didn't know beforehand what she looked like. Perhaps he was surprised by the appearance of this intellectually provocative young writer: he admitted later to being taken with more than her mind, and photographs of West at this time testify to what he might have found so appealing about her. A highly attractive, exotic, dark-haired young woman, with large brown eyes set wide apart (what Wells later called "expressive" and "troubled"), she had a generous mouth and an inquiring expression.

But what exactly was it about Wells that won West over (besides being desperate, as Rollyson cattily implies)? I believe Rebecca West fell in love with Wells's words, as much as he fell for hers, a surprising claim to make given that it was West's *criticism* of Wells's writing that brought her to his attention, not her praise of it. How did she fall in love with a man whose words she didn't appear to like, then?

Whatever West's first feelings about him were, her criticism actually appealed to Wells. He, it could be argued, fell in love with *her* words, even while she was criticizing his. Of their first meeting, he later said, "I had never met anything like her before, and I doubt if there ever was anything like her before." He also later claimed that "I don't think I had any intention of making love to her" when he invited her to lunch. If Wells himself is to be believed, it was West's writing alone that caught his attention. Her professional writing, that is.

Her published words moved him in ways that her personal appeals in letters did not, as we shall see, and it's useful to ask why that was. Was it simply the flattery of published attention that worked on him, the fact that a rather feisty young literary woman had taken him on, in print? Or did her criticism titillate him out of the safety of being a celebrated and commercially successful author, reminding him of the danger of failure that pursuing a writing career could present, the kind of danger he had once faced as a young man?

Whatever the appeal, there is no doubt that the reality of this beginning is almost as confusing as any fantasy version of male power over female insubordination or disrespect might have it. Because it compels us to ask why Wells appeared to enjoy being put down in print, and if that was why he wanted to meet his accuser in the flesh. We can't help but wonder if she was just a challenge for him, or if he wanted to see if he could mold her. Did he agree with what she said about his books? Did he want to see if she had the courage to repeat her claims to his face? And why did she fall for a man whose writing turned him into "an old maid"?

I think the true story of West's falling for Wells, and vice versa, is much more subversive than the biographies and memoirs have so far suggested. They sell us a recognizable fantasy of a young girl throwing away her literary ambitions on a man who possibly doesn't really love her, and with whom she has a child he won't even publicly admit is his. But it can't explain the appeal in the first place of such an affair for a young woman who had canvassed for votes for women in Edinburgh when she was still a schoolgirl, who had been involved in suffragette marches that turned violent, and who had even written about unmarried mothers (before becoming one herself). There is always disillusion and disappointment when ideals and behavior don't correlate, a struggle to understand seemingly inexplicable actions and choices. West's alliance with Wells will, for some, forever contradict her own feminist principles about women's autonomy and authority; it will always be seen as a betrayal of her real self.

Certainly, there were times in her life when West saw her history with Wells in exactly this light, and her regret begs the crucial question each woman in this book must answer: What did she continue to need him for? Why did such a startling and original talent, harnessed to a strong personality and enough determination to see that talent through, attach herself to a relationship in which she was always going to be the less important partner? Why did she put up with the many tiny but daily humiliations that are the lot of the mistress to a married man, the kind of life she detailed so well in *Sunflower*, her unfinished novel about the end of her relationship with Wells? Was it simply because they shared a child? That still doesn't explain why, when she began her writing life with such power and independence, she seemed to give up that very power.

In the five months after that initial luncheon, Rebecca West and H. G. Wells appear to have met up often, but it wasn't until the early spring that they kissed for the first time. The intensity that contact engendered in her seems to have frightened Wells off, though, and he retreated, much to West's anguish. Her mother, who had suspected something was going on between them, couldn't be in any doubt when West had what appears to have been a breakdown over Wells's retreat: living in the same house together, she would have been aware of West's pain over the end of an affair that had scarcely begun. While West tried to hide some things from her mother, Isabella saw a telegram delivered to West from Wells that read innocuously enough: "No hurry about the artichoke, Wells"; she didn't like the familiar tone or the private jokes between the married Wells and her youngest daughter. And so, alarmed at her daughter's deep despondency over Wells, Isabella immediately whisked her away on holiday to France and Spain in an attempt to distract her and help her forget him.

It didn't work. While abroad, West wrote two pieces, both of which would be published in *The New Freewoman*, in August 1913. One of the essays was an astonishing short story, "At Valladolid," which told of a young woman who had tried, unsuccessfully, to kill herself twice, first with a gun and then by overdosing on veronal, a strong sedative, after her lover had rejected her. Like many debut works of fiction, there was more than a hint of autobiography in this story, though West always denied she had ever attempted to kill herself, saying only "I thought of doing all those things."

In March, though, in a letter that perhaps anticipated the feeling behind the short story, and which certainly revealed a great deal more about the emotional torture she was putting herself through, West had written the following desperate words to Wells:

During the next few days I shall either put a bullet through my head or commit something more shattering to myself than death . . . I don't understand why you wanted me three months ago and don't want me now. I wish I knew why that were so. It's something I can't understand, something I despise . . . Of course you're quite right. I haven't anything to give you . . . I always knew that you would hurt me to death some day, but I hoped to choose the time and place. You've always been unconsciously hostile to me and I haven't tried to conciliate you by hacking away at my love for you, cutting it down to the little thing that was the most you wanted . . . You can't conceive a person resenting the humiliation of an emotional failure so much that they twice tried to kill themselves: that seems silly to you. I can't conceive of a person who runs about lighting bonfires and yet nourishes a dislike of flame: that seems silly to me.

You've literally ruined me. I'm burned down to my foundations. I may build myself again or I may not . . . You have done for me utterly. You know it. That's why you are trying to persuade yourself that I am a coarse, sprawling, boneless creature, and so it doesn't matter . . . I would give my whole life to feel your arms around me again. I wish you had loved me. I wish you liked me.

In spite of West's later denials that she had attempted suicide, in this letter she makes it clear how closely she identifies with the heroine of her short story. She understands Wells is frightened of how much she feels for him, that he can't cope with this Big Love that she has to offer (the kind of Big Love that Elizabeth Smart, who would also write similar recriminating yet testifying missives to George Barker, also experienced). But, exactly as Barker did with Smart's letters, Wells simply ignored West's epistolary appeals because proof of how great her love for him was was exactly what he didn't want to hear. He was clearly frightened of it, and of her.

This outpouring of West's feelings of love, her words of hurt at Wells's withdrawal and her disbelief that he didn't love her enough to continue to see her, was perhaps never even sent to him. Yet this seems unlikely, when this cool, three-line letter was sent by Wells, apparently in response to her words: "How can I be your friend to this accompaniment? I don't see that I can be of any use or help to you at all. You have my entire sympathy—but until we can meet on a reasonable basis—Goodbye."

How did she feel when she read this response from him?

West's personal words, changed nothing. Did she despair, knowing that it was finally over? Did she feel gratified that he'd even responded at all? She was very young, only twenty, and the intensity of her feelings here, their sincerity and their lack of equivocation, reflects both her youth and her lack of experience, although not gullibility or simplicity. She believed that telling him how she really felt would affect him, would change the course of their relationship. She didn't want to use traditional "feminine wiles" to woo him, and she was too sharp to play a game that might ensnare him yet undoubtedly make her hate herself. But it seems that she didn't understand she was expected to show less, not more, of her real feelings. West might have been razor-sharp in her articles, but her breakdown after Wells dropped her, and her flirtation with suicide, suggest a vulnerability the professional reviews don't show.

Wells, on the contrary, more experienced as he was in love affairs, picking women up then dropping them again, was worldly and sophisticated, but he could only play the kind of game that similarly experienced and rather cynical adults could play. This is perhaps why her personal words couldn't reach him, and also perhaps why their affair would never have resumed had she not been a professional writer. Because it was her professional words, in the work that she subsequently published in *The New Freewoman*, that did what her personal appeals couldn't. One article in particular, entitled "Nana," was about a café singer West had heard while in Spain with her mother, and whom she described thus: "Now Nana's dazzling body declared it lucidly, 'Here am I, nothing but flesh and blood. When your toys of the mind and the spirit are all broken, come back to my refreshing flesh and blood!'" "Nana" elicited the miraculous response from Wells that West had been hoping for:

"You are writing gorgeously again. Please resume being friends

... Nana was tremendous. You are as wise as God when you write—
at times—and then you are a tortured, untidy ... little disaster of a girl
who can't even manage the most elementary trick of her sex. You
are like a beautiful voice singing out of a darkened room into which
one gropes and finds nothing ..."

Those words—"Please resume being friends"—must have
proved irresistible. How could they not have been? And yet, according to one biographer, "Rebecca ... did not respond." Wisely,
and perhaps at last employing the only kind of "feminine wiles"
she was comfortable with, she resisted his personal appeals, his
praise, his merging of her personality and her writing gifts. Or at
least, she held out for a while—for a few months. By November
1913 they were lovers. And by January, she'd found out that she
was pregnant. Wells later blamed himself, as he should have, recognizing what it did to her career: "It was our second encounter
and she became pregnant. It was entirely unpremeditated. She
wanted to write. It should not have happened, and since I was the
more experienced person, the blame is wholly mine."

Telling her that she was "as wise as God" when she wrote,
though, was perhaps the key. Wells did a good line in praise, but
more than that, he actually meant what he said. There is no doubt
that West was an extraordinary writer at this time: Wells wasn't
a fool when it came to other people's work. He could prove to
be both contradictory and hypocritical in some of his thoughts
about his relationships later in life—he claimed in *H. G. Wells in
Love*, written in the mid-1930s but not published until 1984, that
"we did at times love each other very much. We love each other
still" in a chapter that also painted her in personally crude and
unflattering terms. But he wasn't confused or confusing about
good writing. Wells held out for West the remarkable possibility
that he admired her, loved her even, for her writing. To be loved
for disagreeing, to be adored for defying what everyone else was

saying—this was an unusual reaction for a woman to receive from a male writer, and this is partly what West fell for. But to be loved for one's "gorgeous" writing: that, in this case, was everything.

• • • •

To the many critics and biographers who look back at its history, the only way to explain the longevity of the West-Wells relationship has been to assume that West performed an ultimate act of surrender when she sacrificed herself and her writing—perhaps foolishly—to be with Wells. Fay Weldon's 1985 portrait for the *Lives of Modern Women* series, for instance, depicts West in 1914, on the birth of her son, Anthony, as utterly confused. Weldon imagines how West might have expressed her confusion to her doctor sister, who was quite perplexed by West's choice of man and lifestyle. This entirely imagined voice is alternately submissive and helpless, one minute declaring, "I know what I've given up. But this feeling is so rich and deadly, Letty, you have no idea. Love and motherhood and babies!" and the next crying out in anguish about her writing future: "What about my career? What's to become of me? What have I done?"

If West ever did ask these questions of herself at this point, then she might well have continued asking them for the rest of her life. What *had* she done? And further, she might have asked, what exactly had she done to deserve desperate, demeaning portrayals like this? Her first biographer, Victoria Glendinning, is much kinder, but still refers to West as having been an "ingénue" when she came to the attention of Ford Madox Ford and Violet Hunt in 1912, shortly before she met Wells himself. And we will find out from Jean Rhys's experiences exactly how little power the ingénue wields.

A later biographer, Carl Rollyson, reminds us of the "stinging jab of a style" and the "droll sense of the occasion equivalent to a great actor's timing" that made West's early journalism stand out so well and cause such a stir, but he also implies West was naive in falling for Wells. Bored of his current mistress, Elizabeth von Arnim, Wells simply "needed a fresh turn." Poor, foolish Rebecca, Rollyson insinuates, not to have realized. Possibly he thinks she was just too desperate for a man to have the wit to figure out he was just using her. Again, though, this is a reductive view of West and her interest in Wells. Both Rollyson and Weldon see the writing and the sexual attraction as completely separate things that West must choose between. It doesn't occur to them that they were part of the same package.

And so, in these stories of West's life, we learn that she surrendered; she was weak; she was foolish. Part of our problem with Rebecca West is that she, like every other woman writer in this book, fell in love. And fell in love inappropriately. Because West didn't fall in love with just anybody: she fell in love with a Great Man, a famous author who was already married and the father of two small boys. As Weldon remarked of West's submission to Wells's charms, "If young women lie down in the path of this energy, what do they expect? They will be steamrollered!" Such a simple story, told to women since the dawn of time. She should have resisted better. She should have behaved better. She had no one but herself to blame. She lay down when she should have stood tall.

This is yet another appealing fantasy, one that conforms to our view of women who get involved with inappropriate men, implying that falling in love means weakness. What's more, it's a fantasy that tells us, once their son was born and the relationship was well underway, West and Wells didn't really help each other with their art at all. A long time after their relationship ended, Wells himself said "we did harm to each other as writers," highlighting their artistic differences, and claiming even that "a considerable antipathy developed between us as writers." West herself was to imply that she resisted much of the authorial advice he gave her, and Wells seemed to agree, writing that "I realise I got much the best of our relationship." Was this true?

It's certainly true that West often portrayed herself as the wronged woman in the relationship with Wells, especially in the early days, as the victim of his wife Jane's machinations against her. According to Gordon N. Ray, who conducted interviews with West for his book, *H. G. Wells and Rebecca West*, West viewed Jane as a "hypocrite," a "false goddess, the Virgin Mother, the nonsexual women to whom she as the sexual woman was being sacrificed." West viewed the perfect home that Jane Wells set up at Easton Glebe with suspicion. She believed that if it weren't for Jane, Wells would marry her. She was sensitive to the fact that a prospective marriage to Wells would force him to abandon his two sons by Jane, but this did not make her stop her repeated demands that Wells leave his wife. In this letter from March 1923, Wells writes to West: "I don't think it fair for you to turn on me with this grow-ing mania of yours about the injustice of my treatment of you in not murdering Jane."

There is little in this picture that signifies power. And yet, it was West who wooed Wells, not the other way round. Becoming the mistress to a married man may not seem like a powerful move to make, but West *chose* to enter into this situation. Wells did not woo her and lie to her about his position. West was not the gullible victim of a dishonest man. She knew exactly what Wells's position was, and it made no difference to what she wanted. There is a cer-tain power to be had in going after what one desires most, in spite of the consequences. West did not like to acknowledge the power that she might have held in her relationship with Wells, prefer-ring instead to emphasize her lack of it. It is possible, though, that this was a strategy she believed would ultimately yield her more power, as he conceded it to her.

Rather like Wells in his memoirs, seesawing back and forth

about his feelings for her, West, too, in later years, would veer from this view of herself as a victim to one of her relationship with Wells as a "a union of equals"—insofar as equality was feasible between a young, eager girl and an older, experienced man at the beginning of the twentieth century—"that they were to be two writers living, working and loving together." But, without a doubt, the birth of their son, Anthony, in August 1914 had made any attempt at equality extremely difficult. Wells wrote shortly after the birth to West, "You have got to take care of me and have me fed and have me peaceful and comfortable" in their new home, clearly making her the caregiver in their life together, while granting her authority, albeit only in domestic matters: "You are the woman and you are to be the maker and ruler in all this life." Although he confirmed that "you also write," it was the domestic situation that he stressed, and his own comfort most of all. It was also up to West to make sure Anthony was looked after properly, as well as to make conditions as palatable as possible for her lover. And once this was all done, to get some writing completed, too!

A baby might make calls on *her* personal and professional time, but Wells made it clear that their son could not make any calls on *his*. On one occasion, he wrote to her, "I wish we could fix up some sort of life that would detach us lovers a little more from the nursery . . . Can't you fix up some sort of living with your sisters [and Anthony] with me not about, and me and you have a love life together." West's relationship with Wells, both in its private fantasy world as well as in the public, real world, put her in the subordinate position of the mistress to the married man, the protégé to the mentor, the child-woman to the older man, the newcomer to the established celebrity. Becoming a mother simply reinforced that powerless position, it appears. It didn't give West an extra hold over Wells or make their relationship more equal. On the contrary, it made her more subservient to him, and this reinforced subservience allowed their relationship to continue.

How, then, do we situate this relationship in a book that seeks to show women writers deriving a kind of literary power or benefit from a relationship that appears to be doing them damage? All of the women writers included in this volume made a kind of Faustian pact with the writer men they loved. In exchange for what benefited their art, they took on board certain behaviors, attitudes, or treatment from their male partners, the kind that they very likely wouldn't have stood from anyone else.

But Rebecca West's is perhaps the trickiest case to make here because we're forced to ask, again and again, if this was really how it was for her, with a disheartening feeling that, yes, it possibly was. We are forced to accept that Rebecca West stayed in a relationship that often publicly humiliated her because she had had a child with a married man. Wells was still nervous about public disapproval—he didn't like going to the theater with her in case he was recognized. She let herself down when she pretended that she didn't have a son at all. Wells claimed it was West's mother and sisters who "forced upon her idiotic lies and pretences; for example, that our Anthony was an 'adopted' child; and would not let her be straightforward with her servants"—yet he seems to have been perfectly happy to go along with the idea of West telling people that Anthony was her infant nephew. She let down her writing by having to be a single mother, giving her attention to her child and not to her work. According to Gordon N. Ray, "under the conditions that her life with Wells imposed on her, she could work only half-heartedly and irregularly." By the end of her ten years with Wells, it seems West could claim few literary or personal benefits from her relationship with him.

Yet Ray also says that "a good part of the day was 'given over to work' by both of them, and certainly what West did manage to write during this period doesn't really bear out this idea that Wells was bad for her. Her connection with him did her no harm in the eyes of the literary world—a large number of reviews for prestigious magazines like the *New Republic* were commissioned from her over the decade they were together, and Wells also encouraged her to complete what would be an acclaimed biography of the recently deceased author Henry James. She also found the time to write an extraordinary first novel, *The Return of the Soldier*. Even so, how can we be sure West wouldn't have achieved all this without Wells? It was, after all, the years *after* the end of her relationship with him that saw her output really advance, with novels like *The Fountain Overflows* and the two-volume travel memoir *Black Lamb and Grey Falcon*. These are the works that really made her name stand the test of time.

It's possible to see West's time with Wells, the bestselling writer of twenty years' standing by the time she met him, as a kind of literary apprenticeship that flowered best once that apprenticeship was served, and the relationship—its sexual momentum as well as its literary uses—over. Gaps in the story lead us to speculate on letters West wrote to Wells that we shall never read, because he destroyed them. We may also speculate on the odd lack of a diary or journal that West might have kept throughout the course of their relationship—odd because, as a professional author and critic, she would have been expected to record her thoughts about her relationship with another author in writing—where we might have heard her thoughts about it as it progressed. There are no memoirs from those who were party to the affair, such as friends of the couple or those who assisted the young mother in the early years of her relationship. Her sisters never wrote about her relationship with Wells, nor did her mother. What record we do have is mainly from Wells's side of the story: his own autobiography, an early novel commemorating his relationship with West, called *The Research Magnificent*, and the letters he wrote to her during their relationship. There is also Anthony Panther West's novel about his upbringing, *Heritage*.

West's view of the relationship is far less easily detectable:

some of it can be found in the posthumously published novel, *Sunflower*, and critics have found parallels in her early novel, *The Return of the Soldier*. Her memoir, *Family Memories*, first published in 1987, covers her parents' history and her own upbringing, as well as the period immediately before she met Wells, yet even this memoir cannot be considered completely factual. Its editor, Faith Evans, comments: "It would . . . take a psychoanalytic critic to disentangle her 'real' memories from those which entered her adult imagination from family legend or her subconscious." There is relatively little autobiographical material for such a prominent literary figure, and especially for a key period of her life. And so, assumptions have tended to follow a typical path, to tell a typical story: foolish woman's talent ruined, or at least constrained, by a powerful male genius. But it isn't necessarily true. It's what the gaps have told us, thus far. But they can also tell us something else.

• • • •

"Every mother is a judge who sentences the children for the sins of the father." This was the epigraph to *The Judge*, the second novel West published, and it came right at the end of her relationship with Wells. We know that West chafed against being shut up in the series of houses Wells found for her and their son, miles from London, where they could not be gossiped about. Britain was embroiled in the Great War, but by 1915, London was considered safe enough and she moved from the country into the city. There, West worked on her study of Henry James, while Wells continued with his novel, *Mr. Britling Sees It Through*.

Around this time, in the midst of seemingly endless quarrels about dealing with the servants, inadequate living quarters, and whether Wells was prepared to leave his wife for her or not, something crucial happened. In an important writing moment, West got Wells through a sticky period: "When H. G. foundered in the writing of *Britling* in the fall of 1915, he showed it to Rebecca, who gave him the impetus to complete the novel: 'It does no end of good to get you into my work. I was frightfully *tired* of the old book and now it's fresh and alive again. All because old Panther has read it.'"

Evidence of Wells encouraging West with her journalism and of West helping Wells with his novel is often hard to see. Many have acknowledged it only in passing, preferring instead to see the difficulties of, and hindrances to, writing together the way that they did before Anthony came along. But it was undeniably difficult and stressful for West once Anthony was born. Wells found it easier, with an eager young literary mistress and a complacent wife at home. West needed the literary side of the relationship as much as the sexual side, I think, and if she found the latter easier to indulge in, she found the former trickier to find time for.

Faith Evans writes of West's "lack of discipline" in writing, which "infuriated" Wells, quoting his words in *H. G. Wells in Love*: "She writes like a loom producing her broad rich fabric with hardly a thought of how it will make up into a shape, while I write to cover a frame of ideas." When their relationship had been in its early stages, still very passionate, as some of Wells's more explicit letters from "Jaguar" to "Panther" show, they were clearly extremely supportive of each other's writing. Wells's influence wasn't an illusion West indulged in; we have plenty of evidence that Wells constantly urged West to write more ("get some work done, good work"). While he admits in one letter to not having read *Return of the Soldier* yet, too busy as he is with his own work, in another, much later on, he urges her to finish *The Judge*: "I want dear Panfer with a fresh mind biting on a new world with a sense of something triumphantly finished."

What created problems for West in her relationship with

Wells was not any reluctance on his part to boost her as a great writer. Nor was it even the fact that he was married, in spite of his reluctance to be seen at the theater with her—the literary people West and Wells knew were mostly bohemian enough to accept the "open" aspect of Wells's marriage (especially after the shock of his affair with Amber Reeves, Wells's impregnating women outside of his marriage could cause no more shame). However, she did complain about being shut up in the countryside, secreted away like the mistress she was, and away from everything that was going on in London. So West, possibly chafing against being excluded, would ask him to leave Jane and marry her, but these appeals continued even once she moved to London and could attend the occasional literary party, mixing with the literary people she found so interesting to be with. Wells always felt these continued appeals were at the behest of her mother and sisters, which is possibly true, given how worried her mother always was about respectability (this was a woman who, we should remember, encouraged her daughter to change her name when she began writing to avoid any social embarrassment).

What West and Wells wanted was precisely what they indicated to each other at the very beginning of their relationship: a writing partnership, bonded by strong sexual desire. But in only 1916, West wrote to a friend, S. K. Ratcliffe, "Now I am hardly ever allowed to see the Great Man . . . my life is suddenly empty," fretting that she was not seeing him as much as she had in the beginning when they were two writers, in love, alone with their work.

That particular fantasy had been almost impossible to maintain after Anthony's arrival: "You know it's as clear as daylight to me that you are my love," Wells wrote on one occasion after a problem arose over what to tell the servants about West's status and Anthony's existence. "Mentally, temperamentally, physically, I've never been so warm and close with anyone as with you. And we've been ragging it all to pieces and spoiling it with detailed bothers for which we are both indisposed and naturally not very capable." Even though West had been able to help Wells with his novel, by 1916, he too was feeling that things were not as good between them as they should be, or benefiting them as much as they had at first envisaged: "For two years we have muddled, been uncomfortable and piled up expenditure, your output of work has been trivial, my work has suffered enormously."

That was how Wells saw the years after Anthony's birth, and West too seemed to condemn what the birth of a child had done to their relationship, as well as to her "output of work," which Wells condemned here as "trivial." It seems obvious that Anthony was the reason West produced less during her relationship with Wells, compared to an equivalent period after, but if so, wouldn't this surely confound the notion that it was *Wells* who "harmed" her as writer? Would it not be truer to say it was being a writing mother that caused the difficulty? In that fateful year of 1916, West also wrote to another female friend, Sylvia Lynd, "I hate domesticity" and "what I want now is ROMANCE." By 1917, she was working on *The Judge*, which she hoped would be finished by autumn, but she confided to S. K. Ratcliffe how difficult it was to find the time: "I never now can sleep till 1 and Anthony wakes me several times in the night and finally starts singing comic songs and doing conjuring tricks and otherwise hymning the dawn at 6.30."

That *The Judge* wouldn't appear until 1922 shows just how hard it was for West to fit her child, her journalism, and her fiction into her life all at once. Fitting in Wells on top of it was probably a hindrance rather than a help. By 1920, she had some strong sense of how things were between her and Wells, and of how they might be going in the future: "H. G. says he is coming straight here from America in the middle of March, but men being what they are there may be some other lady in possession by then. I really do like him much more than most other men—besides loving him, as I do. We dined together with your friend Beaverbrook the night before I left. I found him one of the most fascinating talkers I've ever met, full of the real vitality—the geniusy kind that exists mystically apart from all physical conditions, just as it does in H. G."

"Vitality" was what had initially appealed to West about Wells. She seems to have absorbed some of that vitality from other people when she was around them—in 1922, she wrote that her family "vampires me" and that she hadn't "got at any decent writing since *The Judge*." But by this time, ten years on from her first meeting with Wells, she was writing to her sister about the "terrible denunciations of my work" from him, that he had said she "will never be able to write novels" and that she'd "felt his hatred of my work for a year or two." By now, she was determined to leave him. As Wells said later, perhaps by now they really were doing "harm to each other as writers."

There's a temporariness to literary relationships, and the majority of those which figure in this volume testify to writers coming together as a necessity, which does not last. Where writers have children, like West and Wells, or Smart and Barker, a relationship that perhaps should have ended earlier persists, mainly because of the children. Anthony held West and Wells together when they wanted to part, but he also made it difficult for them both to write. And it was the writing that they needed. Their relationship, begun on an antagonistic literary note, persisted through antagonisms over childcare.

In 1969, West wrote to a biographer of Wells, Lovat Dickson, to explain to him that "the real reason I separated from H.G. was that he nearly ruined himself and me by involvement with a lunatic woman, and I got him out of the mess, and received little thanks, and realized that I might run into even uglier situations, to the prejudice of Anthony. Your whole version of H.G.'s life is based on what he wrote about it, which was not true. The woman he loved most of all was his cousin."

The problem with writers of fiction is that fictional techniques slip over into nonfictional forms, like letters and diaries. West was referring here to a young woman with whom Wells had an affair in 1923. She had subsequently turned up at his flat and slit her wrists; Wells managed to get her taken to the hospital but he was worried about the press sniffing out of the story. West agreed to use her journalistic connections to help suppress it, but Wells had told her the affair was merely a brief fling, and that it was in front of Jane Wells that the girl had made her suicide attempt. According to Glendinning, this was the story that Wells gave her. It was only when her first biographer, Gordon N. Ray, was investigating the affair that the truth came to light. "His lies were a sad time bomb," writes Glendinning.

When Anthony Panther West's novel *Heritage* was published in the 1950s, it, too, his mother argued with him, was full of lies. She told one correspondent "my life with H.G. was such unspeakable hell." The many years she spent refuting Anthony's version of his upbringing reads exactly like a battle between fantasy and reality ("you are living in a dreamland"; "this disregards the real and suffering self of H.G."). For the rest of her life she would alternate between versions of her relationship with Wells—that it was a disaster, she never loved him, that she did love him, and so on.

The truth is, in this case, much more mundane. Rebecca West must have known from the moment she met Wells what compromises she would be forced to make by indulging in a liaison with him. She freely chose to enter this relationship, but in later years, long after the relationship was over, she could hardly bear to think of all the petty little humiliations her situation had brought her. In her posthumous novel, *Sunflower*, which portrayed the actress Sunflower's longstanding relationship with the married, bullish Essington, West charted the lonely, antisocial lot of the mistress thus: "They didn't give parties. Essington hardly liked anybody. And she didn't go out to parties much now; she had so often had to break engagements because he turned up unexpectedly that now she hardly liked to accept invitations. Sometimes, indeed nearly always when she was not rehearsing, he would tell her that he would come to her during the day, but that he could not say at what hour; and then she could only go out for a little while at a time, nervous dashes into the park with one eye on a watch, and come back to sit about alone, for he hated to find people out when he came."

These were only some of the many complaints of the mistress of a married man, the woman who wished she were his wife, that she was too often left sitting about "alone," that she was there to function solely to serve his needs. As mistress to the married Wells, West had had a lot to complain about (this portrait of Wells, as Lynette Felber points out, "satirizes the patriarchal values Wells had come to represent for her"), and her resentment grew over the years.

And yet, in the same novel, she also acknowledges what she loved: "She had forgotten that it was all right when Essington did at last come, so great, so cleverly, so childishly dependent on her, even after ten years. He would drop his face into the curve of her neck and shoulder and rub his face against her warm flesh like a baby or a puppy." Just a few pages later, too, West also has her heroine, her alter ego, question what she is to do about it all. "Though she rebelled against him, she was a part of him. How could she leave him? How can one leave oneself?" Indeed. And yet, she did leave him.

It was West who kept wanting to make the break, and West who finally achieved it. By 1922, she seems to have tired of being the mistress. Whether Wells behaved badly is not the point; this is how she felt about it: "Everywhere they went [at this point, early in 1922, they were on holiday in Algeciras], he forced Rebecca to play out painful public dramas as the 'ill-treated mistress' of a man twice her age. He would ask her 'to go and fetch his coat in front of a number of people, which in a Latin country went down very badly indeed." That summer, West holidayed with her sister Lettie, G. B. Stern, and Hugh Hart—without Wells—in Devon, but Wells was jealous of her, so he decided to join the party. Aging poorly and in ill health, the now fifty-six-year-old Wells accused West of wanting to be alone with Hart. Additionally, he savaged her writing, calling *The Judge* "an ill conceived sprawl of a book with a faked hero and a faked climax, an aimless waste of your powers."

This seems to have been the last straw for West. Writing to Lettie in August, she said, "I have told him definitely that I won't live with him any more and I mean to stick to it." She weakened though: it wasn't until March that she got away, and even then, only by literally leaving on a lecture tour to the States. Gordon N. Ray claims that West told Wells unless he was going to marry her, there was no future for them, but that she also recognized marriage was impossible: "I said I thought he was rooted in his domestic routine, that I was sure he felt there was something right about it, that I saw well that Jane's friends would make life impossible, and that I recognized that it would be hard on the two sons."

It's perhaps disappointment at his weakness in not doing the honorable thing by her that infects her letter to S. K. Ratcliffe in March 1923, in which she claims that "I have stuck to him partly for his own sake—mainly for Anthony's sake—but really quite a lot for his own sake as he has, to an extreme nobody quite realizes, not a soul on earth who looks after him," as well as fear of her own weakness with regard to him: "I am dreading another attempt to get me to come back." She was right to dread it—she was back with him again by the summer of that year, and only the Atlantic Ocean could do what she had tried and failed to do so often: effect a real, and lasting separation.

After they parted, West would go on to have a short-lived but intense affair with Lord Beaverbrook, before marrying in 1930. Wells would console himself with a number of women after the death of his wife from cancer in 1927, including a close flirtation with a young Martha Gellhorn. On August 13, 1946, the day West heard Wells had died, she wrote, "Dear H.G., he was a devil, he ruined my life, he starved me, he was an inexhaustible source of love and friendship to me for thirty-four years, we should never have met, I was the one person he cared to see to the end, I feel desolate because he has gone."

West and Wells were a contrary partnership. Never married, they were together for better, for worse, both in fact as well as in fantasy. The reality and the fantasy of the West-Wells liaison have become so intertwined together that they can barely withstand separation, just as West, in her letter about Wells's death, can barely separate her feelings of love and hate, fulfilment and loss. A relationship so dependent on the interplay between reality and fantasy inevitably means serious compromises: it means lies, betrayals, hypocrisies, and double standards. All of those things were present, in abundance, in their affair. And all of it was fuel to their writerly ambitions, too. Neither of them could do without it.

After all, as West once wrote, "how can one leave oneself?

PART II

1920s–1930s: The Paris Set

Top: *Jean Rhys.* Below: *Ford Madox Ford,* left, *pictured with James Joyce, Ezra Pound, and John Quinn in Paris, 1923.*

4. THE "INGÉNUE": JEAN RHYS
AND FORD MADOX FORD

Even the rest of her, the writer, was a child . . . it was also what she wanted: never to grow up . . .

—Carole Angier, *Jean Rhys:*
Lives of Modern Women

★

"After all," remarked Marya, suddenly, "weak, weak, how does anybody really know who's weak and who isn't? You don't need to be a fine bouncing girl to stab anybody, either."

—Jean Rhys, *Quartet*

★

When Jean Rhys, the author of *Wide Sargasso Sea*, and many other challenging, fascinating novels, began an affair with the influential writer and editor Ford Madox Ford in Paris in 1924, she was thirty-four years old. She was also a married woman as well as the mother of a baby girl. She was hardly, in the dictionary definition of the word, any kind of "ingénue" at all. The last thing a vivacious, chic, beautiful, and sexually experienced woman like Rhys was, was an innocent, artless, or unsophisticated young girl.

Yet that latter portrait is the one that has been painted of her, over and over again. In biographies and memoirs, even in her own letters and the novels that portray fictionalized versions of herself, especially in regard to her liaison with Ford, she is talked of as an innocent abroad, a child. "She regularly acts like a seventeen-year-old child bride lost and abandoned in a world she does not understand," one biographer writes rather sniffily of the character Marya from *Quartet*, the novel said to be based on the Ford-Rhys liaison. "It was Beauty and the Beast. Jean was thirty-four and looked twenty; she was slender and delicate, *la jeune fille*," another says of Rhys when she first met her mentor. Her childlike appearance betrayed a child's weakness, according to one feminist critic, who argues that she was "marked by a fundamental passivity," and "desperate and dependent."

In many different accounts, then, Rhys is viewed as the weaker half of an unequal relationship, only able to attain power by sneaky, passive-aggressive, manipulative methods. She was underhanded in her dealings with Ford, some have claimed; she was not what she seemed. She may have looked like a girl, but she was not one. She was a woman, and, according to some, a particularly conniving and dangerous one at that: a "witch-seductress," no less, with a horrifying capacity for "drunken violence."

How fair are these views of Jean Rhys? On the surface, these critical assessments of her character might seem just and appropriate. Rhys was, even by her own account, a "troubled" type, a tortured soul. She strikes us now as someone whose mental state would almost certainly be diagnosed as depressive, and for whom the appropriate medications would be prescribed for her extreme behavior and chaotic ways. In her later years, she relied on the inadequate effect of "pep pills" to treat her mood swings, but these only buoyed her up for a short time. She could lie in bed for days, even as a very young woman, apparently paralyzed to any kind of action in a depressive stupor, especially when something bad had happened to her—usually, it was a love affair that had gone wrong, leaving her feeling abandoned and, more often than not, financially destitute. Alcohol was something she relied on to help her get through life, as it often rejuvenated her and, most importantly, helped her to write. But that effect, too, would only last for a short time: soon, she would become vicious, angry, and violent toward those nearest her. Friends knew to make a sharp exit when Rhys had drunk too much, and those meeting her for the first time could be shocked by her drunken appearance. In her late middle age, she was even arrested for assaulting a neighbor in a drunken rage. One very painful, pitiful example of her alcoholism emerged just after she died, when an interviewer recalled having to help a drunken, elderly, frail Rhys to the toilet, where she collapsed in a puddle of her own urine. During the writing of her fourth novel, *Voyage in the Dark*, which was published in 1934, she apparently got through two bottles of wine a day. Sometimes she would promise herself a drink once she was *finished* writing for the day, as opposed to drinking while writing: "Meanwhile there is nothing to do but plod along line upon a line. Then there's a drink of course which is awfully handy. Or drinks. '*When* I've done that I'll have a drink . . .'" She never got over her dependence on alcohol; some would argue, she never got over her dependence on anything.

But Rhys was a self-aware woman. She knew she drank too much. She knew how horribly self-obsessed she could be, apologizing to one correspondent in 1941, "I *realised* perfectly that my talk of myself, Ford, Paris, 'Perversite,' myself, gramophone records, myself was irritating you. But I couldn't stop." She knew she was needy, as her depressive state of mind forced her to be, and passive in every aspect except when searching for those who could prop her up or look after her. It's possible the real reason for the endless walks both she and the heroines of her early novels took through the streets of London and Paris—walking, walking, always walking, but never finding what they were looking for— was because she was searching for that ultimate caregiver, the one who would look after her.

She was also aware, and sometimes ashamed of, the fact that she took money from her men. She rarely, if ever, exhibited pride: either past lovers or present ones would do, as long as they could provide for her, but novels like *After Leaving Mr. Mackenzie* show an underlying horror at, as well as fascination with, what she was doing. As she herself wrote in her unfinished autobiography, *Smile Please,* "It seems to me now that the whole business of money and sex is bound up with something very primitive and deep. When you take money directly from someone you love it becomes not money but a symbol. The bond is now there. The bond has been established. I am sure the woman's deep-down feeling is 'I belong to this man, I want to belong to him completely.' It is at once humiliating and exciting." Some have argued that she simply exploited her victim status, playing on former boyfriends' guilt over abandoning such a helpless, needy individual, but Rhys's acceptance of checks from her ex-lovers was more complex than that. She didn't see herself as capable of exploiting anybody; what she wanted was someone to take care of her.

Before she found Ford, though, Rhys believed she had married that caregiver. But her husband wasn't quite what she thought he was, and his care of her would never be adequate. Jean Lenglet was a rather shady character, a French-Dutch sometime journalist whom she called 'John'. She married him in 1919 at the end of the First World War; unbeknownst to her, he was still married to someone else, a Frenchwoman named Marie Leonie Pollart. Shortly after Rhys met Ford in 1924 in Paris, she became destitute and penniless because Lenglet, who had ferried her from one European city to another over the last few years, was imprisoned for theft. With her particular kind of fragile beauty, Rhys thus acquired a vulnerable air, a consequence of these and other painful events, and this impression of vulnerability never quite left her. Even in the good times, she could seem weak, powerless. And so the woman who was to write *Wide Sargasso Sea*—a work which would one day make her "the best living English novelist," and which easily rivaled the very best her onetime lover and mentor Ford ever produced—passed from one man to another.

From Lenglet's wife she became, quite simply, in the words of one expat in Paris during this time, "Ford's girl."

"Ford's girl": because the then fifty-year-old Ford was, after all, a "name" when Rhys met him; he was a somebody in the literary world. He was hardly a "beast," but photographs of him at this time show a heavily mustached man with jowly cheeks and thinning hair. Rebecca West described him as "stout, gangling, albino-ish" and said that being kissed by him was like being the toast under poached egg. Photographs of Rhys, by contrast, reveal large, wide-set eyes, with a flapper-style haircut and perfect skin. Rhys and Ford may have made for an incongruous-looking pair, but something important was taking place between them.

It was Ford who first published Rhys; and, in an echo of Pound's initializing Hilda Doolittle into H.D., it was Ford who gave Rhys her pen name. Ford taught her how to write, encouraged her to read certain writers, to learn from them to better her art. He knew the movers and shakers of the expat world of 1920s Paris and threw parties for them all. In comparison to this older, important man who could lift her up (and drop her) as he chose, it appears inevitable that the younger, seemingly helpless Rhys, so much less experienced in literary matters, would be viewed as the embodiment of the "ingénue." What else could a woman in her position be?

Everything about the ingénue suggests charm, but it is charm instead of power. The ingénue has no power at all, except the power to charm with her artless, innocent ways. And it was powerlessness that Rhys felt most after she arrived in bohemian Paris with the husband who would soon let her down so badly. Powerless to prevent her first baby's death, she would soon be powerless to stop her husband's imprisonment, which would leave her to fend for herself. The "girl" is a culturally far less powerful figure than the "woman": Rhys seems to have embraced that powerless aspect of herself which expressed so precisely just how she felt, and projected it outwards, so that everyone around her viewed her as a helpless young girl too, in spite of her age, her circumstances, and her personal history.

The contradiction of "Jean Rhys, Ingénue" permeates her life story as much as it does her relationship with Ford. Indeed, it could be argued that this relationship brought out more contradictions than any other relationship she ever had. So much about it proved so hard to reconcile, and it has led to difficult questions ever since. For instance, one cannot help wondering what exactly it was that Rhys wanted and expected from her relationship with Ford, a man who was living with another woman by whom he had a daughter. Perhaps she expected him to marry her, even though she was married to someone else, and so was he. Maybe she simply wanted him to set her up financially on her own, as a mistress with her own apartment and nice clothes.

It is my belief that she fell in love with him partly because of literary closeness, because he believed in her writing. But many have argued that she never really loved him at all; that, rather, she exploited his feelings for her. It may all beg the question, what did Ford want from Rhys, but Rebecca West may have answered this in part when she once wrote that Ford was a fantasist. Fantasists aren't necessarily lovable Walter Mitty types: they can be dangerous people who encourage those around them to believe and participate in their fantasies as though they are real, and when the truth is finally discovered, it can be shocking, even devastating, for those closest to them. Was Rhys part of a fantasy for Ford? Was he simply indulging in some ego-stroking fantasy when he took her on?

Certainly we can see the damage that had been done once the fantasy was over: Rhys clung on to Ford long after he ended their relationship and made it clear he was no longer interested in her. What her relationship with Ford ultimately cost Rhys was undoubtedly a serious increase in her dependence on alcohol, coupled with a belief that she needed men, not just to help her get through life, but to help her write as well. Ford's fantasies became Rhys's nightmares once he abandoned her. One can only wonder if it was worth it for her, and, most importantly, if she would have become a published writer without him.

• • • •

Jean Rhys was born Ella Gwendoline Rees Williams, the fifth of six children, in Dominica in 1890. Her elder sister, Brenda Gwenith, died nine months before Rhys was born, aged only nine months; perhaps the speed with which Rhys's grieving mother became pregnant again indicates a remedy for the loss of a baby, the kind of remedy recommended to grieving mothers at the time. Rhys herself would know this pain of a lost child when her baby son, William, died when he was only three weeks old. She did not follow her mother's practice, however, by replacing him right away with another baby. Her daughter, Maryvonne, was born a full two years later.

Rhys's childhood on the Caribbean island has been well documented, partly because she used it in many of her novels like *Voyage in the Dark* and *Sleep It Off, Lady*. It forms the background to her most successful novel, *Wide Sargasso Sea*, published in 1966 after a thirty-year hiatus during which many took her silence to mean she was no longer alive. And it plays an important role in *Smile Please*, published in 1979, and unfinished at the time of her death that year. The daughter of a Welsh medical officer and a Creole—that is, a British-descended white Caribbean woman, whose grandfather was actually a Scottish slave owner on Dominica—Rhys was considered to have mixed parentage. It meant she grew up alienated from the other girls at the convent school she attended, who were either white European or black Dominican. In her memoir, she recalls trying to befriend a black girl whose beauty caught her eye. The young Rhys tries to talk to her: "Finally, without speaking, she turned and looked at me. I knew irritation, bad temper, the 'oh, go away' look: this was different. This was hatred—impersonal, implacable hatred. I recognised it at once and if you think that a child cannot recognise hatred and remember it for life you are most damnably mistaken. I never tried to be friendly with any of the coloured girls again. I was polite and that was all. They hate us. We are hated."

So Rhys was a lonely child. She was misunderstood by a mother she tried to make love her ("Even after the new baby was born there must have been an interval before she seemed to find me a nuisance and I grew to dread her") and was extremely frightened by the violence that would occasionally erupt on the island. When she was twelve, a crowd of locals gathered around her family's house, which was next door to the house belonging to the editor of the local paper, who had criticized the power of Catholic priests on the island. Some islanders had objected, and, in Rhys's recall, "they surged past the window, howling, but they didn't throw stones." She would always be disturbed by the racial inequities she saw all around her: the friends whom the black cook would entertain in the kitchen, would become silent if Rhys drew near; the "fear and distrust" of her black nurse, Meta, the "terror of my life" who would scare her with stories about zombies and werewolves.

What helped her during her childhood was writing. Rhys said she found that "writing poetry took away sadness, doubled joy and calmed the anxious questioning that tormented me." when she was young, and confessed later in life that "I found when I was a child that if I could put the hurt into words, it would go. It leaves a sort of melancholy behind then it goes." But writing was always a double-edged sword for her. In a letter to Peggy Kirkaldy in 1949, she declared, "I never wanted to write. I wished to be happy and peaceful and obscure. I was dragged into

writing by a series of coincidences—Mrs. Adam, Ford, Paris—
need for money"; and to David Plante, she exploded, "Oh what
a Goddamn shitty business we've taken on, being writers! Oh
what shit! What shit!" She bemoaned what she believed to be
her "mediocrity" in writing, and told the *Paris Review* interviewer
that she felt "fated to write . . . which is horrible. But I can only
do one thing."

So writing wasn't necessarily easy for her, and its effect
wasn't always cathartic, but it was something she felt compelled
to do from an early age. It is important to remember, when we
consider her relationship with Ford, that from childhood Rhys
was a writer. Yet when she left Dominica for school in England
at the age of seventeen, she forgot about writing altogether. After
her warm, exotic home, England struck her as cold, grey, and
wet, which dampened her enthusiasm for her new country. The
austerity and parsimoniousness endured by the lower-middle and
working classes in 1907 didn't help either: on her first morning,
she managed to upset the landlady of the boarding house where
she lodged with her aunt by running a hot bath for herself. "My
aunt then explained the ritual of having a bath in an English
boarding-house. You had to ask for it several days beforehand, you
had to be very careful to take it at that time and no other, and so
on and so on."

But she left the school where her father had found a place
for her after only one term because she had discovered what she
believed to be her real vocation: acting. This was after getting permission from her father to attend Tree's School, or the Academy
for Dramatic Art (now the Royal Academy of Dramatic Art). She
claimed in her memoir that her father's death forced her to leave
and join a touring company, as there was no more money for her
to continue at the school, but one biographer has argued that her
father was actually still alive at this point, and Rhys's departure
from acting school was partly because she wasn't good enough,

and partly because "when she took the first step out of her sheltered childhood into the demi-monde beyond the pale it was her own choice and her own doing . . ."

But why would Rhys have wanted to hide the fact that becoming a professional actress was her own choice? Was it because it went so badly wrong and she wanted someone else to blame? Often without much money, in cold and unfriendly places, viewed by society still as only a step or two above being a prostitute, the life of a jobbing actress was a particularly difficult one, and unprotected as she was without family to support or shield her, Rhys found it far too challenging. By this time, the summer of 1910, her father really had died, leaving her mother with little money, and the aunt with whom Rhys had stayed when she first came to England wasn't in a position to support her financially either. And the sort of men who expressed interest in young actresses were generally not the supportive type. But Rhys was luckier than most. She fell for a more aristocratic version of this particularly predatory kind of male, when she was spotted by the upper-class banker Lancelot Hugh Smith. He was older, more sophisticated, moneyed, and she genuinely believed that she had found her Prince Charming. She believed, in fact, that he would marry her.

Her devastation when he broke with her in 1912 brought on those paralyzing stupors which prevented her from getting out of bed and carrying on with her work, as she depicted in her 1930 novel, *After Leaving Mr. Mackenzie.* In her memoir, she writes, "When my first love affair came to an end I wrote this poem: *I didn't know / I didn't know / I didn't know.*" She blamed much of her later weakness in life on this extreme response to her first abandonment: this was when she first succumbed to drink, and began to hang around rougher places with harder girls. She became pregnant by an unnamed man after her break with Smith, but Smith came back at this point and told her to have the baby, that they would bring the child up together. It was not to be, though: his cousin, Smith's closest friend, appeared one night and encouraged her to have an abortion, to save her former lover's health, as Smith was worrying himself over the whole matter. Rhys agreed, and Smith paid for the abortion, about which, she simply says in her memoir, she "didn't suffer from remorse or guilt." Smith continued to pay her an allowance after he broke with her, but through solicitors rather than in person, and this hurt her. She began to model for artists, then got engaged to another aristocratic type, the journalist Maxwell Henry Hayes, who went off to cover the war in 1914. The engagement was more or less forgotten. Left to her own devices once again, Rhys went back to acting and had more boyfriends.

These were difficult years, both before and during the First World War, coping on her own with only Smith's allowance and precious little self-esteem, so it is perhaps not surprising that when a handsome, charming, half-French, half-Dutch arrival at her boarding house in Torrington Square proposed to her, Rhys accepted him. Smith tried to warn her that Jean Lenglet was not a reliable proposition, that he had worked as a secret agent for the French. But Rhys nevertheless sat out the rest of the war in London while she waited for him to return from Holland. In 1919, Rhys and Lenglet were married, and moved to Paris, where Lenglet wanted to work (Rhys always maintained he was vague about what his work at that time actually was) and where later that year, their first child was born.

Rhys's recall of the death of her son only three weeks after he was born is characteristically frank, as well as self-accusing. The little boy came down with pneumonia and was taken to a nearby hospital. That night, to calm their worries about their son, Rhys and Lenglet joined a friend and drank champagne. The next day, they were informed that he had died, at the very moment, Rhys was always to say, that his parents were drinking and laughing. Of this moment, one biographer writes, "I think the death of her first child was one of the sorrows of her life, but most of her sorrows were part guilt, and so was this one. Though she was nearly thirty she was still a child herself, because she always would be." This notion of Rhys as "the child," like Bowen's representation of her as "the girl," would persist throughout the rest of Rhys's time in Paris, and beyond. But it wasn't until she met Ford that her ingénue identity was fully realized.

• • • •

Ford Madox Ford was born Ford Hermann Hueffer in 1873 to artistic, bohemian parents. His background was as literary and as artistic as a writer could have wanted: his maternal grandfather was the painter Ford Madox Brown, who was friendly with the famous Rossetti family after Dante Gabriel Rossetti asked him to be his tutor. Although Madox Brown himself was not part of the Pre-Raphaelite Brotherhood, at the heart of which were the Rossettis, John Millais, William Holman Hunt, and other mid-Victorian-era painters, critics, and artists, the family connection did not end with him. Madox Brown's daughter, Lucy, married Dante Gabriel's brother William Michael, who also happened to be the nephew of John William Polidori, author of *The Vampyre* and physician to Byron. Ford himself inevitably sought an artistic career, but it was writing, not painting, which claimed him.

Ford Madox Ford married his wife, Elsie Martindale, in 1894, but that marriage soon ran into problems, especially as the young Ford struggled to make money as a writer. A serious relationship with the rather ubiquitous Violet Hunt followed. She, too, was related to artists, and she published a memoir of the Pre-Raphaelites in 1926; her father, Alfred William Hunt, a painter, had been encouraged by John Ruskin, and his daughter would write a biography of Elizabeth Siddall, the painter and wife of

Dante Gabriel Rossetti. Hunt had also had a relationship with H. G. Wells, who was a friend of Ford's. She would be with Ford for eight years, and would provoke a court case by Elsie Martindale when she publicly referred to herself as "Mrs. Ford" (conscious of his German surname in England during the First World War, he had changed it). Her relationship with Ford broke up partly due to his affair with the almost equally ubiquitous Brigit Patmore (who would also have an affair with H.D.'s husband, Richard Aldington), whom many consider the inspiration for Nancy Rufford, the love interest of Ford's greatest work, his 1915 novel, *The Good Soldier.* But by the time Ford met Rhys in 1924, he had been with the Australian artist Stella Bowen for six years, and they had a young daughter together.

Ford had built his considerable reputation not only on the back of a series of novels, some good, some bad. He was, like his friend Ezra Pound, keen to be at the center of a literary revolution, and he was responsible for publishing some of the greatest writers of the modern era. The first periodical he founded was *The English Review* in 1908; like Pound, he had firmly established rules for what he considered to be good writing (economy was extremely important), and published those who wrote accordingly, with what looks like a surprisingly Victorian list to us now, and not necessarily writers we would associate today with an economic prose style (John Galsworthy, Arnold Bennett, Thomas Hardy, for instance). But *The English Review* barely lasted two years, and after Ford arrived in Paris, he established a new periodical in 1924, this time called, appropriately enough given the number of expats littering the Parisian streets, *transatlantic review.* Ernest Hemingway was its deputy editor and his work would appear in its pages; James Joyce, Ezra Pound, and Gertrude Stein would all write for it too, and its very last edition would publish the work of the ingénue Ford had met via Mrs. Adam, the wife of *The Times*'s Paris correspondent.

But at the moment that he met Rhys in 1924, Ford was at a more desperate point than all of this editorial activity might suggest. The *transatlantic review* was drowning fast, and it wouldn't even last the year. Ford was, on the face of it, a highly successful writer and editor, but both publications he launched lasted for a very short time, and his own books never sold well, not even *The Good Soldier*. In Paris, he was financially stricken: he and Bowen were living largely on the family money that she had independently. He may have given literary parties and surrounded himself with exciting young writers, but he was past his best and felt it. He had published a novel, *Some do Not,* that spring, but felt too old to be that bright young hope of the literary world; his star, if it had ever really been launched at all, was fading.

Life for Rhys was hardly at its brightest either, but she had made some translations of her husband's writing to see if she could sell it to any of the English papers that had a base in Paris. As she tells the story in *Smile Please*, she had no luck with her first approach, the continental *Daily Mail*, but she remembered meeting Mrs. Adam at a party once in London, and so decided to approach her. As Rhys tells it, Mrs. Adam didn't admire Lenglet's work, but she did ask if Rhys herself had written anything and if she could see it. Rhys supplied her with the diaries she had been keeping over the last ten years. "I hesitated because I still didn't want to show them to anybody," Rhys later recalled, but the next day she left her notebooks with Mrs. Adam, who then asked Rhys if she'd "mind" if she "typed it and sent it to a man called Mr. Ford Madox Ford who had been the brilliant editor of *The English Review*, a London magazine, and that he was famous for spotting and helping young authors." When Mrs. Adam asked if she could "change parts of it in the typing," Rhys, ever the ingénue, told herself that "she was an experienced journalist and must know far better than I did." Rhys claimed later that she didn't care very much for the end result. But Ford liked it. Mrs. Adam had called the manuscript *Suzy Tells*; Ford renamed it *Triple Sec*, just as he was to rename its author, who had, up until that moment of her first publication, been going by the name of Ella Lenglet.

There's little to tell us how their affair began, but if *Quartet*, Rhys's novel based on their liaison, is any guide, it seems that she was introduced to Ford and Bowen at the same time, in a Montparnasse restaurant, by Mrs. Adam. Rhys describes Ford, cast in the role of Heidler, his fictional counterpart, in this novel thus: "He looked as if nothing could break him down. He was a tall, fair man of perhaps forty-five. His shoulders were tremendous, his nose arrogant, his hands short, broad and so plump that the knuckles were dimpled. The wooden expression of his face was carefully striven for. His eyes were light blue and intelligent, but with a curious underlying expression of obtuseness—even of brutality." They walk along to a café, the three of them, and when they sit down, Marya, the character based on Rhys, finds that Heidler has placed his hand on her knee.

This novelistic account suggests that it was Ford who first made a pass at Rhys, and given Ford's past behavior to women, this isn't unlikely. What Rhys leaves out, though, is how she appears to men. In the novel, Marya moves her knee and Heidler withdraws his hand, but given that he had already signalled his interest in her, she must have known what to expect from him on further meetings. However, it's tricky to know exactly what went on between Ford and Rhys in the two years during which they conducted their relationship because of, rather than in spite of, a profusion of a certain kind of detail. A great deal of fiction has been written about the affair, and not nearly enough of what is usually considered "factual" material (letters that record events and repeat conversations; autobiographies that detail circumstances which can be backed up by others' testimonials about the affair; diaries that relay feelings and reactions as they happen). Instead, we have novels where after their association was over first Rhys then Ford poured out their experience of the relationship for all the world to see.

Rhys's *Quartet* came out in 1928 and Ford's *When the Wicked Man* appeared in 1930. Both novels were immediately considered "autobiographical." In the absence of any other material, the novel had to stand in for fact, although Rhys protested later in life that her novel wasn't autobiographical at all: "I think it is angry and uneven as you say, but it has some life and it wasn't an autobiography, as everyone here seemed to imagine though some of it was lived of course . . . I was astonished when so many people thought it an autobiography from page 1 onwards and told me it should never have been written. Well, I had to write it."

Critics have tended pretty much to ignore Ford's novelistic account of the affair itself (one Ford biographer considers it little more than "revenge for Rhys's portrait of him as Heidler in *Quartet")* and have preferred to concentrate on his earlier masterpiece, *The Good Soldier.* This was published in 1915, nine years before Ford and Rhys had even met, but many biographers and literary critics view this novel as some kind of prefiguring of the events in Paris from 1924 to 1926, and believe it to be a much better delineation of Ford's character and attitude to extramarital affairs and to love itself. Some have gone even further, and compared both these texts with two others: Rhys's husband Jean Lenglet's novel *Barred*, which appeared in 1932 and which gave his side of the story, as well as *Drawn from Life*, the autobiography of Stella Bowen, Ford's partner of six years and the mother of his daughter. This was the last word on the subject, appearing much later than all the others in 1941, and long after she and Ford had also parted.

How to disentangle the life from the art is never an uncontroversial business, as some would argue fiction should never be used to explain the truth of a situation. However, in this case, it is clear that Ford himself regarded *Quartet* as autobiographical:

the very reason he wrote *When the Wicked Man* was to present his own side of the story, just as Lenglet and Bowen subsequently did. Rhys may have been convinced her book was fiction, but the other three involved in her affair with Ford didn't appear to think so. Hence, a consideration of *Quartet* when trying to dissect the nature of the relationship between Rhys and Ford has held sway as a valid exercise among critics. How much Rhys's novel condemns her, though, as much as any other work, for what happened in this affair is open to controversy and to question. How often she describes the character of Marya as a girl in *Quartet*, for instance, is as revealing a detail as any other.

The "story" of the relationship between Rhys and Ford appears to have gone something like this: Ford made a pass at Rhys, and fell in love with her. In *Quartet*, a concerned Heidler orders Marya a taxi one evening when she complains she isn't feeling well ("She was sure that he knew she was ill and near to tears. He was a rock of a man with his big shoulders and his quiet voice"). Some days later, Mrs. Heidler (who was based on Stella Bowen) voices concern over Marya's husband Stephan's situation and how Marya is managing with so little money, and it is Mrs. Heidler who offers Marya the spare room in their apartment. Stephan encourages Marya to go, presumably because he cannot afford to keep a roof over her head and can manage more easily, for the time being, on his own. According to *Quartet*, Mrs. Heidler tells Marya that her husband is "always rescuing some young genius or the other and installing him in the spare bedroom"—only this time, the young genius wasn't a "him," it was a "her." The novel shows a fictionalized Ford, unhappy, feeling "trapped" in his relationship with Stella Bowen, and only too eager to begin an affair with the helpless young woman he now has staying with him.

For a man who took up so easily with other women, it's quite surprising to learn that Ford wasn't that keen on sex. Or at least, his sexual technique wasn't quite up to the mark. Violet

Hunt called him "a cold, patient man, without fire" and in *Quartet* Rhys writes of Heidler, "He wasn't a good lover, of course. He didn't really like women." In that novel, Heidler makes it plain to Marya that he and his wife have "gone their separate ways," implying that they no longer sleep together. Gradually, by offering the lonely and frightened Marya shelter, warmth, and love, he wins her over and at some point they begin to sleep together, with Mrs. Heidler's knowledge and apparent consent (although in her autobiography, Bowen claims to have known nothing of the beginnings of the affair between Rhys and Ford, simply accepting this attractive young woman as Ford's pupil: "I was singularly slow in discovering that she and Ford were in love").

It was during this time that Ford helped Rhys with her writing, although none of that appears in Rhys's novel. More than helped—he shaped her, showing her how to edit her own work, encouraging her to leave a story if it wasn't working and begin something new. He made her read out her work in front of him and Bowen, and would shout "cliché, cliché!" much to her mortification. He refined her reading, making her read more French fiction, and, arch-modernist that he was, showed her how to write economically, as well as to concentrate on her own experiences. He could see that she was a "modern" type—rootless, alone, romantic—and got her to put that into her prose. He introduced her to other writers in Paris, like Ernest Hemingway and Gertrude Stein, but she seems to have made little impression on them. She was quiet in a crowd, and unsure of herself in a literary milieu. In *Quartet*, Marya is similarly lacking in confidence, and finds herself falling more and more in love with the masterly Heidler. By now, however, his wife has discovered the affair and is making things extremely difficult. Mrs. Heidler plays tricks to get her husband back onside; according to Marya, they are "inscrutable people, invulnerable people, and she simply hadn't a chance against them, naive sinner that she was."

Quartet portrays Rhys as the hapless girl, down on her luck, who falls in love with a man who is simply using her to have some fun, bored as he is in his current relationship. She is the mistress whom the married man eventually rejects for his wife. In real life, Ford and Bowen helped Rhys get a job in the south of France with an extremely wealthy American woman who needed someone to help her write a book. On Ford's recommendation, Mrs. Hudnut—whose daughter was married to Rudolf Valentino—accepted Rhys for the task. The arrangement lasted several months until Ford called her back, by accusing Mrs. Hudnut of exploiting Rhys. Rhys returned to Ford, but by now his interest in her seemed to have disappeared, even though spiking her job would suggest he wanted her. Rhys panicked at his distance, grew more needy, drank too much, and generally made life even more miserable for everyone concerned. In *Quartet*, Stephan is released from prison and Marya goes back to him—Heidler tells Marya he will never share her with another man, and ends their affair. But Marya has been hurt in precisely the way she'd told Heidler she couldn't handle ("If I'm hurt again I shall go mad . . . I can't stand any more, I won't stand it").

But this novel doesn't tell the whole truth of why Ford fell out of love with Rhys. In *When the Wicked Man* Ford's portrayal of Rhys as a drunken harridan is likely a picture of the woman she became to him when Ford wanted no more of her, not what she was when he met her. It is possibly also an exaggerated portrait, a record of Ford's hurt at the depiction of him as the invulnerable, cruel, and insensitive Heidler in Rhys's novel. Nor does *Quartet* explain exactly why Rhys was so furiously angry with him when he ended the relationship. She had a husband to go back to, a husband whom she loved; she had learned a great deal from Ford about writing, enough to stand her in good stead for the rest of her career; and he had helped her out of a tricky situation by putting her up, giving her a roof over her head when she needed it most. Yet her anger was the catalyst for the writing of *Quartet* and it wasn't until much, much later in life that she could say, "Ford helped me more than anybody else." She stayed angry, it seems, for a very long time.

• • • •

Was Rhys's anger that of the victim or that of the predator whose prey has gotten away? Stella Bowen implied in her memoir that Rhys used her victimhood to prey on other people's husbands, but then, given that Bowen always attributed the breakup of her "marriage" with Ford to his relationship with Rhys, perhaps she would say that. Perhaps Rhys was never quite as passive and needy as she and others have claimed. Passivity and neediness can help a person to survive, and as an ingénue, Rhys was portraying herself as the blameless child-woman who was never truly responsible for what she did. Perhaps by investing in this particular type more than in any other, Rhys could dodge that very victim/predator dichotomy.

That Rhys was married no fewer than three times in her life, and had numerous affairs, makes it clear that men desired her. She also formed many close relationships with women over the years, including Diana Athill, Peggy Kirkaldy, and Selma Vaz Dias, to name just a few, so she can't have been all bad. Apart from her striking physical appearance, which allowed her some modeling work in Paris in the early years, friends have testified to her good company when she was on form, and there was undoubtedly something exciting about her, something on the edge.

Rhys wasn't ever the norm; she wasn't the usual kind of woman. She had something different about her—even Stella Bowen, writing from the position of the betrayed wife, had to acknowledge that Rhys's "needle-quick intelligence and a good sort of emotional honesty" marked her out from the crowd. To have

stood out among the expats of Paris in the 1920s——enough
to catch the eye of an enterprising editor and writer like Ford
Madox Ford, Rhys must have been something special. It must
have been obvious; it must have been indubitable.

And yet Rhys was an outsider during those times in Paris;
she wasn't friends with the important people and she didn't hob-
nob with writers, although, encouraged by Ford, she did attend
notorious drinking holes like Les Deux Magots. With little money and few literary pretensions, she didn't hang around Saint-
Germain too often—mainly because she couldn't afford to, but
also because she was shy (although, given that her early career
involved acting and being a chorus girl, it's hard to know just
how shy she may have been; another contradiction, perhaps). The
dingier parts of Montparnasse were Rhys's territory, where her
neighbors were discarded and desperate women who hid themselves away, and were, possibly, the kind of women with whom
she identified most readily.

Her first five books came out over a period of only twelve
years: the short story collection *The Left Bank* was published in
1927, with an introduction by Ford, then *Quartet* in 1928. *After
Leaving Mr. Mackenzie* followed in 1930, then *Voyage in the Dark*
appeared in 1934, and *Good Morning, Midnight* in 1939. They all
recalled Rhys's time in Paris and in London, and they were all
subjected to the same critique, perhaps as a result of her associa-
tions and living quarters. Her books were considered "sordid," a
word used to describe not only the circumstances in which Rhys's
heroines find themselves, but also the mind of Rhys herself, the
woman who was writing about such "unpublishable" things as sex
with married men, sex for money, abortions, poverty, destitution.
Quartet's reviewers were completely divided between those who
deplored its lack of morals, and those who found its peek at demimonde life "powerful." And when *After Leaving Mr. Mackenzie* appeared—a much more "sordid" story in many ways, given that it

mixes details of the breakdown of Rhys's relationships with both
Ford and Lancelot Hugh Smith with details of her abortion and
her acceptance of checks from Smith—even Rebecca West felt
the need to warn potential readers: "It is doubtful if one ought to
open this volume unless one is happily married, immensely rich
and in robust health; for if one is not entirely free from misery
when one opens the book one will be at the suicide point long
before one closes it. Miss Jean Rhys has already, in *The Left Bank*
and *Postures*, quietly proved herself to be one of the finest writers
of fiction under middle age, but she has also proved herself to be
enamoured of gloom to an incredible degree." No one seemed to
understand that if the true modernist was the alienated individual
struggling alone, then surely Rhys had a greater claim to that title
than many of her fellow expatriates. She was an ingénue, though,
an innocent young girl; she shouldn't have been writing about
such things.

It is quite possible that it was this essential contradiction in
Rhys that drew Ford to her: the harsh, "sordid" world of prostitutes and cheats and alcoholics was being conjured up on the
page by a child-woman, a "girl" who seemingly couldn't cope
and needed support. A man with a reputation for finding exciting, new, young writers and launching them on their careers, Ford
must have been aware of plenty of literary young women, the kind
who were hanging about Saint-Germain at that time, no doubt
eager for his help and whatever else he could offer. But there was
something special about this particular young woman. Bowen
has commented on that girl-woman contradiction in Rhys's appearance and behavior: "I learnt what a powerful weapon lies in
weakness and pathos and how strong is the position of the person
who has nothing to lose."

Was it a perceived weakness in Rhys that appealed to Ford?
The hopelessness of her situation? "The girl was a really tragic
person," Bowen wrote in her memoir, "a doomed soul, violent

and demoralised." Rhys, at thirty-four, is not a woman here but a "girl," even though she was actually older than Bowen herself was then. Was it indeed the tragic nature of this "girl" that led Ford on? Was he taking a walk on the wild side, by getting involved with her, indulging in a bit of the sordidness of a world he didn't have to inhabit?

Bowen gives short shrift to something else about Rhys: "Her gift for prose and her personal attractiveness." There is a sense of bewilderment in Bowen's two-page account of the affair that broke up her relationship with Ford, a relationship she viewed as a marriage (Elsie always refused to give Ford a divorce). Bohemian and artistic, Bowen was no doubt open to a certain amount of flexibility with regard to Ford, and even to possible other extramarital affairs. But there's a real sense of puzzlement in her memoir over what it was exactly that Ford saw in Rhys. All she can suggest is a general theory about her husband: that Ford needed "to exercise his sentimental talents from time to time upon a new object," to keep him "young," to "[refresh] his ego," that he "needed more assurance than anyone I have ever met. That was one reason why it was so necessary for him to surround himself with disciples." And, of course, there was Rhys's victim-like status, which appealed to his male ego as he rode to her rescue.

How much of this is truly representative of what happened between Rhys and Ford, of what drew them to each other in the first place? Are we to discount Rhys's later claim to her friend and editor, Diana Athill, that she didn't love Ford at all and he didn't love her? Was it Rhys's own fault? As one biographer writes, "In the end, of course, she lost Ford." There is a great amount of supposition in that "of course," and a great amount of space in that "in the end." Space enough for two; space enough for important questions to be asked. It is a space that needs to be filled. Did Ford not love Rhys either?

• • • •

To remain with Ford, and to keep him in love with her, Rhys would have had to perform an almost impossible balancing act for the duration of their time together. It is clear that Ford either couldn't reconcile the two aspects of Rhys's personality, the child-woman contradiction that first drew him to her, or that he simply grew tired of the very contradiction that had initially so beguiled him. Contradictions are hard to live with—they don't understand compromise. They don't, in Heidler's words in *Quartet*, "play the game."

Disappointment in a lover is a terrible thing: when we find out that the beloved object is not quite what we thought it was, the letdown can be enormous. And there is something of that in Rhys's novel: a sense that Marya has let down Heidler in some way. Rhys hadn't let Ford down by writing poorly; the freshness, the rawness, the nonjudgmental attitude Rhys had as an author toward the underdog, the sympathy for those on the breadline, was all effortlessly "modern" and highly personal. It was brave writing. Rhys was writing about dangerous, unpalatable things.

But this is where the "ingénue" aspect of Rhys begins to ring true: she really doesn't seem to have been ambitious about her work in the beginning, or to have taken herself seriously as a writer, or to have been aware of Modernist fashions. Not until Ford met her. He paid such attention to every word she wrote, discussing it and advising her on what to drop and what to develop, to the extent that she missed his advice massively in the forthcoming years and with every book she subsequently wrote ("There is nobody to talk to and advise me or tell me I am right to stick to what I feel for that is what I hope to do after much worry," she wrote to her daughter in 1958). It's perhaps no accident that after she wrote *Quartet*—without Ford's help, of course—she married Leslie Tilden Smith, a literary agent, recommended, ironically enough, by Ford himself. He, too, was a man who could advise her about her writing.

But Ford couldn't live with his literary find. Part of his account in *When the Wicked Man* is true: Rhys was a depressive and a heavy drinker, and the two don't sit together well. Stella Bowen wrote that Rhys "nearly sank our ship," and I don't think she simply meant her relationship with Ford by having an affair with him. It was more than that; it was the negative aspect of Rhys's personality, the depression that she brought into their world—Bowen's account is full of words like "sordid," "tragic," "shattered," "doomed," "darkness," "disorder," and so on. This is not just a bruised partner speaking; this is someone who really resents the darkness that has been brought into her life, and by the person she least expected to bring it: the "girl," the "pretty and gifted young woman." The dangerous side to Rhys that Ford found attractive was also deadening, harmful, and destructive. He couldn't cope with her. The worldly-wise stories weren't supposed to be quite that real; they weren't supposed actually to *be* the woman who wrote them and who was now living in his house. That woman was supposed to be a girl, an altogether far more malleable ingénue. Where had she gone?

The answer is, she probably never existed in the first place. All the way through *Quartet*, Marya is described as a girl, a "babe in the wood," a "darling child," a "poor little devil" who is "frail," "little," a "doll," like "a child shut up in a dark room." This Marya couldn't also be the author of "sordid" novels, could she? No, that was too much, even for fiction, so Rhys left out any mention of Marya as a writer and of Heidler helping her professionally. It was an unsustainable reality in a novel, and it was an unsustainable reality in life, as Ford came to realize: his ingénue was nothing of the kind. His fantasy of Rhys wasn't matching up to the reality.

To be condemned for being a woman, not a child, results in a childish, yet very womanly, moment of anger in *Quartet* when Marya publicly slaps Heidler's face. This really did happen between Rhys and Ford: six months after their affair ended, Rhys and Ford were both still in Paris, and when Rhys happened on Ford in a Montparnasse café, she apparently slapped him right across the face. Was Rhys's anger simply, then, the anger of a woman scorned?

It is important to note that while Ford encouraged and published writers like Katherine Anne Porter and Djuna Barnes, Rhys was the only one to receive the full treatment of being taken up by him, loved by him, edited and humiliated and remade by him. She must have believed him when he told her that she was special, that he had never met anyone like her before (as he undoubtedly would have, because it was true: he hadn't met anyone like her before), that she was a genius, that she was his girl. How then, if she was so special, Rhys might well have asked herself, could he live without her? Nothing has even been mentioned of the help Rhys might have given Ford with *his* writing—the suggestion has never been made; not even Rhys herself has ever made it, as though it was impossible for her even to imagine such a thing. The ingénue doesn't help others; *they* help *her*.

But given that the facade of the ingénue had worn pretty thin during the course of Rhys's relationship with Ford, especially while they were sharing the same house, and that he was discovering Rhys was, in fact, a woman, it would be very surprising if even unconsciously she had not helped him. It is very unusual indeed for literary relationships to be a one-way street. At some level both Ford and Rhys must have known what she was giving him, in a literary sense; how much she was helping him with his writing.

The same year that he met Rhys, Ford had published the first of the Tietjens trilogy, which he completed in two years, a remarkable achievement. He also found time to write his reminiscences of Joseph Conrad and publish a book of essays, but he was exhausted and worried. It was a contrast to the previous decade:

after *The Good Soldier*, and up until the year he met Rhys, Ford had published poetry, a book of reminiscences and essays, and one other novel, *The Marsden Case*. For a man as prolific as Ford, this could only be considered something of a dry spell—indeed, when he met Bowen, he told her all he wanted to do was live in the country and raise pigs. They did this for three years. Back in Paris, everything changed.

There may be little factual evidence of the kind of literary influence that Rhys had on Ford, but there can be little doubt that his liaison with her galvanized him into writing again. One biographer has gone so far as to comment that "the sexually charged atmosphere of *No More Parades* . . . may have been influenced by the beginning of Ford's affair with Rhys. He was certainly writing again with the force and anguish that new passions elicited from him." Had Rhys known of this beneficial effect her very presence had on Ford's writing, her anger might have been quelled: no cast-off lover wants to think she hasn't left her mark, for good or for ill. It was the woman that Rhys *was* who helped him, not the ingénue he believed her to be.

• • • •

Few critics or biographers have appreciated just how terrifying it must have been for Rhys to be cut out of Ford's life when he decided to end their affair. I do not mean terrifying in a financial sense, or even in terms of a loss of love. Those were things Rhys had experienced before: she knew she could cope with little money, unpleasant as it was, as she had had to do that many times before, both as an actress in England and later in Paris with Lenglet when they were both hard up. She could have done what she did then and become a governess, teaching English to young children; or she could have approached Mrs. Adam for more work.

She could also cope with the pain of rejection, even if in *Quartet* the character of Marya warns Heidler that she couldn't. Rhys had surely experienced the worst of it with Lancelot Hugh Smith; while she may have loved Ford very much, as some believe, it was unlikely she had loved him more than she had loved Smith. The loss of Ford's feelings for her would have been extremely painful, but not as apocalyptic as some have suggested.

What I think really terrified her more than anything else was the loss of her adviser. Ford had shown her more than how to write well. He had shown her a new way of living, of making her way in the world, as a writer, something she had never considered before. He had given her a whole new identity, both literally when he changed her name, and psychologically by making her see what she could be. He had introduced her to writers, most of whom she was, admittedly, too shy to talk to unless she had a drink in her, but he had shown her what it meant to be one. He had made her see what she was good at, and Rhys, from a very early age, had desperately wanted to be very good at something.

Breaking away from Ford meant that she was now on her own when it came to writing: she had to decide for herself what was good and what was bad. She could follow some of his rules and keep putting into practice what he had taught her. But when Ford abandoned her, so did her confidence in her writing: that she could do it, and do it well, without him.

Which is why, perhaps, her first piece of writing after she left Ford was about their affair, and was written in such a mood of anger and despair. It was a piece of writing that had to come out, for good or ill; as she said herself, she had to do it. Not just to expunge her feelings about it, the cathartic method she had used ever since she was a child, but also to prove to herself that she could do it, and that she could do it without him. Few have suggested Rhys's anger might have come from fear: not fear of being destitute or alone or penniless, but fear of writing without his help.

It all suggests, of course, that Rhys would never have become a published writer without Ford, and out of all the women
in this book, Rhys is probably the one for whom that was true.
Rhys's tragedy was that she appeared to continue to think of
herself as a helpless child, even in old age. But this contradiction,
while it may have made her a tricky woman to deal with, was
what made her the writer she became. And it was a contradiction
that wasn't, ironically enough, destroyed by her relationship with
Ford, but rather enhanced by it.

There were more quarrels with him. At the beginning of
1927, Ford managed to get her a job translating *Perversite* by
Francis Carco (with whom Katherine Mansfield had once had
a fling). Unfortunately, when it was published, Ford was credited
with the translation, not Rhys. Rhys was furious about this, but it
wasn't until 1966 that she acknowledged in a letter, "It was Covici
the publisher's fault and I know Ford did his best to put things
right." Part of the reason it took her so long to forgive him was
her feeling that he'd taken her up and then cast her aside. She had
been just a part of his fantasy all along, and as a fantasy, none of it
was real. He had fallen for her because he had fallen for his own
fantasy of helping a weak, powerless young girl, who would in
turn adore him for all he had done for her. Ford's love for Rhys
was, I would argue, as self-interested as Rhys's love for Ford, and
that is also why so many people have been confused about the
authenticity of their affair ever since (did they really love one
another?).

But there is another aspect that the fantasy got wrong. Rhys
had never been a helpless young girl at all; she had never been
an ingénue. In the end, however, that assumption wasn't Rhys's
mistaken fantasy. It was Ford's. And they both paid for it: Ford's
relationship with Stella Bowen never recovered from his affair
and they broke up shortly afterwards. Rhys herself would struggle

all her life with an inner rage she was never able fully to articulate, and which dragged her all too often into a pit of alcoholic despair. The fantasy of the ingénue produced love for a time, and it produced a writer. But it was a horribly high price to pay, and it's arguable that Rhys, the ingénue, paid more than any other woman in this volume for her literary partnership.

Anaïs Nin and Henry Miller.

5. THE "MISTRESS": ANAÏS NIN
AND HENRY MILLER

*Between Henry and me there is the diabolical compact of two
writers who understand each other's human and literary life, and
conflicts.*

—Anaïs Nin

I will stay home and polish my nails like a well-kept mistress.
—Henry Miller

Anaïs Nin had been married for almost nine years when she first
met Henry Miller through a mutual friend in Paris, toward the
end of 1931. Within a short time of that meeting, she had become
his "mistress." But she was the one who paid for his food and
for his clothes; she was the one who bought her lover gifts. This
expenditure was quickly followed by money for Miller's rent and
to print some of his publications, as all the while she struggled to
find publishers for her own work. Nin's extraordinary financial
support even extended to her lover's wife, June, in those first few
months of their relationship. But none of it was Nin's money,
strictly speaking. It all came from the household allowance she
got from the substantial salary of her long-suffering banker husband, Hugo Guiler.

From wife to mistress wasn't the most unexpected path for
an alluring, attractive, still-young woman of twenty-eight like
Anaïs Nin to take. Born to Cuban parents, brought up in Paris

and New York, she was exotic and exciting to be around, intellectually curious as well as sensually open. She was a beguiling-looking woman with dark, almond-shaped eyes framed by long, dark lashes and carefully plucked eyebrows, and with a delicate but sensuous mouth. Her marriage to Guiler had been a good financial move for her. It had secured the furs and comfortable houses she had always wanted, but it had been sexually unsatisfying for her from the beginning. Surprisingly, considering Nin's later reputation for sexually liberated writing, when she married Guiler in March of 1923, at the age of twenty, Nin was almost prudish about sex and had had no sexual experiences. Their marriage went unconsummated for months because neither of them knew what to do. And things, alas, didn't improve very much once they did understand what sex meant. At the point that Nin met Miller, Guiler was largely reliant on pornography for arousal. Any spiritual or creative connection there might have been between them in the early days of their marriage was gone. But Guiler still adored her, and Nin needed to be adored.

It was possibly this need that had kept her physically, if not emotionally, faithful to Guiler, in spite of her disappointment in the marriage. That is, until she met Miller. She had considered an adulterous affair a few years previously in New York, when she had fallen heavily for John Erskine, a literature professor. They hadn't gone beyond some "heavy petting," however, and much to her distress he had eventually rejected her. Now, after seven years in Paris, where she had spent much of her time writing a book about D. H. Lawrence and adding to the ever growing volumes of diaries she had been keeping since she was a teenager, the sexually frustrated, literarily ambitious Nin displayed a much more ruthless approach to getting the man she wanted.

For various reasons, in spite of his unprepossessing physical appearance (as Nin herself acknowledged in her diary), the man she wanted was Henry Miller. Miller was then a forty-year-old, short, balding man with glasses, who had first arrived in Paris from New York two years before. Now, in 1931, he was with his second wife, June, and had earned a reputation as a bit of a hack with grand writing ambitions. So far, he had published occasional articles with the *Chicago Tribune* and the Paris *Herald*, and had also written a much-talked-about appreciation of the filmmaker Luis Buñuel for the *New Republic* magazine. He had completed two novels: *Moloch*, about his first marriage to Beatrice Wickens, and *Crazy Cock*, about his marriage to June and her close sexual relationship with a female friend, Mara Andrews. Both were yet to be published. What he was really doing, haunting the demimonde of the French capital, was gathering material for the book that would later make his name, *Tropic of Cancer*. That, though, was all to come.

But if it is less easy to understand Nin's attraction to Miller, the rather unprepossessing *man*, it is quite evident what attracted her to Miller, the ambitious *writer*, especially when we see how much a literary career meant to her. It wasn't just a sexually unsatisfying relationship with her husband that caused Nin to take up with the "warm, joyous, relaxed, natural" Henry Miller when she met him, although the strains in her marriage produced by a lack of physical rapprochement no doubt contributed to her eagerness to be intimate with him. Nin does focus, in her diaries of the early years of her relationship with Miller, on how good the sex between the two of them is, and their letters are unsurprisingly explicit: in one March 1932 letter, Miller wrote Nin, "Come quickly then and screw me. Shoot with me. Wrap your legs around me. Warm me." She also focused in those diaries on the sexual tension of the ménage à trois she enjoyed with Miller and his wife, June ("Henry and June change as I come near to them. I destroy the worlds I want to enter. I arouse creativeness in Henry, romanticism in June. June, by her voluptuous body, her sensual face, her erotic voice, arouses perversity and sensuality . .

. We are two contrasting forces. What will be our effect on each other?"). It is clear from her descriptions of this experience how Nin's later emphasis on sex and the female body would infuse her writing. But Miller was much more for her than a conduit to some kind of sexual self-knowledge that would make her diaries more interesting reading; or to the kind of "writing of the body" she employed, which some argue prefigures the "écriture feminine" of French feminist theory forty years later. He was also a means of gaining entry to the literary world she was desperate to join.

• • • •

Anaïs Nin was born in Paris on February 21, 1903, to Cuban parents Rosa Culmell and Joaquin Nin. Between her birth in the French capital and her move to New York with her mother and two younger brothers when she was eleven years old, she lived in a variety of locations: Havana, Berlin, Brussels, Barcelona, as well as several different parts of Paris. Her father's musical career directed this itinerant existence, as well as their varying financial situation. Rosa had come from a more socially respectable Havana family—her father was actually Danish and he had made a great deal of money through trade. Rosa's husband was eight years younger than she when they married, the son of a Spanish soldier who had grown up to become a professional pianist, and Rosa's wealthier family were understandably not keen on the match. But Rosa was a headstrong woman and possibly worried about being left on the shelf—she was thirty-one when she married Nin. The couple soon left for Paris, where they lived comfortably at first, and their first child, Anaïs, was born. Anaïs Nin was close to Thorvald and Joaquin, her two younger brothers, during those early years, possibly because they moved around so much, depriving them of the chance to establish good friends at the schools they attended briefly, and also possibly because their temperamental, moody father was fond of corporal punishment. They could sympathize with each other in the Spanish or French they spoke all the time, after each had received a beating or two for some trivial offense.

The family's fortunes went up or down depending on Nin's concert appearances, and by the time Nin was ten, her father had been supplementing his income with teaching. It may have helped financially, but private tutoring was disastrous for the Nins' marriage: Joaquin Nin ended up abandoning his family for a fifteen-year-old pupil of his, Maruca Rodriguez, while they were residing in Paris, in 1914.

Nin records that she was devastated when her father left them, and that she began her diary on the boat to New York, where her mother had finally decided to set up home, as a "letter" to him, to let him know how she was getting on. It's possible to argue that her accusations against him in later life, of the sexual abuse that she claims she suffered at his hands when she was about ten years old, may have come from anger at her perceived rejection when he left them all. Where this leaves the explicit account she gives in her diary of the later passionate affair between father and daughter, begun, she says, in 1933, just after her father had called out of the blue to say he was coming to see her, is anyone's guess. According to Nin's account, she dressed in silk negligees when she visited him in his apartment; he made the first move, fondling her feet. Two weeks of "unbridled" sexual activity followed this initial gesture, a "nonstop orgiastic frenzy," as described in her journal. For some, this account is a traumatized "remembering" of possible child abuse that plays out in an incestuous relationship in adulthood; for others, it is the "heavy-breathing prose of a cheap romance novel." It's possible, too, that it's a fantastical account that bears no relation to reality, but is the result of her venture into psychoanalysis, as she attempted to understand its narrative theories by constructing a much more literal story for herself (these interpretations, though, are less important for the subject of this chapter, as I do not believe Nin's troubled relationship with her father is quite as crucial to her relationship with Miller as some have stated).

With her mother earning money in their new city by giving singing lessons and investing in the property market (Rosa borrowed from her wealthy family to buy property, fix it up, then sell it on at a profit), Nin found herself once again moving from one home to another, from West 75th Street in Manhattan to leafier Richmond Hill in Queens. She persuaded her mother to let her leave school at sixteen and educate herself at home; never having developed the knack of making school friends, she had been a lonely child, and the diary she had started keeping was the only friend she had.

But then, early in 1921, it seemed she had finally found a partner in life. She had been invited to a dance in Forest Hills, Queens, by the sister of one Hugo Guiler. The Guilers were Scottish, and had originally been living in Puerto Rico. Hugh Guiler had sent his two sons, Hugo and Johnny, to Ayr Academy in Alloway, a small town southwest of Glasgow in Scotland, which both boys had hated, but he then brought them back across the Atlantic when the family moved to New York. It was a long courtship between Nin and Guiler—he apparently didn't attempt to kiss her for a year, possibly fearing disapproval from his Protestant Scottish parents of his dalliance with a Cuban Catholic girl. And indeed, when they finally married in March 1923 in defiance of Guiler's parents, Nin's new husband was disowned, all funds cut off.

But Guiler had a good job with the National City Bank of New York and could afford to finance his marriage and his new lifestyle. Guiler had ambitions like Nin to be a writer, and in the early days of their marriage, these joint literary aspirations helped to bond them, and blur the disappointment of their un-satisfactory sex life. They would often write together in the same room, assessing each other's work, as Nin cultivated her diary en-tries. But they were living with Rosa, in Rosa's house, which was tricky. Nin and her mother were close, but they were both strong characters, and now, Guiler was finically supporting Rosa as well, which she, a proud woman, found difficult to accept. But when Nin and Guiler moved to Paris at the end of 1924, after Guiler had been transferred there by his bank, Rosa buried her pride, and she and Nin's two brothers followed them.

It is interesting to note that 1924 was the same year Jean Rhys began her relationship with Ford Madox Ford, also in Paris. There is no evidence that the two women ever met—indeed, their social circles would have been very different, with Rhys on the breadline and Nin enjoying greater wealth, not yet hobnob-bing with artists and down-at-heel writers. But Nin's first apart-ment was in Montparnasse, an area Rhys knew well. It's tempting to think of them passing each other in the street, Rhys hurry-ing on foot on her way to Ford's parties in the more salubrious Saint-Germain, and the now-famous Les Deux Magots bar, Nin scouring the better shops for the "Moroccan furniture and cop-per tables" she would purchase to decorate her new apartment.

Rhys's and Nin's paths to publication took slightly different routes, too. As in Nin's case, it was a diary of Rhys's that caught attention; but for Rhys, her materials were immediately passed on to Ford, leaving their author with little need to promote herself or to get a passport into the literary world of expatriate Paris. Nin's diary, meanwhile, would remain unpublished for a long time, and she would have to work hard to gain acceptance into the literary world. Arriving back in Paris with her husband, Nin could only fantasize about being a female Proust. She had had very little literary success so far, having only published a few poems in a school magazine. Her interest in journal-keeping seems to have been shored up by biographies and published diaries of women like Eugenie de Guerin and Marie Bashkirtseff, but she also tried her hand at publishing poems in magazines, getting one accepted by her favorite woman's magazine, *The Delineator*. It seems that reading popular classics by authors like Robert Louis Stevenson continued the education she had dropped out of as a teenager; her brief attendance in 1921 at non-credit courses at Columbia University, paid for by her mother, was her only other experience of formal education.

So it wasn't until 1931 that Nin had the satisfaction of seeing her first adult, published work: an article on D. H. Lawrence for the *Canadian Forum*. This small success would see her try her best to make the right contacts with other women authors, writing to Djuna Barnes and Rebecca West, while sending copies of the Lawrence article to the likes of Janet Flanner and Sylvia Beach. However, all these attempts to break into an exclusive literary club would fail miserably and leave her feeling as isolated as ever (although West did respond, apparently, to Nin's third letter to her).

When she first met Henry Miller, ready to be fascinated and dazzled by him, she exhibited a certain amount of self-doubt, which might have been the consequence of the many rebuffs she had received from the woman writers she had contacted. She was sure that he wouldn't be much interested in her and noted in her diary that, partly because of what he considered to be his wife June's "lies," he was "suspicious of poetry and beauty . . . truth lies only in people and things stripped of aesthetics." This aspect of Miller's personality was quite different from Nin's—she noted that for Miller "illusions and lies are synonymous," but that "in this I feel remote from him, totally in disagreement with him." She told him that what concerned her were not secrets and lies themselves (Nin thrived on creating fiction out of fact). It was *"what makes them necessary"* that mattered to her.

This attitude toward truth and lies is at the heart of Nin's diaries themselves, diaries which would eventually total some thirteen volumes and run from 1920 to 1974. Most of them began to be published in the 1960s (the first volume was published in 1966 and reviewed by *The New York Times Book Review*, bringing her the kind of fame she had always craved, with radio and TV appearances and a deluge of fan mail) when Nin was gathered up by the feminist movement, and her explicit sexual accounts formed part of the new sexual revolution for women. Her many novels, like *House of Incest* (published in Paris in 1936, then in the States in 1947)—strictly speaking, a "prose poem," not a novel—*Winter of Artifice* (1943), and *A Spy in the House of Love* (1953), are impressionistic, experimental works, less accessible than her erotic novels, like *Delta of Venus* (1976), and were always less popular than the diaries. But everything she wrote was infused with this mixture of truth and lies.

Nin's biographer, Deirdre Bair, makes great play with the "mensonge vital" or the "necessary lie" that she believes Nin constructed repeatedly throughout her life about every aspect of it: about writing, about men, about women, about her father. Feminist critic Elizabeth Podnieks, echoes Bair by calling Nin "a consummate liar," and refers to Nin's diary as a deliberate "act of self-invention," drawing attention to the "heavily excised, edited and rewritten" diaries that she kept from 1931 to 1966. "Let us admit then, as Nin was wont to do, that her diaries are not factually genuine. But let us also admit that they are a genuine self-portrait." Academic Lynette Felber counters, though, that these accusations of lying ignore the "generic innovation of Nin's tactic" in her diary, which was the "bold fictionalization of autobiography."

One person's lie is another person's fictionalized autobiography, it would seem. But this particular opposition (lie versus fiction, factual versus psychological truth) implies another one: that of the reactionary, conservative impulse (the old-fashioned lie) set against a revolutionary one (the "fictionalized biography"); and it seems likely to me that Nin was capable of being both reactionary and revolutionary at the same time. She was someone who liked to hold opposing views simultaneously, who knew she lied but said it was for the sake of the truth. Bair points out that she would construct an alternative "self" in her diary from the earliest days, a self that did, and did not, reflect who she really was, what she was really doing, how she was really feeling.

For some critics, this split personality was a survival strategy that came out of her experience as a stranger in a foreign land, when her mother left France for New York when Nin was only eleven years old. For others, it was the response to possible sexual abuse at the hands of her father, just a year or so previously. Either way, this contradiction corresponds perfectly to Nin's endless battle between the safer, more reactionary bourgeois claims on her life, and the dangerous, revolutionary, bohemian role of the poet: she liked too much her husband's nice, bourgeois banker's salary and the comfort and luxury it could give her to ever think of giving it up, even for Henry Miller. But she forever hankered after the more bohemian lifestyle of the demimonde Miller introduced to her, believing that to be a poet, one must live in that bohemian cliché of the starving artist in a garret. That contradictory impulse informed much of her fascination with Miller's wife, June, who seemed perfectly at ease with no money, no home, and no comfort, much to Nin's amazement.

How much did such a contradictory impulse inform her feelings for Miller, though—wanting him one moment, dismissing him the next; moving, as she did in 1933, from his bed to her analyst Rene Allendy's, when she began an affair with him (or Otto Rank's, whom she also began seeing, or her husband's), sometimes even all in one day—as she makes out in the diary? Did she love Miller or not, or was she capable of feeling both at the same time? Did this contradictory impulse enable Nin to view her relationship with Miller more simply, as the equable one she wanted it to be of two writers sharing their thoughts about each other's work, advising and encouraging in equal measure? Or did it enable her to ignore much of the reality of that relationship, the complexity of it, the less satisfying parts of it? Contradictions abound in Nin's life and the reporting of her life (her first feelings about June, for instance, note a fascination with June's "face and body which promises so much, but hating her invented self which hides the true one"; one would have thought that Nin, of all people, would have appreciated such an "invented self" and all that went into creating it), which have long puzzled readers of her letters and her diaries, and which have occasionally undermined her posthumous reputation.

But contradiction was as necessary to Nin as food and water are to the rest of us, and contradiction formed the basis for her literary partnership with Henry Miller. The question of whether she would have become a published writer without him, however, is not so riven with contradictions. It is perhaps clearer in this instance, in more than any other example from this volume, that a woman with her ambition, self-belief, and ruthlessness would eventually have achieved her literary aims without the necessity of a male literary partner. So why, then, did she need him? And was her relationship with him good for her, and for her writing?

· · · ·

The concept of adultery presented no moral problems for Nin, a delicate but striking woman who always took great care of her appearance with regular facials and careful makeup, and who prided herself on looking even younger than her twenty-eight years. If at times it was logistically tricky, keeping her husband in the dark, once her affair with Miller was underway, that was nothing to the game she would play when she first made overtures to Miller's wife, the "chaotic" June. It was June she fell for first, she would claim in her diary of that year; only after June went back to the States did her sexual relationship with Miller fully begin.

The marriage between Henry and June was a complex one: they had fallen out several times over the years, and both of them had been sexually unfaithful, he with prostitutes, she with Mara Andrews. There was a further problem at this point in 1931, because Miller had fallen in love with Paris and wanted to stay; his wife kept flitting back to New York, which she preferred. It seems to have been June Miller who encouraged her husband to see Nin: although she was invited along with her husband to meet Nin, she stayed behind; one biographer suggests that she wanted Henry to "cultivate the wealthy Nin as a good milk cow." What she hadn't expected was the impression Nin would make on him, and June's response to Miller's interest seems to have been to try to seduce Nin herself, to pull her away from her husband.

The tension of this ménage à trois couldn't last long, though, and sure enough, by the end of 1932, after June's return to Paris in October, Nin would see off at least one of the players in this troubled trio. The stormy, passionate "literary fuck fest" that she and Miller had already embarked on, though, would last for a surprisingly long time, almost ten years in total. It would be continued by Miller even when he no longer needed money from her; even when she turned down his requests that she leave Guiler and live with him instead. Nin herself would find it hard to break from Miller, even when she was conducting affairs with other men and had fallen out of love with him.

In the final analysis, though, it was Nin who resisted complete commitment to the man she described, on first seeing him, as "a man whom life intoxicates." Most commentators assume it was mainly financial reasons that held Nin back from committing to Miller: that she could never quite bring herself to abandon the loyal, wealthy husband she could be sure of for an unpredictable, unfaithful, often impecunious writer. Yet something else had been established between Nin and Miller. Something that ensured that, long after the end of the Second World War, when their relationship had stopped being a sexual one, they would remain friends and supporters of each other's work. Miller would carry on using his influence to help Nin publish her diaries, no matter that by then she had stopped discussing them with him, or asking for his advice.

He was the most important man in her life, she often told him, and he was almost certainly the most expensive. Anaïs Nin may be best known for her erotica and sexually enticing diaries, but she is also notorious as Henry Miller's "mistress." And yet, in spite of her own comments on her "mistressing" ways, this description of her really belies the nature of their relationship. Miller professed himself ashamed of his financial dependence on her: "It hurts me to know that you are pinching and scraping to aid me. I think sometimes I am nothing but a big bum. Damn it, if I could find a way to earn a living I'd sell myself for the remainder of my life." The traditional gifts and handouts of a married man to his mistress were Nin's prerogative, not Miller's. In every respect, Nin managed to fulfill the double dictionary definition of a mistress as "a woman in authority over others" by being the one with the checkbook as well as "a woman (other than his wife) with whom a married man has a usually prolonged sexual relationship."

But this doubleness was part of Nin's makeup: she liked playing with readers, both of her fiction as well as of her diaries, and she once wrote, when working as an analyst in the States, that on her desk she had a photo frame into which she would soon be inserting a picture of her husband—on top of the one she had of Henry, which was laid on top of one of Otto Rank, another lover (also known to her as "Huck"), which was laid on top of a picture of her cousin, Eduardo Sanchez, who was her first love. That way, she said, "to each one I can write truthfully, according to the hour,

'I have your photograph before me.'"

Being the mistress of many men as opposed to a single man may be just one more subversive tactic Nin employed to overturn the traditionally subservient aspect of the role. But by allowing Miller to play his designated part (a part that many others played, too) in her crucial subversion of what being a mistress meant, she was also denying Miller his importance to her (that he was "the one"). This ploy—turning what may appear to make her weak and deny her power into what can give her control and author-ity—is what defined Anaïs Nin's whole approach to life and art, and she needed Miller to do it.

It is an approach that she refined in the adult diaries, which continually assured her that every man and woman she came into contact with, including her closest relations, desired her; that eve-ry intellectual she encountered was envious of her brilliance; that every artist was in awe of her work. What Nin displayed in her adult diaries was more than simple narcissism, though; in them, she turned an unpublished author who was effectively paying men to have sex with her into an irresistible woman and success-ful artist. It's uncertain whether Miller, convinced of his contribu-tions to her artistic as well as her sexual life, was ever fully wise to this strategy of hers, in spite of being privy to what she wrote in the diaries. Both of them, he admitted, were egotists; both of them were artists, after all. But did he ever realize how much she used him, if indeed she did use him? Did he believe that she needed him for her art, for her life? Did *she* believe she needed him? Just what kind of an investment was he for Nin? Did hav-ing a relationship with another writer give legitimacy to her own claim to being a writer, too?

• • • •

Miller may not have been much more successful a writer than

Nin when they first met, but he was at least considered a professional one, trying to live off his earnings with his words. He also represented a type that repulsed yet attracted Nin, contradictory as ever. Miller may have been short, but with his swagger and his wit, he had the kind of forceful personality that made up for what he lacked in physical presence, and he had the kind of exterior confidence Nin appears to have lacked, for all her self-belief and sending of her work to important figures like Flanner. Nin always had her doubts about what writing could do for her: "I am not sure that being a writer will help me escape from Louveciennes." She may always have been sure that she was a writer—from the age of eleven, writing in her diary, she knew that was what she wanted to be—but she wasn't sure that it could work for her. So when she first read Miller's article on the Buñuel film, *L'Age d'Or*, shown to her by their mutual friend, Richard Osborn, she found it evidence of what writing could do. It was "as potent as a bomb"; even better, his writing reminded her of Lawrence's.

What more could she have wanted? Nin needed above all someone who knew about writing and whose work she could admire. Was this because such a genius would surely reflect her own greatness back at her? In this, Miller perfectly obliged, telling her in February 1932, after he'd read her manuscript of the book she had written about Lawrence: "Certain passages are of an inestimable beauty. Above all, a sureness, a grasp, a mature dexterity which I, alas, will never attain . . . You are essentially the artist . . . You have a power, through sheer feeling, that will captivate your audience." Even his reservations and advice—"Do not attempt to resolve . . . Don't preach. No moral conclusions"—could hardly have dampened down such praise, such flattery.

It wasn't yet the flattery of a lover for the object of his love—they wouldn't sleep together until the beginning of March 1932, three months after they'd met—but rather, the flattery of a writer for his patron. Nin seems to have overlooked the fact that she was paying for him at this point (she was giving him a monthly amount of at least \$200 from her housekeeping money, to pay for the apartment she had found for him, as well as its furnishings), and any suggestion in her own mind that his flattery wasn't to be trusted was simply never raised. That same month, in her diary, she says she is "grateful" for the "avalanches" of letters she gets from Miller, and it's not all flattery. She is getting literary advice, too: "I have learned from Henry to make notes, to expand, not to brood secretly, to move to write every day, to do, to say instead of meditating . . . I write against and with him." It cannot be overstated how beneficial Miller was to Nin's writing career at this point in their relationship. She was paying for more than a room and nice furniture for her "bit-on-the-side": she was paying for a good teacher.

Even when Miller sometimes made fun of her words—usually when she misused a word, English not being her first language—she forgave him because what she loved about him was the writer in him. Yet at this early stage, it was not quite everything: "Henry gives me a world of writing, June gives me danger. I must choose and I cannot." Nin was not completely won over: she would become "tired of his obscenities, of his world of 'shit, cunt, prick, bastard, crotch, bitch,'" yet she also understood there was something there that she needed: "I want to be a strong poet, as strong as Henry and June are in their realism."

According to Nin's account of the ensuing ménage à trois, it was June she fell for first, describing her the first time she saw her as "the most beautiful woman on earth." Nin seems to have operated doubly here, too, however. She was attracted by the idea of a lesbian relationship, if not quite by the hard realities of it—she would later reject lesbian sex altogether after she had a bisexual threesome with Donald Friede and another woman called Mary in 1936. It was her first experience "tasting a woman's vagina," as she put it, and she didn't like it. After the episode, the unimpressed

Nin declared, "I would never have asked to see her again. I did not know if my body had value in that fucking world."

But in 1931, Nin had yet to come to these conclusions about a physical lesbian relationship, and claimed in her diary to have fallen hard for June. In her diary, she talks of how fascinated she is by *Miller's* fascination with June, and she adopts it: in comparison to June, she says, "Henry faded." She wants to understand these new, complex feelings she claims she has for June—"June does not reach the same sexual center of my being as man reaches . . . what then does she move in me?"—and decides that "June's elusiveness, her retreat into fantasy, suddenly enrage me, because they are mine." She feels like a lesser being in the face of June's "strength" and talks of June also feeling lesser in the face of Nin and Nin's love for her. She turns her obsessions with June into June's obsession with her: on one shopping expedition that the two women undertake, for instance, "she refused . . . anything that was not symbolic or representative of me." In love with June, she says it is not to Miller that she shows her "true self" but to his wife ("before her I repudiate all I have done, all that I am. I aspire to more. I am ashamed of my writing"), and she faithfully records, in a betrayal of Miller, June's distress over Miller's representation of her in the book he is writing, *Tropic of Cancer*: "It's not me, it's a distortion."

What was really going on here? Nin found relationships with other women difficult, much as she had tried to establish contact with other women writers in Paris, and prior to June there is little from her expressing any kind of attraction to women's bodies. A kind analysis of her adoration of June would see it as a mirroring device: that Nin used June to reflect her own strengths and weaknesses back at her, for it almost seems as though Nin was determined to talk herself into this adoration.

But her relationship with June, which played out as more erotic than sexual, had several other functions. Nin reveals on one occasion that "then we return to Henry with an incandescence which frightens him. Henry is uneasy," and this is key. Nin's encounters with June never went much beyond touching—they never slept together, and it's doubtful just how much did happen between them. Nin's later repudiation of lesbian sex would seem to indicate some falseness in her claim to be so physically attracted to June (a woman who wore "black or bilious green lipstick"). But it made Miller jealous, and, in doing so, prevented Nin from being "the other woman" in her relationship with the married Millers. Sexually involved with both husband and wife, she was the one at the center, not at the margins, of the relationship. Nin worked all of this expertly—in letters to Miller in October 1932, nervous about June's return to her husband in Paris, she starts to operate against the very woman she says fascinates her the most, and reminds him that "I gave you gold and bread, and you resuscitated, until the next upheaval. And upheavals won't come from me. We need each other to nourish each other."

Feminist accounts of Nin's relationship with June Miller tend to downplay Nin's essential treachery here, preferring to view Miller as the patriarchal presence attempting to obliterate one or other of the women involved, or blaming Miller for co-opting Nin into his betrayal of his wife. But that is to ignore Nin's divisive strategies—she was frightened that she would lose Miller. June was a rival, and, I would argue, always had been, right from the beginning. Nin needed Miller as a writer; she didn't need June. Furthermore, she was terrified that June, the wife, would triumph over Nin, the mistress. It was essential to Nin that she pass from position of married man's mistress to married man's one true love, or it would have undermined her writing relationship with Miller, one that she believed, or purported to believe, was founded on an equal basis. Bair argues that, having won out against June, Nin did realize that "two fragile ties, sex and a monthly stipend, bound Henry to her," and feels that that her diary entries from 1933 are "often angry, bitter and cynical." Possibly insecurity about the poor reception to her book on Lawrence made her need for Miller even greater. Rather reminiscent of Katherine Mansfield's and John Middleton Murry's shoring up of each other's egos when they reassured themselves they were both geniuses, there are many references in the letters between Nin and Miller during this year to their both being artists, almost as though Nin needed to hear it to be sure.

But 1933 was also the year that Miller really got stuck into Nin's writing, when he critiqued "Alraune," the early draft of the novel that would eventually become *House of Incest*. Nin's initial reaction to such a brutal reading was surprisingly accommodating—she seems to have appreciated that this was what being in a literary relationship meant. It was what she had been seeking all this time. When Miller lays in with "You have gotten ingrown, more and more protected, more and more sensitive . . . I want to be harsh now, I want to liberate you. I don't ever want to see you write another Alraune . . . What I did sometimes, in changing your language, was to work for a more universal tone—thus cutting through those 'femininities' I referred to in Louveciennes," Nin responds with a meek "I have been working over your corrections of 'Alraune' which prove to me what a gorgeous poet and imaginist *you* are."

But this meekness may have given Miller the wrong impression, if he thought that what Nin wanted was a bruising critique of her work on a regular basis. For if we contrast this reply with her response to his criticism of her *diary*, just six months later, we see what happened when something that really mattered to her came under attack. After telling her that he completely understands why his agent, William Aspenwall Bradley, to whom he has recommended her journal, didn't like it, Miller writes, "I insist on your showing me what you are writing as you go along. You must let me help you. You must toughen up for criticism . . . The hours

that go into the journal are an evasion, fundamentally, of the im-
minent, the ever-impending problem—that of mastering your
medium . . . In general there is too staccato, too jerky, too hectic
and hysterical use of the sentence. Too dramatic, all highlights,
and little or no relief. Too much use of abstract terms, of abstract
emotions. Often culminating in slightly ridiculous hyperboles . .
. You see, I am aiming seriously at the destruction of this diary. It
is good only if you recognize it for what it's worth—otherwise
it is dangerous, poisonous, inclined to make one lazy, facile, self-
centered . . ."

Not content with attacking her writing style, Miller goes
for the whole diary as a project here ("I am aiming seriously
at the destruction of this diary"), forgetting, or perhaps jealously remembering, that the diary is the most important thing in
Nin's life. But Nin isn't going to sit back and take that, the way
she has his previous criticisms. She responds immediately, firing
back: "You have it in for the diary, you know . . . A certain re-
writing of another's writing can be dangerous and go beyond
criticism." She tells him he is encouraging her to write as he
would write, and that that isn't any good for her. She also accuses him of ridiculing her and says she won't send him anything more to look at—"you're not serious." She tells him that
he "reads coolly and without sympathy," and reminds him that
she expects from him what he gets from her, "that is, response,
and an appreciation of what is good, with the emphasis on the
good." She accuses him of being disloyal, of writing under the
influence of Bradley, of not being true to himself and to her,
and upbraids him finally, "Let me know when you are ready to
accompany me again, to come along with me. Otherwise, leave
me alone."

There's a real sense of a battle being waged here by each
writer for the integrity of their writing souls, of which I think
Nin is much more aware than Miller. As much as Miller was a

help to Nin, he was also extremely dangerous. He was sexually demanding, he wasn't above teasing her with the possibility of letting her husband know all about their affair, he was bigger and louder and brasher than she was, and far more willing to frequent sexually transgressive places like brothels and sex clubs, showing a fearlessness of the world that Nin never possessed. Throughout their correspondence, Nin's physical fragility is countered by Miller's sheer virility, which he liked to exaggerate at all times. She was never frightened of him, but he could have done her real harm if he'd wished to, causing Guiler to leave her, perhaps, or even just lashing out at her in an angry temper. Much of this sense of a torturous battle was taking place in October 1933, less than two years after they had first met. What could have happened between them in that short time, to bring them to such a desperate all-or-nothing point?

• • • •

Miller's criticism of Nin's diary felt to her like an all-out personal attack. And it presented her with a problem that none of the other women writers in this volume faced in their literary partnerships: an injunction to destroy her work. No other woman in this volume is ever told to forget what she is writing by the man she is in love with; almost a condition of their love is that they respect the artist that each woman is. Criticism is welcomed and encouraged; destruction is not. In trusting him with her literary soul, Nin was placing far too much power in the hands of a man, and the hands of a man like Miller, who was ruthless enough to use it and to abuse it. Now it seemed she was reaping the effects of giving away too much of that power. The Faustian pact she had made with her literary partner was becoming clear: if she did not resist what he was telling her to do, she would lose the very thing that gave her her writing identity. I don't think any other relationship in this volume poses quite such a literary threat as Miller does to Nin here. There are many personal threats that women experience in this book, such as sexual betrayals that cut too deep for them to survive, or abandonments that leave them financially floundering, unable to find the time or energy to write. But nobody else actually tells them to destroy their work. Nin had destroyed a fetus by allowing a very late abortion to be performed on her. What Miller was telling her to do was, I believe, like asking a mother to kill her living, breathing child.

Miller was no less than a real danger at this point, and if he had succeeded persuading her to destroy her work, we almost certainly wouldn't know the name of Anaïs Nin now. But it's easy to see how seductive the dream of a literary partner with whom she was also sexually compatible had been for her. In the early days of their relationship, Nin was aroused by Miller's passion, both for his work and for her, but she held on to power. The day after their first night together, she wrote to him about his "engulfing kiss," and told him that before the previous night she had contemplated suicide. But, she added, it was her love for June that held her back. She was willing to praise Miller ("I love this strange, treacherous softness of you which always turns to hatred"), but not to let him think he had much power over her—it was June who saved her from self-destruction, not Miller. Whether this was true or not, she recorded in her diary that Miller had praised a manuscript of her first novel (which would remain unpublished) thus: "Says it is the most beautiful writing he has read lately."

This was the kind of literary relationship she wanted. From her childhood days when she first began the diary, she had always envisaged sharing it with someone, fantasizing about her cousin Eduardo, "he who will write in my diary with me." After she married, she encouraged Guiler to read her journal, and he would annotate it, too. It was a site of reconciliation between them, both of them working on the reporting of her life, her feelings, her interpretation of events. Guiler was playing along, keeping his wife sweet, possibly, although his own poetic aspirations may have found some succor in encouraging his artistic wife's writing.

But Nin could cope with this level of interference—adding to what she had already written, or praising what she had done. Her relationship with a professional writer like Miller was a different deal altogether. Apart from the fact that he didn't always offer unalloyed praise, there was the nitty little problem of two artists feeding off each other. Their days, according to her diary, were spent having sex with each other (Bair records one afternoon where Miller "was preparing himself for sex by shaking sandalwood on his penis"), drinking whisky, and writing feverishly: it seems that the moment a sexual encounter occurred, Nin immediately transcribed it into her diary. Not living with Miller meant she could do this at his place, or leave and write at home, or if they were both at hers, she could throw him out when she wanted—she would often sneak Miller into her house while Guiler was out at work, then sneak him back out again just as her husband walked through the door. She had also begun a sexual relationship with her analyst, Rene Allendy, which she somehow managed to fit into her day of writing, sex with Miller, and drinking. It's clear that many of the diary entries are meant to titillate Miller (she even claimed to have had a sexual relationship at this time with Antonin Artaud, the surrealist poet, who was homosexual), and it's during this year that she begins to describe the sexual revelations about her father, although one wonders how much of this was meant to titillate Allendy, as her notes about that affair were also discussed during her analytic sessions with him.

The letters between Miller and Nin during 1933, however, do not give any hint of other sexual liaisons: it seems that they are the only two in the world, and that their days are spent reading (Miller liked to recommend books to Nin, and on one occasion advised himself, "make her read *Magic Mountain* and *Gay Neck*, read *The Inferno* of Strindberg, borrow or steal for her Hamsun's *Wanderers* and *Mysteries*, buy Stokowski's 'Love Song' for the piano. And Fletcher's *Gaugin* and van Gogh's *Letters* and the first volume of Elie Faure in French. Etc. Etc."), writing, becoming artists. But there are huge rows, tantrums from Nin (which Bair puts down to sexual exhaustion and too much drinking) and impatience from Miller over Nin's mood swings, her tearfulness, all through this close writing year, this dancing between partners, between rooms. Nin should have felt more secure—she had seen June off by now—but her book on D. H. Lawrence had received some bad reviews. She had established Miller in Paris with her own money and begun analysis, but this was counteracted by the fact that she had supplied Miller with her diary notes on June, which he incorporated into his novel, *Tropic of Cancer*, a book Nin would subsequently help to publish.

In March 1934 Nin wrote in her diary that her analyst, Otto Rank, had read the now-completed *Tropic of Cancer*. "'I owe all this to you,' says Henry. I answer, 'You owe it to what you are yourself.'" When it was published later that year, this thinly veiled autobiographical novel about a down-at-heel writer struggling to make a living amongst the demimonde of Paris, with very little plot but much sexually explicit material, often conveyed through a stream-of-consciousness, was hailed by Samuel Beckett as "a momentous event in the history of modern writing." It caused offense as it was meant to—Miller had famously written in the pages of his debut novel: "This is not a book . . . No, this is a prolonged insult, a gob of spit in the face of Art, a kick in the pants to God, Man, Destiny, Time, Love, Beauty"—and both the United Kingdom and the United States immediately banned it for obscenity (it would not be published in the United States until 1961). It made Miller an instant celebrity—thanks to Nin's money, which paid for the publication of his book, and thanks to her diary as well, which provided notes on June.

Previously, in the summer of 1932, Nin had not been feeling quite so generous about Miller's potential achievement and her part in it. In fact, she had accused Miller of leaving her with "nothing left to do," and worse than that, of downright theft: "While I was working, I discovered that I had given away to Henry all my insights into June, and that he is using them. He has taken all my sketches for her portrait." Her "insights" show a more sensitive psychological as well as poetic consciousness in Nin than in Miller, which he possibly recognized, hence his "borrowing" of them—and it's interesting that Nin, the outsider, the "third wheel" in the Miller marriage, had a better understanding of June than her husband had. But this literary exchange of equal artists doesn't seem to have turned out the way Nin had in mind at all. That crucial phrase "given away" tells us exactly what was bothering her. "I feel empty-handed and he knows it because he writes me that he 'feels like a crook.'"

Sure enough, Miller had written to her in May 1932, after reading the first volume of her journal, asking: "Have I permission to refer to your Journal? I never stopped to consider that! If not, I will give my remarks to you, not to any book, I promise!" As he had already told her that he found the journal "one of the most beautiful things I have ever read" and that "it makes me love you beyond words," it's possible that sheer flattery blinded Nin to what she was doing. Certainly, by July she was very worried: "As each page of it reaches me, in which he does more and more justice to [June], I feel it is my vision he has borrowed. Certainly no woman was ever asked so much." The next day, though, she sounded more reconciled, and seemed to have forgotten her "literary rebellions."

Lynette Felber argues that this "theft," albeit one permitted by Nin, compelled her to devise a new way of writing, after Miller left her with "nothing to do." She says that Miller "introduced Nin to new kinds of subject matter"; certainly Nin herself claimed in January 1933 that "we have much influence over each other's work, I on the artistry and insight, on the going beyond realism, he on the matter, substance and vitality of mine." Felber also argues that Miller parodied Nin's writing style in a "dream-book" called "Into the Night Life," where he "exaggerates her staccato style," and she claims that Nin "was offended by this piece." But in her diary, Nin responds well to this book. To Felber it seems that their writing styles "were certainly not complementary," given Miller's concern with realism and Nin's for the dreamlike, but this interpretation is contradicted by the letters between Miller and Nin, which tell a different story.

I think what was troubling Nin about Miller's use of her descriptions of June was not just that it left her with "nothing to do." Her worry didn't stem from the problem of writing styles that weren't complementary—quite the opposite, in fact. I think Nin was nervous about Henry's use of her words because their styles were so complementary, because her writing fit so easily into his own prose. Reading the letters between them can sometimes be a confusing experience, they sound so similar. For instance, on August 14, 1932, Miller wrote to Nin, "I feel the greatest peace and joy sitting in the dining room listening to you rustling about, your dress like the goddess Indra studded with a thousand eyes. Anaïs, I only thought I loved you before; it was nothing like this certainty that's in me now. Was all this so wonderful only because it was brief and stolen? Were we acting for each other, to each other? Was I less I, or more I, and you less or more you?"

Miller's writing style here recalls Nin's romantic, self-analytic prose, her own stylistic emphases of the kind she uses in her letter to him of the previous month: "Your pages on my journal move me . . . to see you bending over it so tenderly, taking so much time to understand me, writing such beautiful things about it. It makes me wish I had a much more tragic childhood . . . It is so terribly sweet now to be given what you give me in exchange for the calendars and handkerchiefs . . ."

There's a mirroring here in the intertwining of "you" and "I"; in the emphasis on feeling ("peace and joy" and "move me"); in the hyper-reality of words like "wonderful" and "beautiful." Their sentences are long and flowing, there is no "staccato" style here, none of Miller's trademark curses. The mirroring that takes place here could be because they are lovers; it could also be because they had surprisingly similar tastes in writing. Both loved the work of D. H. Lawrence, having devoured his work before they met each other. Miller had responded to Nin's book on Lawrence with a desire to write one of his own, but he would struggle to complete it his own after the publication of Nin's. Both had torn through Proust and many of the modernist writers that were just becoming known, quite separately, but as they grew closer, they would read more and more of the same writers (Nin would also suggest writers for Miller to read, such as Alain Fournier and Eugene Jolas). At the heart of Nin's writing enterprise were, Elizabeth Podnieks argues, the modernist literary concepts of "sex, self and psychoanalysis." Exactly the same could be said of Miller.

So when Nin, nervous of the complementary aspects of their writing styles, told Miller that he was simply advising her to write like him, she did him a disservice—to a certain extent, she was already writing like him. What was the basis for Miller's criticism of her diary, then? Is it possible that he, too, was blind, and couldn't see how much they were already like each other?

Feminist critics tend to argue that Miller felt threatened by the "feminine" sentences of the diary, or that he couldn't appreciate the innovative project Nin had embarked upon. His urging her to give up the diary took place in mid-October, 1933. But Nin's angry response isn't reflected in her diary for the same month, however much of a breach her letter to him suggested. On the contrary, far from staying away from Miller and rejecting what he has to say, she appears to have actually taken his advice: "Dropped the diary and wrote first twenty pages of June story objectively. Conscious order. Excision of irrelevant details." But she also shows a glimmer of recognition about what their writing has in common: "Henry tries to restrain my exuberance in writing, while yet allowing himself complete exuberance."

In November 1933, Nin began analysis with Otto Rank, who also advised her to give up the diary—the result, she writes, makes her feel "deprived of my opium." But she begins to feel that "I still have something to say. And what I have to say is really distinct from the artist and art. It is the woman who has to speak." She used Rank to talk about Miller, almost to undermine the power she had handed over to him ("we talked about how Henry 'deformed' and never understood people"). By February 1934, she was insisting that the diary was "dead" one minute, then asking herself, "has the diary truly died?" It was indeed a trial for her, being without the diary, even though Rank was telling her that it damaged her creativity, channeling her energies away from fiction where they would be much better used. Like Miller, he felt it was "withdrawing from the world."

It's fair to say that Nin presents this advice from both men as a life-and-death struggle to keep her diary—the threats from outside in the shape of men like Miller and Rank, and the threats from inside, in the shape of her own insecurity. And yet, of course, the very fact that she is writing all of this—in her diary—no matter how belatedly after the fact, proves just how little notice she has taken of their advice. No wonder her voice is so meek at this point, so agreeable. Contradictory as ever, she knows that she is disobeying what they have said. The very act of writing "dropped the diary" is a contradiction, when it is being written in a diary. It is a lie. It is also a rebellious action. And so, inevitably perhaps, the diary becomes her site of rebellion, of her stance against Miller and Rank.

Did the diary ultimately defeat Miller? Was Nin forced to make a choice between the diary and Miller, to make a choice between art and love? Was the contradictory impulse in her one that ultimately made art and love incompatible for her?

· · · ·

One of the problems with Nin's diaries is that she revised and rewrote them extensively, so it's hard for us to get a sense of her growth as an artist, apart from the development she tells us herself that she is making. After Miller urges her to destroy the diary, advice she ignores, she does become much more sure of herself, writing on March 19, 1935, while in New York at the same time as Miller: "My faith in Henry as a writer is absolute. All the others are wrong. But I know, too, that Henry would not have been a writer without me. The inner and poetic illumination of his life came from me." The month before, Miller wrote to her from his hotel room, begging her not to "push me away"; in March he tells her that "you took me, a broken man, and you made me whole" and shores up exactly what she has written in her diary by confiding, "You are an artist—in life—and what greater compliment could I pay you? I was only the artist in words, and in life a bitter failure . . ."

He possibly sensed her hostility toward him and feared he might lose her, and he was right to feel wary—in her diary she records her sense of being put-upon by both Henry and June, of being used by them. There is often an underlying feeling in Nin's diaries that the Miller marriage fed on and needed the extra complication she provided it, and one can't help wondering just how close she came to being discarded by them both after they'd used up her money, or after Henry had filched ideas off of her. Nin would never admit that possibility to herself, just as she would never admit that there might be someone who didn't find her attractive, but it's a tantalizing thought just the same.

By June 1935, though, Nin was back in France with Miller, and putting in her own money for the purchase of a printing press. She had ended her affair with Otto Rank, which she had been conducting while in New York that year, and she and Miller were both at Louveciennes, her home in the French countryside. Guiler was in London at this point, so the lovers were safe to work together in freedom. But it wasn't all as harmonious as it seemed: the woman who once said she disliked Miller's use of words like "bitch" and "crotch" was by now calling him "a whore by nature" in her diary and claiming that everything Miller learned about writing he learned from her. By the following summer, she had fallen in love with Gonzalo More, a half-Scottish, half-Peruvian Indian political activist and journalist, and was making excuses to avoid Miller.

The criticism that both Rank and Miller made of Nin's activity of diary-keeping was that it made her withdraw from the world—that is, from the world into herself. Nin's narcissism is what maintains all the diary volumes: even when she is writing about Henry and June, she is writing about herself (as Miller points out to her on one occasion, she is self-centered). In some cases, she writes about herself physically interposed between them as they argue; she links their existence in the world to her, just as she does with everyone she meets. In February 1936, she notes in her diary a rare occasion, supper with some friends, from which Miller is absent, and wonders, "Is it possible I have enjoyed myself for two hours without him?" The minute she realizes that she can enjoy herself without him, that she doesn't need him constantly, is the beginning of her separation from him.

What is remarkable about her diaries is her ability, and her willingness, to drag up from the depths of her being the most unattractive, unappealing aspects of herself and show them to the world. All her insecurities and jealousies, all her manipulations, both conscious and unconscious, are there for public view, because these diaries, as many have pointed out, were written to be read. As quoted by Podnieks, she says, "I want to know the inner self . . . That is why I am fascinated by journals and biographies. Nothing holds so great an interest for me now than the study of the human heart seeking to express itself in life," and then remarks on her great interest in the journals of Katherine Mansfield. Contradictory once again, she took a private form, the diary, and made it public.

• • • •

Through her tempestuous, often devoted, often overwhelming literary and sexual relationship with Miller, Nin was able to enhance the contradictions of her life, and realize them in art. She had begun this artistic realization as an eleven-year-old on the boat to New York, when, at the exhortation of her mother, she began a diary. But it was, ironically, her contact with the outside world, and the outside world represented by Miller in particular, as well as the battle he forced her to wage, that made her turn the diary from a self-absorbed collection of personal thoughts and feelings into a work of art. A dubious work of art, perhaps—many of Miller's literary criticisms of her writing still stand: the grandiose language, the rhetorical flourishes, the profusion of abstract nouns, and the never-ending "I"—but a work of art nonetheless. Nin is rightly celebrated as a woman who brought female sexuality to the fore in her writing, at a time when female sexuality was still considered a morally dubious subject, just about suitable for discussion by male scientists and psychoanalysts, but certainly not by women themselves. It is unlikely, as narcissistic as she was, as aspirational as she was, that she would have become the kind of writer she did without her relationship with Miller. He was necessary, after all.

Jean-Paul Sartre and Simone de Beauvoir, Paris, France, 1940.

6. The "Long-Termer": Simone de Beauvoir and Jean-Paul Sartre

"Look," he said with sudden vehemence, "why don't you put yourself into your writing?" . . . To put my raw, undigested self into a book, to lose perspective, compromise myself—no, I couldn't do it, I found the whole idea terrifying. "Screw up your courage," Sartre told me, and kept pressing the point.

—Simone de Beauvoir,
The Prime of Life

So your letter this morning made me doubly happy, by assuring me that nothing would ever separate us. We'll both go back to the Hotel Mistral, my love, won't we? We'll live together again? Promiscuously? Little being, dear little creature, I love you so much . . .

—Letter to Sartre, October 1939

Writing and sex bonded Simone de Beauvoir and Jean-Paul Sartre longer than any other couple in this book. And yet, they stopped having sex with each other quite soon after they became a couple, and it took them almost ten years after they first met to produce a single publication between them. This seeming contradiction is only one of the many mystifying aspects of this literary and sexual alliance that spanned a total of fifty years.

But there is a good argument to be made that writing more or less *became* sex for both of them, after a fashion, given their predilection for titillating each other with written details of their love affairs with other people. Not for nothing has the epistolary aspect of their relationship, with all its subterfuges and maneuverings, been likened to that of Choderlos de Laclos's devilish pair, the Vicomte de Valmont and Madame de Merteuil.

However, before we consider the complex nature of their particular Faustian pacts and sexual bargains, their manipulation of minors and their deceit of trusting friends that all took place between their initial meeting in 1929 and Sartre's death in 1980, there was, in the beginning, the birth of a romance. It was a romance that wouldn't be like any other, as they both determined from the outset, but a romance nevertheless. It began during daily discussions in the Luxembourg Gardens in Paris, where two remarkable young philosophy students discovered not just a meeting of minds, but a mutual need for stimulation as well as a lasting identification. There is something of a mirror-recognition in this moment when Beauvoir writes in her memoir many years later: "Sartre corresponded exactly to the dream-companion I had longed for since I was fifteen."

When her "dream-companion" suggested that theirs would be an "essential love," one that would survive and exist alongside other, lesser "contingent loves," this unusual young woman, who had only recently realized she didn't want the husband and children and home in the suburbs that her bourgeois upbringing had designated for her, was only too happy to agree.

Did she know what she was letting herself in for? In her second volume of memoirs, Beauvoir admitted to feelings of anxiety, a "flicker of fear," "some qualms." Sartre proposed a "two year lease" of intimacy between them, followed by two or three years apart, abroad teaching perhaps, before coming back together again. But there was never any question in her mind of refusing him. There was an "identical sign on both our brows" she wrote—they were marked for each other; they were meant to be.

••••

Can sheer force of will keep a couple together? In spite of a poor sexual relationship and intellectual viewpoints that differ as they grow older? What else does a relationship need? Questions like these, though, didn't come until after Sartre's death. "Why is a nice girl like Simone wasting her time sucking up to a boring old fart like Jean-Paul?" asked Angela Carter in 1981. "Her memoirs will mostly be about him; he will scarcely speak about her." After Beauvoir's death in 1986, Toril Moi wanted to know this, too. "To explain fully why Beauvoir fell in love with Sartre, however, is not the same thing as to explain why she never left him. What possible good did the relationship with Sartre do her after the first seven or ten years?" Beauvoir's letters to Sartre, which she had always denied keeping and which were discovered in 1990, as well as letters to her much younger lover Jacques-Laurent Bost, which were published in 2004, were full of shocking revelations. At least one biographer was prompted to voice what many had been thinking since the moment of Sartre's death: "Why on earth did she stick with Sartre?"

All these questions point to a raising of Beauvoir's reputation in the world during the latter part of the twentieth century and a falling away of Sartre's (what did *she* see in *him*?). But they also demand an answer to the puzzle of the longevity of this sexually arid relationship that had also stopped being intellectually nourishing. Indeed, Beauvoir's latest biographer, while talking of the "potential good" of their relationship, also points to its "dangerous potential for evil." This relationship turned them into more than an unattractive couple, she argues; they harmed people. Not only did Sartre not do Beauvoir any good (whether after seven years or not, as Moi asks), he was actually bad for her.

Beauvoir, though, had already acknowledged their joint

potential for harm. They had lied to the young women they knew, played games with them, led them into despair and destruction. The memory of the wrongs they had done one young woman in particular caused Beauvoir pain—Bianca Bienenfeld, the student whom she and Sartre had "shared." Bianca was Jewish, and Beauvoir and Sartre had not taken care of her or protected her when the Nazis invaded France. On the contrary, they had done everything they could to shake her off, with the result that the friendless Bienenfeld had ended up in a concentration camp. The guilt of what Bienenfeld suffered there haunted Beauvoir, as she wrote to Sartre at the end of the war: "She moved me . . . because she's suffering from an intense and dreadful attack of neurasthenia, and it's our fault, I think. It's the indirect but very profound aftershock of the business between her and us. She's the only person to whom we've really done harm, but we have harmed her . . ." Beauvoir's admission of guilt here is somewhat disingenuous, however, in claiming to have harmed only one person. It is clear that many who came into contact with both Beauvoir and Sartre, who were the subject of their games, were harmed, too.

But for the mother of second-wave feminism to admit to "harming" even just one young woman is damaging enough. Perhaps Beauvoir didn't need Sartre at all. Perhaps he was the last thing she needed, if closeness to him meant an urge to harm other people. And, increasingly to critics and academics over the years, it looks as though she didn't need him to be a great writer or a great polemicist, or even, as some claim now, to be a great philosopher. Was it, then, all for love? And a debased and debasing kind of love at that? What kind of woman was Simone de Beauvoir, who caused harm to other young women, all in the name of love?

The words of one of her letters to Sartre, written ten years after they first met and quoted at the beginning of this chapter, would seem to confirm that, yes, she loved him very much and she always would. And yet, that "promiscuously" is a clue to what she meant by it. In 2004, the world learned that Beauvoir had also been seeing Sartre's student, Jacques-Laurent Bost, a man with whom she fell deeply in love, and with whom she had a much more satisfactory sex life than with Sartre. How seriously were we meant to take the protestations of love then, the repeated urges to kiss her "little man," as she called Sartre, in an echo of his mother's endearment? Especially once we discovered that there was this other love, and not at all the kind of "contingent" one they'd agreed each would be allowed, taking place at the same time? Have we spent the last two decades since her death, ignoring that "promiscuous" warning in her letter to Sartre, and if we have, what does that say about our idealization of this couple, of the nature of the love we want to believe they shared?

Two bodies of opinion have grown up around the Beauvoir-Sartre relationship: those opinions which were formed after the deaths of both parties but before Beauvoir's letters to Sartre were published in 1990, and before her letters to Bost were discovered and published in 2004; and those opinions formed after both these publications. For those before this time, it was a struggle not to see the author of that pioneering feminist work, *The Second Sex*, of numerous novels and a four-volume autobiography, as the inexplicable victim of an ugly, squinting, controlling little man who cheated on her relentlessly with other women, and to depict her victimhood absolutely. Moi, for instance, could talk easily of Beauvoir's "masochism" and use terms like "hysteria" and "primary narcissism" to explain her "compulsion to repeat her cycles of depression, anxiety and fear of abandonment throughout her life . . . and all for the sake of a man." One of Beauvoir's first biographers, Deirdre Bair, sympathized with her subject's predicament and spoke of her reluctance to press the tape recorder during her conversations with Beauvoir in old age, lest she disturb a rare happy memory for the poor, downtrodden, aged writer.

For those after 1990, though, after the revelations of Beauvoir's affairs with women as well as with men, including some of her own students, and her perceived "passing on" of those young women to Sartre, leading some to accuse her of "procurement," the perception is less one of victim and more of predator. Her most recent biographer, Carole Seymour-Jones, even accuses Beauvoir of "paedophile tastes," particularly when she took up with one of her teenage students, Nathalie Sorokine. Seymour-Jones argues that Sorokine was a "nymph, whose childish ways spurred the teacher to take the initiative when they went up to Sorokine's room in Saint-Cloud"; possibly because Sorokine was older by the time she got sexually involved with Sartre, Seymour-Jones avoids accusing him of "paedophile tastes" as well. How valid is this accusation? Had Beauvoir been a man, there is no doubt her behavior would have been seen as criminal, worthy of prosecution. Certainly it all makes for uncomfortable reading, and it is even harder to view Beauvoir's cruel physical descriptions of Bianca Bienenfeld (for instance, "If I'm to tell you everything," she wrote to Sartre on January 12, 1940, "in addition to the usual rufous odor of her body she had a pungent fecal odor which made things pretty unpleasant") and conclude that she was any kind of victim. As a result, the question—What did Beauvoir see in Sartre?—has almost become redundant after this time. Beauvoir didn't need to see anything in him, not sexually at least, because her love life was largely satisfied with her liaisons with other people.

The much bigger question has therefore become: Did Beauvoir and Sartre stay together because they really loved each other? And it provokes further questions: Did those "contingent loves" in fact work to keep them together? What was Beauvoir, in particular, getting from this relationship, when even the charms of the young Bost in the early days, or the passion of Nelson Algren in later years, could not pull her from Sartre's side for long? And was the love they shared a "bad" kind of love, one that only existed because of the pain they caused to others?

More than any other couple in this volume, Beauvoir and Sartre played with the biographical tools of memoir, letters and diaries, as well as autobiographical fiction, withholding information, planting red herrings, masking the truth, and misleading the unwary. There are many different versions of their love story: while they employed all the means of telling the truth about it, they created instead a series of fictions. We know that Beauvoir had ambitions to be a great writer from an early age, because she tells us so in her memoirs: "Yet at the age of fifteen when I wrote in a friend's album the plans and preferences which were supposed to give a picture of my personality, I answered without hesitation the question 'What do you want to do in later life?' with 'To be a famous author.'" But how far can we trust what she says in those memoirs, especially when they exclude the details of her relationship with Bost, and blur the nature of her relationship with Olga Kosackiewicz, the young woman she and Sartre both fell in love with, and whom she immortalized—and murdered—in her first published novel, *She Came to Stay*? The letters to Sartre and Bost, now published, contradict what she tells us in the memoirs—can we trust the letters themselves? Or did she lie to Sartre and to Bost as well?

What is important to remember, and can seem contradictory, is that truth was important to both Beauvoir and Sartre. A crucial part of the "pact" they made, beyond allowing for other loves, was that they would tell each other everything. And so, it appeared, they did. Sartre's letters to Beauvoir, especially when he was away during military training at the start of the Second World War, are filled with detail, most often about what he is doing, thinking, writing. Her letters to him are equally voluble, mostly full of information about the people they know back in Paris. Beauvoir backs up this fascination with gossip about other people when she acknowledges in her second volume of memoirs, "Whether in Paris, Rouen, or Le Havre, however, our main topic of conversation was the various people we knew . . . when we made new acquaintances we set about turning them inside-out in every sense of the phrase, and worked like beavers to produce our own definitive version of them. All our various colleagues were subjected to this process."

This appropriation of other people's stories, other people's lives, was to "fill our day-to-day existence" and "insure against any monotony," Beauvoir argues, but it clearly served other purposes: it maintained the intimacy between a couple who in many other respects had lost that intimacy; it allowed them a feeling of control over other people, and in turn, over their own lives and their own relationship. Other people's lives occupied an area they could both be truthful about; indeed, sometimes it seems as though they were in competition with each other over who could be the most truthful, because they also told each other frankly when they fell in love with other people. Beauvoir would have to read that Sartre was in love with Kosackiewicz; Sartre would be teased about the lack of letters Beauvoir had received from him, compared to the number she had received from Bost.

Where the letters and the memoirs back each other up, then, we can assume that the truth is being told. But what about the autobiographical novels? And what about other people's perceptions of the couple, people who may have been lied to over a long period of time? How do we verify those versions of their relationship? The true nature of the liaison between Simone de Beauvoir and Jean-Paul Sartre matters because they set themselves up as an example, as a living alternative to the bourgeois, married, monogamous couple long considered the social norm. Few have looked at Sylvia Plath and Ted Hughes or Rebecca West and H. G. Wells and seen a recipe for an ideal, artistic, free way of living. So many of the relationships in this volume involve pain and compromise and Faustian pacts of one sort or another, especially for the women concerned. Not Beauvoir and Sartre, though—or so it seemed. Instead, those who wanted to live a different kind of life saw a model in the Beauvoir-Sartre relationship that they could copy for themselves: "Didn't we all want an intellectual partner with whom we could share our work, ideas, and slightest thoughts? Didn't everyone want to write in Paris cafes amid the clatter of coffee cups and the hubbub of voices, and spend their summers in Rome in complicated but apparently harmonious foursomes? Who wanted monogamy when one could have freedom *and* stability, love affairs *and* commitment?"

Such idealism, though, is little equipped to deal with accusations of lying and manipulation, and many of those who had originally seen in Beauvoir and Sartre a real recipe for an alternative way of living felt a genuine sense of disillusionment and disappointment when new truths were revealed after 1990 and 2004. So deep did that sense of disillusionment go that many doubted the love between the couple at all, never mind the project that the two had initially embarked upon. Were Sartre and Beauvoir ever really a "couple"? Or were they just friends, albeit of an extremely possessive and intense sort? Did Beauvoir really "pimp" for Sartre, grooming her "girlfriends" for him in order to maintain some kind of hold over him, and over them? And if so, did this strategy work? Did Beauvoir ever experience a final disillusionment in her literary partner, as so many women in this volume have done? Was Sartre necessary for her artistic success, after all, or is that another smokescreen? Could she have done it all without him, or did she need to be told to "screw up her courage," and be shown how to do it, in order to become the writer she did? And above all, did she mean any of what she told him through the years?

• • • •

Simone de Beauvoir was born, as she tells us herself in her first volume of memoirs, at 4 a.m. on January 9, 1908, in Paris. She was the elder of two girls, and her little sister, Helen, or "Poupette," as she was called, became Beauvoir's essential partner in made-up childhood games. Recalling those early days, Beauvoir writes, "A partner was absolutely essential to me if I was to bring my imaginary stories to life." But it was more than that—this young girl, who identified herself as masochistic, who loved to play the victim in her own stories ("often I found myself revelling in the delights of misfortune and humiliation. My piety disposed me towards masochism"), also needed to control someone else, in this case, her younger sister: "What I appreciated most in our relationship was that I had a real hold over her."

Writing this memoir when she was approaching fifty, Beauvoir had of course identified certain traits that would be of interest to biographers of her life with Sartre, hence there is doubtless some self-consciousness about noting her desire to be a writer so early, her need to play the victim, and her desire for control over someone else. One of the many questions biographers after 1990 have asked, though, is why Beauvoir did not publish her letters to Sartre in her own lifetime, when the perception of her as a victim of her partner's cheating ways would have been challenged. Perhaps the answer lies in this memoir of childhood: that Beauvoir *liked* being thought of as the victim. Being thought of as a victim is wholly different from being a victim, of course: as in her childhood games, Beauvoir was no victim at all. It titillated her to play the role of one. It also, paradoxically, gave her power.

Growing up with a love of reading and writing, though, meant that the young, bookish Beauvoir was also antisocial and shy. She felt herself to be "an outcast from childhood," and recalled getting pleasure from her reflection in the mirror and wanting to please adults, especially men. This desire to please contrasted with her tendency to furious tantrums when she didn't get what she wanted, and one wonders how much of that was due to her parents' relationship. Her father, Georges, was a lawyer's secretary who had intended to marry money—Beauvoir's mother, Francoise Brasseur, was the daughter of the founder of the Bank of the Meuse—but his wife's parents went bankrupt and her father was sent to prison. A dowry promised to Georges never materialized, and the lack of money was to be a sore point between the couple. Georges responded by staying out late, taking up mistresses, even prostitutes; Francoise would cause big scenes—meanwhile, they became poorer and poorer. It can't have helped the intellectually precocious Simone de Beauvoir that her maternal cousins were much better off, and when she spent holidays with them, the contrast between her own impoverishment and their wealth was a difficult one to manage.

Lack of wealth might have meant poor marriage prospects, but Beauvoir had other interests by the time she reached her teens. Books took her out of herself, and her father encouraged her reading, possibly understanding that he would never be able to provide enough of a dowry for his daughters to marry well, and that they would be dependent on their own abilities. Beauvoir responded to this intellectual encouragement, and as an adolescent, she found that erotic tales suited her growing sexual awareness. But it was when she read George Eliot's *The Mill on the Floss* that she made her first real identification: "Maggie Tulliver, like myself, was drawn between others and herself: I recognized myself in her." This recognition went further, though. Finally, Beauvoir realized that she didn't want simply to play the kinds of roles in life that she had played during her childhood with her sister. She wanted to create those roles, and create them in writing. She wanted to be a writer: "the scholar, the artist, the writer and the thinker created other worlds, all sweetness and light, in which everything had purpose. That was where I wished to spend my life."

To become a creator of lives in fiction was historically considered a god-like aspiration, to be associated with male artistic ambition. (It is, after all, Joyce's Stephen Dedalus in *A Portrait of the Artist as a Young Man* who likens the artist to "the God of the creation . . . within or behind or beyond his handiwork, invisible, refined out of existence, paring his fingernails.") Beauvoir was picking up on that association when she sought a female artist like George Eliot, who wrote under a male pseudonym, to follow. She wanted to be like Eliot, to be a female artist who could do what male artists did—to be a creator of lives, too: "By writing a work based on my own experience I would re-create myself and justify my existence."

It sounds from those words as though she hardly needed Sartre's later urging to "screw up her courage" and put herself into her work: she had already partly realized herself that that was what she had to do. But that "re-create myself" has a ring of fiction about it, of reinvention. At this point, Beauvoir wanted to present herself in fictional form; Sartre encouraged her to present the truth of herself, not some made-up version. Whether she achieved that, though, remains to be seen.

Contradictions also needed to be reconciled when it came to her views on love. Growing up with her wealthier cousin Zaza, to whom she was devoted, the two girls would discuss romance and love (both girls had by then enrolled at the Cours Desir, where they also studied less romantic subjects like philosophy and mathematics; Beauvoir would graduate from this school to the Sorbonne in 1925, to study for a teaching diploma). Beauvoir would say that what she wanted from a man was "someone more accomplished than myself, yet my equal, my double." She claimed that this need for superiority wasn't a desire for a father-figure as such, but she did acknowledge the influence of her feelings for her father, a man she loved very much, in spite of his infidelities to his wife and the part he played in the fall of his family's fortunes.

As her studies developed and it became clear what a gifted student she was, she decided that her life "would be a beautiful story come true, a story I would make up as I went along."

. . . .

Meanwhile, Jean-Paul Sartre grew up without his father, who died just fifteen months after his son was born. Sartre developed a close early relationship to his widowed mother—until she married again. This second marriage resulted in him being pushed aside as the primary object of his mother's attentions. It traumatized him almost as much as the discovery one day that he wasn't a golden-haired, beautiful little boy any more: rather like Ernest Hemingway, Sartre had been treated as though he was a little girl by his mother throughout his earliest years. One day his beautiful blonde curls were cut off and revealed not a feminine little angel, but an ugly boy with a squint.

Much has been written about Sartre's adult need for as many women as possible stemming from this dual blow of his mother's marriage and his own unattractiveness, and it's possible that Beauvoir herself was well aware of this, as she never teased him about his appearance. Throughout their relationship she would use the maternal term his own mother had used for him: "little man," and it's hard not to believe she did so deliberately, to shore up his ego.

Like Beauvoir, Sartre, too, showed superior ability at school. While studying for entry to the prestigious Ecole Normale Supérieure, though, he fell for a distant cousin named Simone Jollivet, who worked part-time as a prostitute. He was to lose her to the theater manager Charles Dullin, but by this time he was at university and had noticed the young woman who hung about with his friend René Maheu. It was Maheu who gave Beauvoir the nickname "Beaver" ("BEAUVOIR = BEAVER. Vous êtes un castor . . ." he wrote in her notepad, and said that he chose the name because of the closeness of the English word for "castor," beaver, to her surname, as well as the fact that "Beavers like company and they have a constructive bent"), and who largely replaced Beauvoir's cousin, Jacques Champigneulles, in her affections. Champigneulles's family did not believe Beauvoir was good enough for him—she would note with a little satisfaction in her memoir his later sad decline after he went off and married someone else.

In *Memoirs of a Dutiful Daughter*, Sartre makes few appearances, blocked as he is from view first by Champigneulles, then by Maheu. But gradually Beauvoir noticed him more and more: chiefly, his intelligence, which she claimed in her memoirs was vastly superior to hers, although it didn't stop her from trying to outdo him in philosophical arguments. "From now on, I'm going to take you under my wing," she reports Sartre's telling her, and during their exams at the Ecole Normale, when she was twenty-one and he was twenty-four, she began "to feel that time which was not spent in his company was time wasted." More than this, he encouraged her in her writing ambitions: "not only did he give me encouragement but he also intended to give me active help in achieving this ambition." We read of how they helped each other in their work for many years afterward, reading and writing together, assessing what each other did every day. What Beauvoir admired most about Sartre was his single-mindedness about his writing, and he taught her how to be single-minded, too. He lived only to write, she said. Nothing else got in the way: everything was made to serve this need.

When the results of their exams were announced, Sartre came first and Beauvoir second. Two biographies have since disputed the outcome, claiming that Beauvoir was actually considered the better philosopher, but the judging panel couldn't give the top prize to a woman. If Beauvoir felt any injustice

had been done, she certainly never showed it, acknowledging from the start Sartre's rightful superior position ("Day after day, and all day long I set myself up against Sartre, and in
our discussions I was simply not in his class . . . it was something serious to discover that I wasn't the One and Only, but one
among many, by no means first"). And so it would go over the
next few years: it would be Sartre who proposed the terms of
the "morganatic marriage" between them, and Sartre who was
published first.

But the power relations between them were confused by
certain realities: Beauvoir was the beauty, not Sartre. And Beauvoir
was bisexual, whereas Sartre liked only women. These factors
were to prove just as important as exam results and the glorifica-
tion of one mind above another. They were factors, however, that
neither Beauvoir nor Sartre ever acknowledged. It suited both
of them to pretend that it was Sartre who always had the upper
hand. Beauvoir would never have hurt his feelings by implying
Sartre was ugly, just as she offered up her relationships with both
men and women for his delectation. There were never any power
shifts when Beauvoir wrote to Sartre of her relationships with her
young women students: he never claimed she had an unfair advantage over him because she liked women as well as men. They
wanted to believe that theirs was a relationship of equals; only, to
paraphrase Orwell, one was more equal than the other.

The relationship between Beauvoir and Sartre really began
after their exams in the summer of 1929. Beauvoir then left to
spend the summer at her cousins' home in the Limousin countryside, and a day or two later,, as one biographer tells it, Sartre
followed her there, booking a room for himself in a nearby hotel. He "courted" Beauvoir persistently over the following days,
and finally they had sex outdoors, in the lush countryside. Her
family were alarmed by his constant presence, though, and her
parents caught them one afternoon in the fields together—her

father subsequently ordered Sartre to stay away. Their initial passion, combined perhaps with injunctions from her family to keep away from her, was enough to prompt Sartre to propose marriage, which Beauvoir, long opposed to it after witnessing her parents' struggles, rebuffed. Interestingly, though, she also slept with Maheu once Sartre had departed for Paris, as he had also followed her to Limousin. Her recollection of Maheu and their time in his hotel room together is all physical: he is a "tender lover," a "sensual man." Sartre, however, is a "great man."

As an alternative to marriage, which Beauvoir kept resisting, when they were back in Paris together Sartre proposed instead his famous "essential loves" idea, and she agreed to what they both decided to call a "morganatic marriage" (although they never actually married). They were then immediately separated by their respective jobs—Sartre was in Saint-Cyr, and Beauvoir in Paris—but this distance only served to heighten their desire for each other, as expressed in their early letters. Sartre was not the sensual man Maheu was, though, and it soon became clear that the two lovers were not, in fact, sexually compatible. Sartre liked foreplay; Beauvoir wanted much more, and one biographer has argued that "Sartre was bewildered by the sexual demands made of him, which he found impossible to meet." He preferred to kiss and stroke; penetrative sex gave him little pleasure. It's not clear if Beauvoir ever actually complained to Sartre about his "coldness," or spelled out what she found inadequate about his lovemaking. It seems that both understood what was going on, without having to spell it out to each other.

That a relationship can exist and grow in spite, or perhaps because, of what is never spoken out loud is hardly a new concept. But when two people so professed to telling each other the truth ("We made another pact between us: not only would we never lie to one another, but neither of us would conceal anything from the other") make a point of not voicing secret thoughts, never mind actually pinpointing the obvious, questions are inevitably raised. In *The Prime of Life*, Beauvoir misdirects her readers, telling them that their promise to tell each other everything wasn't easy, that it raised all kinds of problems for her, not least her shyness about revealing everything about herself, but also her ability to deal with everything Sartre had to tell her. At no point does she consider that he is not telling her everything, or that she herself is deliberately withholding anything from him about their relationship.

And yet, eleven years after their relationship began, Beauvoir could write the following to Sartre: "My God! At the start of our own love affair I always tried to understand how I was placing myself in your life, from your point of view. And how, if I loved you more than you loved me, this meant I found more riches in you and was the more advantaged—in view of what I was receiving, and also by the very plenitude of my feelings." In this letter, Beauvoir is discussing the pressure she feels from Bianca Bienenfeld, a rather fragile young woman with whom she has been conducting an affair. Bienenfeld was Beauvoir's student when the older woman was teaching at the Lycée Molière, and by 1938, at the age of seventeen, she was sleeping with her teacher. By the time of this letter in 1940, however, Bienenfeld had also become involved with Sartre. It is interesting that here Beauvoir is paralleling her own position with Sartre when they began seeing each other with Beinenfeld's position now, vis-à-vis both herself and Sartre.

What does this tell us about the unequal power balance between Beauvoir and Sartre, right from the very beginning? Her words, "tried to understand . . . from your point of view," imply that Beauvoir felt herself to be in the weaker position, obliged to work hard to see things from her lover's point of view. Earlier in the letter, she shows how she has admonished Bienenfeld for not doing the same thing ("she [Bienenfeld] explained . . . she'd tried to look at the affair from my viewpoint . . . Perhaps I've a heart of stone, but I wasn't moved in the least. I think it was her own fault—anyway placing yourself in the other person's shoes is elementary"), but Beinenfeld is in the weaker position with *two* people, not just one. She is trying desperately to juggle two other people's feelings, trying to situate herself somewhere in the trio where she is the weakest member.

Yet Beauvoir has forgotten something of her own "trio," the one in which she was involved right at the very beginning of her relationship with Sartre. In spite of her protestations in her memoir that by the time she and Sartre came together in October 1929 she had "jettisoned all past attachments," she writes to Sartre in January 1930, a full three months after making this claim, that Maheu wants to speak to her about *their* relationship, which is going downhill rapidly as a result of her affair with Sartre ("For you must understand that I have had my fill of the pretty situation that now exists, as a result of that September of yours and the two months of lying which followed it, and that I deserve something better than the crumbs").

Beauvoir seems to have been involved in trios or foursomes for most of her life, an inevitable consequence of never giving up Sartre. She was never a singular entity, always a double, and so any more partners had to take on board that doubleness. But she began with the upper hand: she was the one with two lovers, Sartre and Maheu, and it was Sartre who had to play catch-up. Her recognition of Bienenfeld's position is a misleading one: Beauvoir was never in the position in which Beinenfeld now found herself. Beauvoir's complaints about Bienenfeld not recognizing how she should behave are disingenuous.

It was the disingenuousness of the multiple setup that kept Beauvoir and Sartre together, in spite of its dangers. And at no point was that setup more dangerous than when the young Olga Kosackiewicz became involved with them. Like Jean Rhys's *Quartet* and Anaïs Nin's *Henry and June*, Beauvoir's 1943 novel,

She Came to Stay, is concerned with the cuckoo in the nest—the one who comes between a couple, in each situation a young woman. In both Rhys and Beauvoir, the young woman effectively moves in with the older couple, but whereas Rhys narrates her story from the girl's viewpoint, Beauvoir's does so from the viewpoint of the older woman, effectively the "wife." Sartre, too, wrote up his version of the relationship in his trilogy, *Roads to Freedom*, which was made up of three of his most famous novels, *The Age of Reason* (1945), *The Reprieve* (1945), and *Iron in the Soul* (1949) where he cast Kosackiewicz as "Ilvich." She was also the inspiration for his 1944 play, *No Exit*.

Unlike Rhys, though, Beauvoir provided two accounts of this relationship: in her autobiographical novel and in her memoir. Olga Kosackiewicz was a seventeen-year-old Russian émigré when she first met Beauvoir in 1932. Beauvoir was teaching her in class at the Lycée Jeanne d'Arc in Rouen, and at this time she and Sartre were particularly close, although their sexual relationship was in dire straits, as they rarely slept together, leaving Beauvoir frustrated. Self-conscious about his body, and apparently less than enthusiastic about the naked female form when it was presented in front of him, his lack of enthusiasm led directly to a "space which the admiration of her pupils began to fill," and at the end of the second term Beauvoir noticed Kosackiewicz, and began to coach her privately and to take her to lunch. Seymour-Jones disputes Beauvoir's account of the beginning of the relationship, arguing that "Simone, nine years older than the withdrawn, uncertain émigré, took the initiative." By 1934, Sartre was heavily involved with another woman named "Marie," whom both he and Beauvoir called "the lunar woman," and there is some argument to be made that Beauvoir's love for Kosackiewicz was a reaction to feelings of jealousy about Sartre's affair with Marie. Sartre, however, became seriously ill and depressed, and in March 1935, Beauvoir sent Kosackiewicz to help look after him. Sartre quickly fell in love with her.

Some have seen this move on Beauvoir's part as an attempt to control whomever Sartre fell for, and after Kosackiewicz failed her exams in July, they proposed taking her on board together. They became a threesome, Kosackiewicz taking a room in the same hotel as Beauvoir, which was paid for by both Beauvoir and Sartre. Letters to Sartre during this period, from 1935 to '36, are largely absent, with only one mention of Kosackiewicz by Beauvoir to Sartre ("She was overcome with regret that you could have misinterpreted things, and is thinking of writing to you. She said with a meaningful smile that she hadn't changed her feelings since Saturday, 'on the contrary'"). A few years later we hear much more in the letters about Kosackiewicz, because by then, in the small, local setup—in the close circle of lovers and friends that Beauvoir and Sartre liked to maintain presumably for reasons of power—Kosackiewicz was seeing Jacques-Laurent Bost, while Beauvoir was also seeing him, in secret, and what we hear is mainly how Beauvoir would dodge her to meet up with Bost without Kosackiewicz knowing.

Biographers, then, have been forced to turn to less reliable means than letters; in this instance that means the memoir and the novel. The novel *She Came to Stay* is an account of a relationship between Françoise (Beauvoir) and Pierre (Sartre), both writers for the theater, and Xavière Kosackiewicz, initially a friend of Françoise. Throughout the book, we are reminded of the couple's closeness ("It's true that we are really one"), but when Pierre takes up with Xavière, Françoise cannot cope with the feelings of jealousy their affair arouses in her, or their marginalization of her. As Pierre and Xavière get closer, Françoise becomes more desperate, hating Xavière for impinging on even the smallest amount of time she can spend with Pierre. This was not in the rules: as always in threesomes, someone is getting less than the other two, someone has less power. Françoise imagined she and Pierre would remain "as one" while they both enjoyed being with Xavière, alone and together. But she cannot stop imagining what they are doing together when she is not there ("she had the painful impression of being in exile. In the ordinary way, the center of Paris was wherever she happened to be. Today everything had changed. The center of Paris was where Pierre and Xavière were sitting").

She Came to Stay is a powerful novel of disillusionment: the idea that two people can remain together when one of them falls in love with someone else is taken up and ripped to shreds: "they had built beautiful, faultless structures in whose shadow they were sheltering, without giving any further thought to what lay behind them. Pierre still repeated, 'we are but one,' but now she had discovered that he lived only for himself." Xavière becomes such a threat to Françoise that she feels by the end she has no choice— she leaves Xavière sleeping in her room, turns on the gas in her kitchen, and leaves, the door locked behind her. The ideal of the three of them, "a real trio, a well-balanced life for three in which no one would be sacrificed," has been shown to be the basis for murder, no less, prompted by the basest of emotions: jealousy and fear.

In her memoir, Beauvoir reveals little of this. What she is "open" about is her own worry about reaching the age of thirty without having anything substantial to show for it, and envying Olga Kosackiewicz her youth and beauty. There is no hint of the devastation Kosackiewicz wreaked on Beauvoir's relationship with Sartre: on the contrary, Beauvoir says that "twenty-five years later, she still occupies a privileged place in my heart," claiming that it was Kosackiewicz who wanted the relationship with her in the first place and who "brought it into being." She describes Kosackiewicz's relationship with Sartre as "uneventful" and says that he "had no intention of giving any kind of physical embodiment" to his "wholly platonic" feelings of jealousy toward her. Yet she does admit that she found the new importance Kosackiewicz assumed for Sartre difficult to handle, and she describes how she pulled back from them both, partly to concentrate on her writing. The most she admits is that Xavière is "to some extent" modeled on Kosackiewicz.

Why didn't Beauvoir tell the whole story in the memoir? Was she frightened of the world knowing about her lesbian affair, something she had blurred in the novel (there is little physical interaction between Xavière and Françoise)? We must remember that it was only when her letters were published after her death that we learned about her sexual relationships with her female students. The publication of Sartre's letters to Beauvoir, *Witness to My Life*, in 1983, did not show her involvement with Sartre's loves, that they shared women between them. Was she reluctant to show how much Sartre loved Kosackiewicz, even though the extent of it, and the hurt it caused, is depicted in the novel? Why draw this distinction between the memoir and the novel? Writers usually argue that their depiction of an event in a novel bears little resemblance to that event in real life, and are eager to maintain and emphasize where the barriers between real life and fiction should be raised. But it is Beauvoir's memoir that is the fiction here, and the fiction that is telling the truer story.

What is also unusual is that this dangerous "contingent" love that almost became an "essential" one, didn't dissuade either Sartre or Beauvoir from trying it all over again with Bianca Bienenfeld, and then later with Nathalie Sorokine. Even though Beauvoir found the idea of a long-term trio terrifying with Kosackiewicz, and admitted to feeling "vexed with Sartre for having created this situation and with Olga for taking advantage of it," she didn't stop, or try to change the makeup of the threesome. She carried on introducing her lovers to Sartre, letting him, encouraging him even, to fall in love with them. The lie of equality between the three members of the trio at any one time was perpetuated throughout, though it is clear from the letters between Beauvoir and Sartre that, from now on, they believe they are the two who are in charge. When Beauvoir criticizes Bienenfeld to Sartre—"It was the first time I'd ever felt that: a real hatred of sleeping with a woman I don't love. I articulated it to myself even as she was marveling at the tender expression on my face"—one wonders how much of this was said to deter Sartre from falling in love with her the way he had with Kosackiewicz. Beauvoir clearly was by this time locked into a power game that required subterfuges, lies, and, more than that—an ability to predict the future, to see how things would go.

And yet it was a game without any explicit rules or ideology behind the promise to "tell each other everything." Surprisingly, for two philosophers who set out to live in the anti-bourgeois, anti-monogamous way that they both wanted, there is little in the way of an agenda or a manifesto from them in their letters to each other. The nearest Beauvoir gets to it is in comments to Sartre, like the one she made in a letter to him on November 10, 1939, while he was away fighting the "phoney war": "I worked away assiduously," she writes, "to persuade [Bienenfeld] as far as possible to accept a life without us, instead of rejecting it; to make her solitude into a strength and seek an emotional independence." Sartre's reply is more philosophical in content, but also devoid of any sense of a manifesto agreed on between them, with regard to their multiple partners: "What you say about Bienenfeld is interesting though somewhat nebulous. What I ultimately deduced is that she had a Platonic concept of the human condition as a form including happiness in its essence. Actually that's rather more Aristotelian, it's even what they call eudaemonism."

Beyond their notion of "contingent loves" there is little of philosophical content in the letters they shared about the nature of their lifestyle. Anyone looking for a philosophical manual on the day-to-day practice of sharing lovers will be disappointed. Gossip about lovers is the order of the day; being explicit about their affairs the main content of their discussions. In her memoir, Beauvoir declares that what attracted her to philosophy was "that it went straight to essentials. I had never liked fiddling detail; I perceived the general significance of things rather than their singularities." Yet her letters to Sartre are all "fiddling detail." A philosophy of a way of living resides only in "singularities"; there is rarely any "general significance" to be drawn from what she describes in her letters.

• • • •

The picture that is drawn of Beauvoir over these years is a sympathetic one, if you believe the memoirs; an intimidating one, if you believe the letters. The truth about who Beauvoir was is probably somewhere between the two. The memoirs show a precociously gifted child as well as a young woman who lacked some confidence in herself—she talks of having "fits of disquiet" when a child, that only books could reassure her. Later, at university, a friend's boyfriend describes her as a bluestocking and predicts she'll turn into an "ugly little spinster"—his judgment has her rushing out straightaway to the hairdressers in a panic, buying hats and new dresses. Meeting Sartre seems to have given her the confidence she lacked, and a proper sense of her place in the world.

It is perhaps a sense of gratitude to Sartre that prevented Beauvoir from extracting from her lover a better acknowledgment of what *she* had given *him* when he published *Being and Nothingness* in 1943. Academics Edward and Kate Fulbrook spend a great deal of time proving that Sartre subsequently borrowed for his philosophical work Beauvoir's philosophical development, in *She Came to Stay*, of both the "Social Other" ("the mechanism that explains the social oppression of women"—the philosophical concept Beauvoir would develop further in *The Second Sex*, which posits women as the "other" in relation to men) and the relationship between the mind and body, which has to do with subjectivity and objectivity. (In *She Came to Stay*, this latter concept is illustrated when Françoise notices the lack of consciousness with which a woman in a bar has placed her bare arm on a table, and Xavière suddenly comments, "It's extraordinary, the impression it makes on you to touch your eyelashes . . . You touch yourself without noticing. It's as if you touched yourself from some way away." The body is being experienced here in a variety of different ways, depending on whether one sees oneself in an objective or subjective way.) Sartre admits this debt he owes her in letters, but not in the final, published version of the book itself.

The Fulbrooks blame institutionalized sexism for both Sartre's and Beauvoir's reluctance to show that a woman was capable of coming up with a philosophical system first, and doubtless there is a great deal about many of the relationships in this volume that is due to patriarchal oppression of women: West, Mansfield, and H.D. were all involved in relationships with writers at a time when not only was the possibility of female creative genius denied, but women's entitlement to vote wasn't even a fact of life.

All of the women in this volume found that their relationships were subject to patriarchal laws, as women today still do, if to a lesser degree. But it was really only Beauvoir who attempted, in her personal life, to overturn those laws. Anaïs Nin was perhaps nearly as unconventional as Beauvoir in her relationships with men and women, but she was still married. Only Elizabeth Smart refused George Barker's offer of marriage, but that was after many years—in the early days, she desperately wanted to marry him and even called herself "Mrs. Barker." Simone de Beauvoir, however, resisted official designations and sought a new way of living with a man, a way that would guarantee her artistic and personal freedom.

What was the cost of that freedom? Beauvoir writes in *The Prime of Life* that she was "devoted to Katherine Mansfield, the *Journals* and *Letters* no less than the short stories." She says, too, that she found her "obsessive concept" of the "solitary woman romantically appealing": "When I lunched at the Canebiere, upstairs at the Brasserie O'Central, or had dinner at the back of Charley's Tavern—a cool, dark place, its walls covered with photographs of boxers—I told myself that I, too, personified this 'solitary woman' . . . I would gaze out at the sky, at the passers-by; then I would lower my eyes to the exercise books I was correcting or the volume I was reading. I felt wonderful."

Given that these are Beauvoir's memoirs, where performance matters and the truth is not always told, it is not surprising that the loneliness of being the "solitary woman" is not betrayed here, nor is the reflection that Mansfield herself was scarcely "solitary," given her dependence on John Middleton Murry and Ida Baker, as Beauvoir would have known from poring over those journals and letters as she admitted doing. Rather like Mansfield and Murry, though, Beauvoir talks to Sartre in a baby voice in her letters (hinting at the same real lack of sexual intimacy between them, possibly), and she constantly complains, as Mansfield did, that she isn't getting enough letters from him while they are parted from each other. Beauvoir's reassurances that she still feels passion for Sartre can sound as hollow as Mansfield's for Murry, too, especially when they are repeated almost verbatim, and the real excitement in her letters often comes from the intricacies of the relationships she was conducting with Beinenfeld and Sorokine, while still juggling Olga Kosackiewicz and her sister, Wanda, in Sartre's absence.

But it is yet possible to take Beauvoir's desire to be a "solitary woman" entirely seriously, and to use it as a way of viewing her long-term relationship with Sartre. How to be solitary yet not alone was at the center of her relationship with him, I would argue: it was only with Sartre that she was able to maintain that contradictory notion of solitariness, of being alone yet not alone, a kind of solitariness that neither the more conventional Jacques-Laurent Bost nor the more insistent Nelson Algren would likely have permitted her.

Almost every scrutinizer of the Beauvoir-Sartre relationship has argued that Beauvoir introduced her female lovers to Sartre as a way of binding him to her and maintaining her own control over him, but what if it wasn't like that at all? What if introducing her lovers to him was actually Beauvoir's way of *keeping Sartre at arm's length*, while still remaining connected to him? When he grew too fond of the Kosackiewicz sisters or Bianca Bienenfeld, she understandably panicked that she had pushed him too far away. But it is very possible to argue that Beauvoir used those young women not to bring him closer at all, but to push him from her, to give her the space to be the "solitary woman" she needed to be, the space she needed to be an artist and a philosopher.

It seems contradictory indeed to argue that a literary partnership should flourish when one half of the partnership is actually doing better, and believes she will do better, by pushing the other half of that partnership away from her. But in spite of their close reading of each other's work, their daily visits to the same cafés, their shared friends and lovers, it's possible to see that a certain solitariness, for the female half of the partnership, was essential. Beauvoir did not live with Sartre: she lived alone, in her own hotel room or apartment. Everything about her letters to Sartre, especially when he is absent during the early days of France's preparation for war against Germany, points to closeness on the surface. But underneath, there is that crucial pushing away.

This may seem willfully contradictory. After all, how else is one to read the following, from one of Beauvoir's earliest letters to Sartre, in January 1930? "My love, I never felt our love more strongly than that evening at Les Vikings, where you gazed at me so tenderly I felt like weeping. And what a delightful train took us to Saint-Germain, my love! If I weren't so uncomfortably positioned for writing, I'd spend pages telling you how happy I am and how much I love you." Yet we have already seen that often when Beauvoir was writing her fondest regards for Sartre, she was also with someone else, like Maheu or Bost. In this letter quoted above, she goes on to describe Maheu's jealous little love note, and this is just after establishing how much she loves Sartre. Rarely in her letters does she focus on Sartre alone—even after she has just left him at the end of their holiday together in 1937, describing how "distraught" she is at their parting, she talks of her neighbor at the cinema playing "footsie" with her and reminisces quite happily about the days before, when "you didn't yet love me quite as much."

I don't believe these are conventional games a woman plays with her lover, attempting to tweak his interest in her, or making him jealous by mentioning other men or strangers who fancy her. Beauvoir wasn't playing that kind of game and Sartre knew it—on July 1938, she wrote to "my dear little husband" while on holiday with Bost ("he likes to read me extracts out loud while I'm writing to you or sleeping"). Sartre wrote to her to tell her in great detail of his night of passion with Martine Bourdin ("It's the first time I've slept with a brunette, actually black-haired, Provençale as the devil, full of odors and curiously hairy, with a little black fur patch at the small of her back and a very white body, much whiter than mine"). His letter includes a compliment to Beauvoir, and a reassurance of a kind: "In the morning she said, 'I'm not jealous of Tania [another of Sartre's flings] . . . I'm jealous of Simone de Beauvoir.' A reasonable feeling, in my view. You see, in her eyes you don't seem at all a dupe or some old well-trod path . . . You must realize, my darling Beaver, that I'm muddling through in the midst of all these storms to stay as one with you."

I don't believe, as many do, that Beauvoir's affairs were a re-action to Sartre's entanglements with women, a way of balancing things between them. Nor did she maintain a distance in order to keep him interested—Sartre's commitment to her is quite clear from this letter, and he reiterates it many times, without her need-ing to make him jealous with little tales of her own dalliances. Possibly the only time his feelings for her came under real threat was when he wrote to her that Wanda Kosackiewicz had taken a central place in his life, but that was almost certainly an angry reaction to the new, far more serious feelings she had developed for Bost.

One of the things that Beauvoir and Sartre were doing in these letters was providing each other with material: their letters to each other are so full of other people's business, stories of what other couples they knew were getting up to. That they were able, and keen, to provide each other with this kind of information testifies to how clearly they saw themselves as writers—not for nothing did Sartre say that everything else in life must be made to serve that one occupation, being a writer. By now, Beauvoir was taking up that invocation and behaving accordingly.

But she was still the "solitary woman" and I believe Sartre knew it. On October 27, 1939, Sartre wrote to Beauvoir, "you are on the horizon of my every thought. Everything I think or feel or write is for you. Even my novel and my journal, which other people will eventually see, are first for you, and only through you for others." On October 29, Beauvoir wrote (possibly not having received this letter yet, although she had received letters from him dated October 23, 24, and 25 on the 28th of that month, so it's quite possible she received this one from the 27th two days later), telling him of her delight, not only to receive his letters, but also for what they contain: "you haven't left me for an instant. How you've managed to stay with me! How precious and necessary that is to me!"

What, if anything, about this suggests that she is pushing Sartre away? Very little—until we come to another paragraph and read that she has received a note from Bost, too. This relationship had begun in the wake of the disastrous threesome between Sartre, Beauvoir, and Kosackiewicz in the summer of 1938, when Beauvoir and Bost went on a camping trip together (she immediately informed Sartre of the event, and that it was she who had propositioned him). Bost, one of Sartre's students, wasn't intellectually any kind of partner to Beauvoir, but he was a handsome man, and a brave one, who had volunteered to fight against the fascists in Spain. Her relationship with him mattered a great deal to Beauvoir, which she was happy to let Sartre know. But she also records here that Kosackiewicz has received a letter from Bost, as well, and that distresses her. "It gave me a jolt to see how tender it was," she tells Sartre. "I accept the idea abstractly—indeed he told me expressly he was involved to the hilt—but when I really feel that he loves her, I can no longer believe he loves me too." Beauvoir goes on to describe how miserable this has made her feel, and ends her letter by telling Sartre that she loves Bost "more passionately than I thought."

What can we make of this? Beauvoir has not written to Sartre about Bost to make him jealous, or as a reaction to anything he has said—Sartre hasn't mentioned any other women in his letter to her. It seems clear that Beauvoir is not living out the concept of "essential and contingent loves" here, as many presume. Nor is she playing a victim (what is victimized about her statement of passion for another man?), nor is she a predator. What she is, so clearly in this instance, is the "solitary woman" par excellence. After seeing Bost's letter to Olga Kosackiewicz, what does she do? "I left her pretty hastily and went off to the Coupole." She went off to be by herself, in the midst of company; to be alone, but in public.

. . . .

The secret to the longevity of the Beauvoir-Sartre relationship lies ultimately, then, in Beauvoir's acceptance of the mantle passed to her, not from her male writing partner, but from a female writing antecedent, another "solitary woman," Katherine Mansfield. It was by viewing herself as a solitary woman that she was able to maintain a lifelong connection with the other being in her life who could stimulate her mind and urge it on to new creativity, without having to give up her independence, her need for time and space alone. In the years that followed, Beauvoir would produce the work that would make her an icon: after early novels, *She Came to Stay* (1943), *The Blood of Others* (1945), and *All Men are Mortal* (1946), which finally brought her to the French public, her feminist critique, *The Second Sex*, was published in 1949, still surprisingly early for a work that remains fresh and relevant today. Her award-winning novel *The Mandarins* followed in 1954, and in 1958, she published the first of her autobiographical volumes, *Memoirs of a Dutiful Daughter*. She carried on publishing through the 1960s and '70s, a much sought-after figure for students of literature and philosophy, who would come from all over the world to spy her sitting in Les Deux Magots, her trademark turban holding up her hair.

Through all this time, her reputation was linked with Sartre's, whose first book, *Nausea,* had launched him in 1938. *Being and Nothingness*, his greatest philosophical work, followed in 1943 (with those crucial insights from Beauvoir's *She Came to Stay*), and the first of the *Roads to Freedom* volumes appeared in 1945. Sartre published voraciously throughout the '40s, with theories of existentialism appearing alongside novels and a biography of Baudelaire. Plays like *Huis Clos (No Exit)* were also published during this decade. Remarkably, though, he showed few signs of slowing up after this extraordinary period, publishing throughout the '50s, '60s, and '70s. As Beauvoir and Sartre aged together, they maintained, if not a philosophical closeness, certainly a political one, with their Marxist views taking them to Cuba, and in Sartre's case, leading him into an affair with a possible KGB agent. Students of radical politics loved their left-wing stance, their embrace of communism (which incidentally managed not to interfere with Sartre's lifelong love of the United States), even if many others deplored their support of Stalin long after the dictator's acts of genocide against his own people had come to light. To the very end, Beauvoir backed Sartre, attending to him when he was ill and dying, and making sure the world didn't forget him by publishing his letters to her.

And yet, in spite of this closeness, these political intimacies and final caring moments, Beauvoir was always her own woman. And as contradictory as it may seem to see the maintenance of any relationship as reliant on apartness, on distance, on solitariness, in this particular instance, it was what Beauvoir needed in order to be a successful artist. In Jean-Paul Sartre, she found the person who could accommodate that contradiction. No other man or woman she met was able to do that for her, and it's clear from this that writing and sex did not substitute each other in their relationship as it first appears they might have. Sex didn't become writing for them, either, simply by way of recording their affairs with other people. Sex and writing were part of that contradiction that kept them together—in sex, Beauvoir was the solitary woman, as she was in her writing, while all the time both conditions, sex as well as writing, necessitated the presence of other people. It wasn't an easy balancing act to maintain; it hurt her, it hurt Sartre, and it hurt those around them who couldn't understand. But it was a necessary balancing act.

One biographer has written of Beauvoir and Sartre that "we can't think of one without the other," the perfect endnote to their own insistence that they were, really, one and the same person.

But that was, in the end, just another little story. Beauvoir was always Beauvoir. Solitary women don't become someone else. It was a necessary fiction, just like their literary partnership. And we all believed it.

PART III

1930s–1950s: The Transatlantic Chasers

Martha Gelhorn and Ernest Hemingway in 1940.

7. The "Survivor": Martha Gellhorn and Ernest Hemingway

We are, basically, two tough people and we were born to survive.
—Martha Gellhorn,
May 1944

Nothing is better for self-esteem than survival . . .
—Martha Gellhorn, 1978

Mother said to me once, "What interested you was France, and you found or were found by the most complete Frenchman available. Then you were interested in writing, so you found or were found by what you thought the finest writer . . . But some day you will find a man, and not someone who represents something."
—Martha Gellhorn,
April 1950

How does one survive a romance that the world has covered in newspapers and magazines? Of all the relationships in this volume, Martha Gellhorn and Ernest Hemingway's literary partnership comes closest to what we would understand today as a "celebrity romance." They were each celebrities in their own right; together, they were a literary Richard Burton and Elizabeth Taylor, the Posh and Becks of American letters.

Surviving the death of such a public, starry romance isn't easy. In 1950, a full six years after she had left Ernest Hemingway,

Martha Gellhorn read an installment of her former husband's latest book, *Across the River and into the Trees*, which offered up a
rather cruel caricature of her. Despite the time that had elapsed,
she was moved enough to write the following to a friend: "I weep
for the eight years I spent, almost eight (light dawned a little earlier) worshipping his image with him, and I weep for whatever
else I was cheated of due to that time-serving, and I weep for all
that is permanently lost because I shall never, really, trust a man
again."

As an indictment of a marriage, and of a literary partnership,
there are few more final words spoken, few more sincerely felt
regrets or vicious, self-wounding swipes at the past. Certainly, the
pain of two writers who have ended their relationship is not quite
like any other, given that both parties can record their feelings
in print for all the world to see and judge—and with writers of
Hemingway's and Gellhorn's celebrity status, far too many people
were all too eager to read what each really thought of the other.
Hemingway had been a literary star in the States since the success
of his second novel, *The Sun Also Rises*, in 1926, a book about the
"lost generation," expats like himself who had fled to France and
Spain after the First World War. The subsequent *A Farewell to Arms*
(1929), based on his experiences working for an ambulance unit
during that war, was enough to immortalize him, but Hemingway
was never satisfied: in later years, short stories like "The Snows of
Kilimanjaro" (1938), and the novels *To Have and Have Not* (1937)
and *For Whom the Bell Tolls* (1940) would all get the Hollywood
treatment and be made into films. But it was his 1952 novella, *The
Old Man and the Sea*, that would win him lasting literary gold: he
was awarded both the Pulitzer and the Nobel prizes.

Gellhorn couldn't compete with a Pulitzer and a Nobel, but
her first book, *The Trouble I've Seen*, published in 1936 and based
on the areas she had covered as a journalist during the Great
Depression, caused a sensation. Greater literary success would

evade her, but it was really as a war reporter that she made her reputation, gaining even more respect and admiration for her reports from Spain and Europe during the Second World War than Hemingway did. She was there, minus Hemingway, at the D-day landings and when Dachau was liberated, a shocking experience that she would always claim changed her forever. And she continued reporting long after she and Hemingway had gone their separate ways: she filed reports from Vietnam, from the Six-Day War in the Middle East, and from Nicaragua. She feared very little. At the age of seventy-nine, she was attacked and raped early one morning while out walking near her house in Nyali outside Mombasa. She simply dusted herself down, walked back to her house, treated her cuts and bruises, and then drove herself to a nearby doctor. When she was diagnosed with terminal cancer, she sorted out her affairs, tidied her London flat, took a pill she had been saving in the event of such a catastrophe, drank some whiskey, and simply went to sleep. She knew when it was time to go and she wasn't scared of death.

This fearlessness made her possibly the most famous war reporter of her generation and her country, certainly the most famous woman war reporter, a remarkable achievement given how few women entered into that area of the profession. War reporting was dangerous, grubby, dirty work, but Gellhorn combined her lack of fear with compassion, as well as an eye for detail, that few could rival.

Because of their joint celebrity, Gellhorn and Hemingway would always be mentioned together, even after they broke up, something with which Gellhorn professed great irritation (although she did contradict herself here, as we shall see). Even without Hemingway's caricature of her—a caricature so damaging that, according to one biographer, his publisher actually feared it would prove libelous—Gellhorn still felt she had good cause to regret the long relationship. In 1990, only eight years before her death, and almost thirty years after Hemingway himself had committed suicide, she would write, "Hell hath no fury like E.H. scorned and I'll never escape from him."

And yet, in 1978 she published an account of the trip to China she undertook with Hemingway, just after they were married. It is an affectionate portrait of the man she called in the book "Unwilling Companion," or U.C. for short, a man she described as "heroic" and whose patience and courtesy she praised. Their trip was a journey of horrible discomfort and unpalatable meals, but their humor pulled them both through—that and their mutual affection. A mere four years after this event, however, she would be telling a friend that her marriage was over, its "amputation" horrible but necessary, because of that magical word which would surface again and again throughout the rest of her life when she thought of him: "escape." She needed to escape from Hemingway, escape from herself, escape "from this personal life which feels like a strait jacket."

The downward spiral in which Hemingway was fatally caught for years had a grim effect on Gellhorn herself as well as on their marriage. Sex between them had never been great—Gellhorn is quoted as having told a friend that Hemingway's lovemaking was "short and sharp"—but toward the end of their relationship, sex was entirely nonexistent. Furious rows would rage through the night, when Hemingway would prove capable of anything from throwing glasses to firing bullets through windows. The presence of others wouldn't stop him from calling his wife a "bitch," and as his drinking increased, so did the violence. On one occasion he slapped her, after she took the wheel of his car, when his drunken driving threatened to crash them both. Hemingway's unmanageable behavior has been attributed to the genetic propensity for a repeat mental condition and a repeat outcome (his father was a manic-depressive who shot himself). His treatment of the women in his life has also been linked to his mother, however, who dressed him as a girl when he was little, and to his own complex sexual makeup and depressive tendencies.

Whatever the reasons for his behavior in the latter stages of his marriage to Gellhorn, there is no doubt that it was a truly sordid time for them both, although an exact picture of what really went on between them is not easy to construct. Gellhorn burned all of Hemingway's letters to her shortly before she died. The diaries that she kept appear to skim over what she endured, what brought her finally to leave her husband. Perhaps the fullest account she ever gave in print was in a letter to a lover, David Gurewitsch, in April 1950, where she says of Hemingway, "I left him because he became contemptible, apart from me; and I could not stop him or protect anyone and I despised him. I beg you to understand this. Ernest had a theory that brutality was all women understood; if they seemed recalcitrant (like me) they only needed to be beaten more . . . I had honestly thought that Ernest would drive me mad with cruelty." However, this letter was also meant to reassure her new lover, who seemed to feel nervous about being in Hemingway's shadow ("You said E. was a king in something; and you are a king in nothing. Darling, listen . . ."), so it's hard to know just how much of it represented what she had really gone through and how she really felt about it.

Hemingway had cheated on both his previous wives, Hadley Richardson and Pauline Pfeiffer, so it is perhaps surprising that there was no hint of sexual infidelity in his relationship with Gellhorn, by either party. Not until the end, when their relationship had pretty much irretrievably broken down, did Hemingway find some comfort in the arms of Mary Welsh, and Gellhorn with the handsome young army general James Gavin. This lack of sexual betrayal says something quite important about how they viewed each other (Hemingway would tell others, including his son, Patrick, that Gellhorn begged to come back to him after they broke up, although there is no evidence from Gellhorn that this was true, and it seems unlikely, given how eager she was to get away from him), something that complicates the vicious treatment Hemingway dished out to Gellhorn toward the end, and the reason she took it for so long.

It must have been bad. Gellhorn could not, by any stretch of the imagination, be called a coward. A lover of luxury perhaps, capable of frivolity, and vain, certainly, but she was a brave, even fearless woman who had faced enemy fire with equanimity. During the Spanish Civil War, for example, she refused to run away when Barcelona came under repeated bombing, and instead visited hospitals to speak to the injured there. She was also taken by republican soldiers to view their trenches. On one occasion the hotel she and Hemingway were staying in was bombed. And when the Allies left England to land on Omaha Beach on D-day at the end of the Second World War, Gellhorn managed to join them on a hospital ship, without permission, an action that allowed her to cover the landings but which also got her arrested. Hemingway had not made the journey.

So if there had been any woman who could take on the larger-than-life figure of Ernest Hemingway, it was Martha Gellhorn. More comfortable in the company of men than she was with women, Gellhorn could drink and smoke and curse and sing along with the best of them, and her pioneering work as a journalist—first in Depression-torn America, then covering the fight against fascism in Spain—was the product of a strong-minded, determined, and resourceful individual not easily scared.

Given this image we have of her, it is almost shocking to read of the impact that marriage to Hemingway had on her well-being: "I doubt myself terribly, and in a way I doubt life. I have E. to thank a bit, for there was such an investment of illusion and it paid off so shabbily, that I am frightened and doubtful, and everyone who touches me must suffer." It's easy to interpret her "investment of illusion," one that "paid off so shabbily" as being her own investment in him; but there is also a sense here that she possibly feels theirs was a mutual investment that let them both down, a mutual disillusioning process. She had let him down; she wasn't up to the job. It's a lack of self-confidence that only ever makes itself apparent in her life when she talks about her fiction writing. The link between them, though, is hardly coincidental, as this chapter will show.

Setting aside questions about how and why their relationship ended, we come to why it began it the first place. It seems enough for Hemingway's biographers that Gellhorn was ten years younger than him, blonde and pretty. And while she is not generally considered by biographers and critics to have been a great literary influence on him, she was in fact initially compared to him, and more favorably, too, when her collection of stories *The Trouble I've Seen* was published in 1936, a few months before she met Hemingway. "Who is this Martha Gellhorn?" wrote critic Lewis Gannett. "Her writing burns ... Hemingway does not write more authentic American speech. Nor can Ernest Hemingway teach Martha Gellhorn anything about economy of language."

Gellhorn's impact on Hemingway's emotional, psychological, and intellectual life is similarly considered negligible. But Gellhorn and Hemingway were two novelists and journalists with similar political outlooks and similar approaches to life, and appeared, in many respects, to have been a match made in heaven. While there are many who would argue that such romantic phrases as a "match made in heaven" are inappropriately facile, we should remind them of the period of the Hemingway-Gellhorn relationship from 1936 to 1944. This was the golden era of Hollywood, the age when Hemingway's novels could be made into full-color films with stars like Ingrid Bergman, Gary Cooper, and Gregory Peck. Gellhorn herself, in photographs from that time, resembles nothing less than a film star, her golden hair fashionably curled, her flared trousers the height of fashion for dynamic, glamorous women like Katharine Hepburn and Bette Davis. Together, Gellhorn and Hemingway made a publicist's dream, and the glamour attached to their pairing may have had much to do with its demise, as well as with their mutual distrust after it was over.

But whatever did bring them to the end point matters just as much as what brought them together in the first place, because their relationship itself mattered for both their careers. If some questions seem particularly prurient, their celebrity status demands that such squeamishness be quashed. We must examine their relationship properly and fully, and ask the awkward questions. For instance, was it simply Hemingway's alcoholism that became too much for Gellhorn to cope with? Were they never, as Gellhorn maintained to friends, sexually compatible, given his poor bedroom technique? Was he jealous, as many have claimed, of her international reputation for journalism, the prestigious assignments that sent her across the world, often leaving him behind?

Or was it that Gellhorn simply had no more use for him, as some of Hemingway's friends have implied? Was she just the original literary groupie, hanging around with one of the biggest literary stars, hoping a little of his glitter would rub off on her? Was her relationship with Hemingway simply a good career move, as some of their friends insisted it was? One biographer quotes a friend of Hemingway's, Winston Guest, that Gellhorn "implied to me that she married him as a practical matter; it might help her improve her writing." An unspecified "friend" of Gellhorn's is also quoted, although one struggles to understand how a friend could have spoken thus: "she was more excited by Hemingway the writer than Hemingway the man, that ambition rather than passion had inspired her marriage."

Was Gellhorn really the one who chased him and caught him, as many have claimed, then? And if he was so terrible to be with, why wasn't she simply glad to get away from him, instead of remaining bitter for years after they broke up? Is it possible to argue that she, in fact, needed him a lot less than he needed her, even if she had initially sought him out? Most importantly, did the relationship do Gellhorn no good at all, personally or professionally? Was it really the disaster she always claimed it was?

Their mutual feeling that their marriage was a great mistake occupied both Gellhorn's and Hemingway's thoughts long after the relationship came to an end: it seems fair to say that neither of them ever really got over it, and one biographer argues that Hemingway's separation from her "was the most 'traumatic' of all his marital disturbances." Some prefer to argue that other experiences in Martha Gellhorn's life mattered a great deal more to her. It's true that she never fully recovered from the defeat of the republicans in Spain, or from witnessing the release of survivors at Dachau at the end of the Second World War. But for her, the greatest of all these disasters, some horrific, some with global impact, was a much more personal matter: the failure of her relationship with Hemingway. It was the thing she regretted most: not its existence, but its failure.

Like so many other women in this book, Martha Gellhorn had ambitions to be a writer from an early age, and seemed to sense that a relationship with another writer was what she needed to complete her, in some way. Ever doubtful of her own writing abilities, she needed advice and encouragement, and she was brave enough to face that need and accept it. The failure of her marriage to one of the greatest writers of the time, someone who provided her with all the advice and encouragement she could have hoped for, was a source of constant pain for her. She survived it, but she hadn't planned on needing to.

The constant claim that Gellhorn made in later years, that Hemingway had been bad for her, is not a clear-cut one when we consider the affectionate portrayal of him in *Travels with Myself and Another*, or the contradictory claims she would make that she never read any biographies of Hemingway (she did), that she would never again read a word he wrote (she did), or that she would silence anyone who spoke about him to her. In his intro- duction to *Travels with Myself and Another*, Bill Buford says that, in spite of stating that she didn't want to talk about him at all, she in fact "talked about him at length" and often. "Yes, she resented him for all sorts of reasons," writes Buford, "but he was the only man she talked about." Most crucially, she continued to praise his writing, almost twenty years after his suicide ("I do not forget the good he did in freeing the language; we are all his debtors"), even while picking holes in his grammar or delighting in noticing tiny mistakes.

It was Hemingway's writing, after all, that Martha Gellhorn fell in love with first. Given the prize-winning, innovative, and best-selling quality of that writing, it is perhaps not surprising that the man himself could not live up to it: what human being could? But Gellhorn's literary career was well underway when she first met Hemingway. She was hardly a beginner looking for a more experienced partner to show her the way. She had pub- lished a novelized version of her journalistic forays into the Great Depression, *The Trouble I've Seen*, as well as a novel, *What Mad Pursuit*, whose epitaph was a line from Hemingway's *A Farewell to Arms* ("Nothing ever happens to the brave"). She was on close terms with the wife of the U.S. president, Eleanor Roosevelt, with whom she regularly confided both her impressions on her jour- nalistic assignments as well as her personal situation. While not quite as dazzling a star to the extent that the celebrated author of *A Farewell to Arms* was, there is no doubt that she was considerably further on in her career than any of the other women in this vol- ume by the time she met her literary partner. That fact is of some significance to the relationship she had with Hemingway, and to the outcome of it. When she wrote that they were both tough, they were both "survivors," she was talking, sadly for Hemingway, only of herself. That she had some star status of her own before mingling with an even more glittering light is possibly what destroyed their relationship, while ensuring that she survived it, and as hardily as she did.

• • • •

Martha Gellhorn was born in November 1908 in St. Louis to two half-Jewish parents, a German-born doctor, George Gellhorn, from Ohlau near Breslau in what is now Poland, and his well-educated wife, Edna Fischel, a Bryn Mawr graduate. They met when George Gellhorn set up a practice with Edna's father, Washington Fischel. Both parents were culturally aware, socially minded, and liberal to the point of progressive. They had four children altogether; Martha was the only girl, but she attended the same progressive school as her youngest brother, Alfred, and she also helped her politically active mother on her many suffrage campaigns. Like Rebecca West, Gellhorn was educated by her mother on the value of female independence. Her subsequent career in journalism and her desire to go where no woman had gone before were both linked to this early feminist teaching. St. Louis, however, would soon prove to be too small and too provincial for a girl with big ambitions like Martha Gellhorn. One biographer records her feeling isolated at school because she wanted to go live in France, and a short holiday there in 1925 when she was sixteen convinced her it was where she belonged. She went on to attend Bryn Mawr, her mother's alma mater, but found it "stodgy and genteel." She stood out, nevertheless, as a confident student, dismissive of rules and unengaged with school life. But poetry interested her, and she also reported on the Fourth Annual Congress of the National Students' Federation of America for the school's magazine, *College News.* Gellhorn seems to have developed a bit

of a reputation for college journalism at this point, and one biographer believes that it was at this time that she "read Ernest
Hemingway and tried to write like him." Perhaps it was his tale
of life as an expat in Paris that finally decided her: she left Bryn
Mawr in 1929, determined to become a journalist.

She headed for New York and somehow managed to get a
summer job with the *New Republic* reading galley proofs, which
bored her to tears (she only worked there for a month). She followed that up with stints on the *Albany Times Union* newspaper as a
junior reporter and also wrote book reviews for the *New Republic*.
It couldn't have been easy at this time, even though newspapers
had gone through a boom period during the '20s and there were
jobs aplenty in the industry. Women were still expected to marry,
as a career—and as liberal as her parents were, they seemed to
think so, too, and wanted her back home. Gellhorn obeyed them,
but she used her time at home to practice her writing, not her
husband-hunting, skills.

By the end of that year she had made another decision: she
would go to Paris. According to Carl Rollyson, she "borrowed
the money from her family's cook and boarded a bus for New
York City," but according to Caroline Moorehead, "Edna lent
her the money for her train ticket to New York." Whether it was
bus or train, her mother's money or the cook's, Gellhorn made it
to New York, and a shipping line apparently offered her a cabin
berth on a boat across the Atlantic in exchange for an article
about them. She arrived in Paris with either one or two suitcases,
depending on which biography you read, but with only seventy-
five dollars to her name—on that everyone seems to agree.

How did this young woman with little experience of the
world at large make her way in a city she had only visited twice
before, with no friends there and little money? With remarkable
prescience and self-confidence, she talked herself up. First she
tried the *New York Times*, which turned her down, then she found

work in a beauty parlor. A chance to write a little advertising copy came her way, and she seems to have signed up with a news agency, too, and even managed a short stint with Paris *Vogue*. This little foothold in the world of fashion seems to have encouraged her to write fashion pieces to send to newspapers back home, which were happy to take her word on the latest Paris fashions. Finding people happy to take her word for things would happen throughout Gellhorn's career. She carried, even at that young age, an authority and confidence that would later take her into dangerous places and make her the journalist she became.

France was not only the beginning of Gellhorn's freelance career, though: it was also where she met the first love of her life, Bertrand de Jouvenal, a journalist and the son of an important Paris newspaper editor. Jouvenal had been the teenage lover of the author Colette, his father's wife, who had seduced him, and their affair had scandalized 1920s Paris (which must have taken some doing). Unfortunately for Gellhorn, he was married now, and over the next three years, as he chased her and pleaded with her, she would repeatedly give in to him, in spite of what appears to have been an initially poor sexual experience with him. Nevertheless, she would get pregnant twice and abort each pregnancy over the course of their long affair. There is no evidence that Gellhorn regretted her decisions: she also had an abortion while married to Ernest Hemingway, although she did adopt a child after that marriage failed, a little boy she called Sandy.

Gellhorn's abortions during her relationship with Jouvenal may have been more about concerns that children would hamper her career, which flourished during this period: she was attending political meetings at the League of Nations and making connections with other foreign correspondents in the city. It was probably not so much about the scandal of being unmarried and pregnant, even though she didn't want to shock her parents. She and Jouvenal behaved as if they were married and she would in-sist that friends and family refer to him as her husband. When she later divorced Hemingway, it would even be written up in some newspapers that she had been married twice.

But even at the beginning of this relationship with Jouvenal, a relationship that lasted for four years, Gellhorn, trying to find her way to writing fiction as well as journalism, was aware of Hemingway. In 1930, she was back in St. Louis, possibly prefer-ring to have her abortion in the States than in France, and work-ing on the novel that would become *What Mad Pursuit* (this was a work of juvenilia she tried to disown and dismiss in later years). But the pattern of her thinking about her fiction never changed from this beginning: there is a lack of confidence in what she is doing, a fear that she is not good enough to be a great writer ("I just can't make it jell"). She even blamed Hemingway, then unknown to her personally, who at this point was being feted as America's answer to James Joyce after the huge critical success of his 1929 novel, *A Farewell to Arms*. Gellhorn writes to her lov-er, Jouvenal, in exasperation: "I think Hemingway is pretty bum from what he did in *In Our Time* [his first publication, a collection of stories from 1925]: the story about skiing is written about an ex-beau of mine who used to ski with him. Hemingway makes him inarticulate simply because Hemingway doesn't know how to talk, and as a matter of fact that guy can talk in 9 syllable words all night long. So I'm not impressed. Anyway Hemingway has af-fected my style which is really too bad . . ."

Gellhorn's healthy lack of respect for those who were con-sidered to be gods is appealing at this early stage of her career, and it's a testament to her own integrity that she didn't automatically assume a literary star could teach her how to write. But the link between her lack of faith in her own writing and the mention of Hemingway's work is all too revealing: that he has "affected" her own "writing style" means that she has up until this point been reading a great deal of his fiction—*A Farewell to Arms* had been published in 1929 and had made him very famous indeed. Gellhorn wasn't the kind to be a groupie, but it's clear from this that she was, in spite of her criticism of his work here, something of a fan.

Later, in 1931, Hemingway crops up again, this time in a letter to a friend and in a much more complimentary way: "Meantime, I take my code out of Hemingway. Unbelievable, isn't it? Do you remember *A Farewell to Arms.* The hero talks to the woman; she is worried about something; and he says: 'You're brave. Nothing ever happens to the brave.' Which is somehow enough—a whole philosophy—a banner—a song—and a love."

Five years before she even met Hemingway, Gellhorn was allowing his work to furnish her with a style, a "philosophy," even "a love." In the world of celebrity romance, this match was clearly meant to be. Jouvenal meant a lot to her, but as the relationship progressed, she could see what he couldn't give her. In the midst of what was lacking—divorce from his wife and marriage to Gellhorn—was literary advice. At the end of the relationship, she wrote to another friend, Campbell Beckett, to explain her literary worries, while also discussing her relationship woes. She was struggling with the first-person voice, she said—interestingly, Gellhorn would hardly ever use the first-person voice in her novels even after she met him, whereas Hemingway used it all the time—and writing was "hell," it was a purging of the spirit and the mind. She was fearful of "not finishing or finishing badly," one minute, she said, then convinced that she would "write—and maybe even write better than before," the next.

This was all communicated from France in the spring of 1934—by the autumn of that year, she had been recruited (along with other journalists) by Harold Hopkins, Franklin Roosevelt's director of the newly set-up Federal Emergency Relief Administration, to report back on how the Depression was affecting the poorest across the country. Gellhorn was assigned to mill areas of North Carolina like Gaston County, as well as poverty-stricken parts of Massachusetts, where she spent her days interviewing families on the breadline, reporting on their individual incomes, needs, and sufferings. She found whole families infected with syphilis, poisoned drinking water, and rats everywhere, and those individuals who had managed to get work in a factory or store almost too weak to stand, never mind work. Proper relief wasn't getting through to nearly enough people, and the anger she felt at what she witnessed fired her writing and inspired her lifelong campaign against injustice.

By this point, she had completed and found a publisher for *What Mad Pursuit*, which was considered "crude" but "refreshing" by kinder reviewers, but it had come too late, really—Gellhorn was now moving ahead with her journalism. Her fiction wasn't, at this stage, developing quickly enough to keep up with her. Eventually, though, she found a way to bring it on, and it was through her journalism that she achieved it. The sights of people suffering without money, health care, proper food, or sanitation inspired her next book, a collection of four long short stories called *The Trouble I've Seen*.

It was also while on one of her visits to the White House—Eleanor Roosevelt had become a special correspondent for her by now—that she met H. G. Wells, the then sixty-nine-year-old former lover of Rebecca West, a writer Gellhorn admired. One biographer views Gellhorn's later outraged refutations of suggestions that she had an affair with Wells with some cynicism (Wells had written her some passionate letters and made some comments to his son to give the impression they had slept together), but Gellhorn's cry of "Why the hell would I sleep with a little old man when I could have any number of tall beautiful young men?" has a ring of truth to it. Rollyson's assertion that she was on the lookout for a writing helpmeet, a role that Wells all too willingly played when he wrote an introduction to *The Trouble I've Seen* and helped her to get it published in the U.K., overlooks the fact that she probably didn't have to sleep with him to get him to do that for her. Yes, Wells put her up when she came to London; again, he would have done that just for the company of a pretty, clever young girl like Martha Gellhorn. While she was certainly ambitious about her writing, it is doubtful she would have had to sleep with Wells just to win a few literary favors from him.

The publication of that book and its favorable reception, though, didn't help get Gellhorn the jobs or the commissions she wanted, and a couple of unsuccessful love affairs left her kicking her heels. An affair with another married man, Allen Grover, a *Time* magazine journalist, which had begun the year before in the summer of 1935, was coming to an end that August—"I think I can definitely consider you as the cream in my coffee, but not my breakfast," was a characteristically bitter-free comment from Gellhorn at the end of this affair. In this letter to him, she also talks of an "English lad" whom she is seeing and who is also married, but it has not been discovered whom she meant by this. Most importantly, though, she reveals to Grover: "A man is no use to me, unless he can live without me." It would come to be an important dictum for her in her marriage with Hemingway. Her father had died in December 1935, too, and possibly this first Christmas without him made the family—that is, Gellhorn, her mother, and her brother, Albert—embark on a family trip to Florida.

Biographers disagree over who suggested the location, but it's important for the accusation that Gellhorn "chased" after Hemingway. They headed for Key West because they didn't like Miami, where they had arrived first, and which had "bored" them all. In a bar called Sloppy Joe's, "the bar that Ernest Hemingway made famous," they came across the bulky shape of America's most famous literary son. Was Gellhorn's claim that she didn't expect to meet him "suspect," as one critic claims? Her later insistence that it was her brother who wanted to go there—and her ignorance that it was where Hemingway drank—sound to some too much like answers to the accusations that she chased him. It seems unlikely that she would not know these details about Hemingway, especially given her feel for investigative journalism and how much she had read of his work. Caroline Moorehead claims that "Martha Gellhorn was not the only young writer to pin a photograph of him on her college wall."

Gellhorn later also disputed that she began an affair with Hemingway while he was still with his second wife, Pauline; she was friends with them both, she said, although only a few weeks later, she was writing almost intimately to Eleanor Roosevelt of her meeting with the famous writer, saying that he was "an odd bird, very lovable and full of fire and a marvelous story teller." She is at pains to stress that she didn't chase him, didn't break up his marriage—why? A decade later, Elizabeth Smart would be quite open about "chasing" after George Barker and breaking up his marriage; fifteen years after that, Sylvia Plath wouldn't hide her quest for a writing partner and shouting out lines of his poetry at Ted Hughes at a college party, even while he was there with another woman. Were they just more liberated about what, and who, they wanted than Gellhorn was?

The charge that Gellhorn "chased" Hemingway clearly bothered her, given that she made such an effort to deny knowing well-established personal details about him, such as where he liked to drink, later in life. Perhaps the reason it bothered her so much is partly to do with personal vanity. Gellhorn hardly had to chase her men. Blonde, beautiful, stylish, she probably didn't have to do very much to catch Hemingway's eye once she entered that bar. Perhaps it's more tragic than that, however, and more to do with the subsequent failure of their marriage. The accusation that she chased him puts more of the responsibility for its failure on her shoulders. That may have been more responsibility than she could bear.

But in the first days in Key West, they hit it off straightaway. Gellhorn told Eleanor Roosevelt that she would "sit about" and read "the mss of his new book." She spoke of the negative effect this had on her own writing, making it seem "a think-book in which everyone sits down all the time and talks and broods and nothing happens." From the beginning, it was all about the writing—for Gellhorn, at least. Here was the man whose words she had quoted in her own publications; here was the man she'd been trying to take lessons from when writing her fiction. It is hardly surprising that she would have approached him when she saw him that night in that bar, perhaps even set up the entire trip. But Gellhorn's literary aims, her needs, for all her later explanations and excuses, made her the chaser in this relationship by most biographical accounts.

• • • •

Ernest Hemingway was born on July 21, 1899, the second child of Ed and Grace Hemingway. As in Gellhorn's case, Hemingway's father was a doctor and he, too, died when his son was still in his twenties. Ed Hemingway died, though, by his own hand, putting a bullet through his head one morning on December 6, 1928. It haunted his son, who blamed his overpowering mother for his father's death. Suicide would run in the family—in 1982, Leicester Hemingway, the writer's brother, would kill himself, as would his sister, Ursula, in 1966, after being diagnosed with a terminal illness. Hemingway himself would, of course, die by his own hand in 1961, after a long struggle with depression and alcoholism.

Hemingway's life story reads almost like one of the tragic romances that made his name. Like Gellhorn, he started his writing career in journalism, to which he attributed certain skills that lasted him throughout his life, like the ability to pare down sentences, to write clearly and concisely. Toward the end of the First World War he enlisted as an army ambulance driver, and was badly wounded—the skirmish he survived was recalled in *A Farewell to Arms*, the novel based on his wartime experiences and his affair with his first love, Agnes von Kurowsky. When he came back home after Agnes left him for another man, he met his first wife, Hadley Richardson, and in 1920, shortly after the death of her father, he proposed marriage. He took her to Paris, where there was a large expat community of Americans, including Gertrude Stein and F. Scott Fitzgerald, both of whom Hemingway befriended, as well as Ezra Pound, who edited his work, as Pound did every writer's he came into contact with. Hemingway also began working for Ford Madox Ford's *transatlantic review* as its deputy editor. Trips to Spain where he watched the bullfighting were also something he undertook during his time in Europe. His experiences during this period, and his record of some of them in the 1925 collection *In Our Time* helped set him on the road to becoming one of the world's most famous writers, even if his personal life was a mess. His marriage to Hadley Richardson was failing badly by this time, the birth of a child something he clearly wasn't ready for, and he had fallen for another woman, Pauline Pfeiffer. He soon divorced Richardson and married Pfeiffer: she bore him two sons.

By the time he met Martha Gellhorn, Hemingway may have published eight books, but he had also been married twice, fathered three children, seen action in a world war, and been at the heart of the modernist literary revolution in Paris. Whatever else could be said about his troubled private life and peripatetic lifestyle, it couldn't be said that he'd wasted his time. He was only thirty-seven when a youthful twenty-eight-year-old Gellhorn walked into Sloppy Joe's that December evening—what was there left for him to achieve?

It's possible that, feeling slightly dejected and bored, very unhappy by now in his second marriage, which seemed to be going the same way as his first, Hemingway was just waiting for something, or someone, exciting to come his way and rev him up again. It does beg the question, without Gellhorn's intervention in his life at this point, would later novels like *The Old Man and the Sea* even have happened for him? Perhaps he would never have roused himself from his despondency without her. And certainly, after meeting in Key West, he seems to have grabbed at this rejuvenating person who had, literally, walked into his life, and was extremely keen to stay in touch with her after they went their separate ways home. He telephoned her constantly in St. Louis, and they were also writing to each other (Gellhorn, though, was maintaining an air of innocence about the whole thing, and also writing friendly letters to Pauline). Both had decided they wanted to go to Spain to cover the civil war there, and at the end of February 1937, she headed for New York at Hemingway's behest. According to one biographer, she met him there but perhaps surprisingly didn't enjoy his "world," which was public and "odd and glamorous"—it is doubtful much of anything happened between them at this time, even though his wife was not present. She needed money for her boat ticket, and *Vogue* commissioned a beauty article from her, which gave her the money for her journey. Hemingway had already left for Paris and Spain.

From the beginning, though, Hemingway immediately did what critics of Gellhorn believe she wanted him to do all along— he helped her with her writing career. He had recommended a short story Gellhorn had written, to editors at the prestigious *Scribner's Magazine*, on his return to New York from Key West, and they had accepted it. And it was Hemingway who encouraged Gellhorn to come to Spain, too, no doubt flattering her about her writing and the journalistic opportunities it would create for her. The war in Spain was almost unique in that it attracted combatants from all over the world. Those with no connection to the country, like the Glasgow Communists who walked almost the whole way from Scotland, and whose contribution to fighting fascism is honored with a special monument in their home city, were typical of many of the International Brigades: men and women who traveled for the cause of an ideal which they felt was under threat. Both Gellhorn and Hemingway predicted that defeat in Spain would mean a greater battle against fascism, one that would immerse America, too, although few listened to them.

By April 1937, though, Gellhorn had completed her journey and was in Spain. And it was in Spain that she and Hemingway really fell in love—a war their backdrop, just as in his novels. The romance of the situation might be tempered by scenes of slaughter, surviving on food barely fit for animals, dodging bullets and bombs, but for both of them it was nevertheless a romance, and one that everyone knew about—when one shell exploded outside their hotel, people came running out of their rooms, including Gellhorn and Hemingway together. As Hemingway would write many years after they parted: "Funny how it should take one war to start a woman in your damn heart and another to finish her." It has been pointed out that Gellhorn should have been warned about his real feelings for her, if the play *The Fifth Column*, which he published in 1938, and which was largely based on his time in Spain, was anything to go by. The "tall handsome blonde girl," a "lady journalist" from Vassar, Dorothy Bridges, has always been read as a version of Gellhorn, and the Hemingway character's, Philip Rawlings's, ambiguous feelings for her ("She may be bad for me and I may waste time . . . but she's absolutely straight") eventually culminate in the kind of unpleasant scene ("Because you're useless really. You're uneducated, you're useless, you're a fool and you're lazy" as Rawlings says to Bridges) that would be played out between them in real life over and over again.

For instance, it was only in 1941, a mere three years later, that Gellhorn would be confiding in a female friend, "he thought nothing of greeting her at the front door . . . his drawers down, ready for sexual play"; typical evenings between them would begin with Hemingway drinking, running out of ice, shouting for servants, drinking more; his lack of personal hygiene ("he considered it manly to be dirty") put her off having sex with him; he would rage at her into the night when she wanted to sleep. According to Moorehead, toward the end of the marriage, Hemingway "talked about her freely, finding coarse and tawdry stories with which to entertain his entourage of hangers-on . . . ."

But before all that, there was love and romance and a mutual understanding. Hemingway genuinely admired Gellhorn's courage and daring in Spain. They shared a similar sense of humor, too, and both were physically active people, happy to be outside doing something. By the time they returned from Spain, his marriage to Pauline was more or less over, and by February 1939, Hemingway and Gellhorn were living happily together as a couple at Finca Vígia, in Cuba, just outside Havana. She met his sons, who liked her, found her to be good fun, and it's clear too that in the early days Hemingway enjoyed her company. Whatever else he said about her, he never accused her of being boring. On November 21, 1940, four years after they first met in Sloppy Joe's, Gellhorn and Hemingway were married. Reporters besieged them in New York as newspapers ran the story of their wedding; Robert Capa had taken photographs of the couple earlier that month for *Life* magazine. Their celebrity life together had begun.

From a writing point of view, though, equally important things were happening. Gellhorn's dispatches from Spain had given birth to a new kind of journalism: Gellhorn was unsure of writing about the technicalities of war, so Hemingway encouraged her to do what she did when visiting North Carolina previously—to write about the effects of it on ordinary people's daily lives. Her first story for *Collier's* magazine launched her as a particular kind of war correspondent that was much more than simply "lady journalist," and she was subsequently asked to go to Finland for them, to report on the beginning of the war in Europe.

Hemingway was right when he said of his relationship with Gellhorn that it took "another war to finish her." From the start of her career as a roving reporter on the war front, he was deeply unhappy and insecure, mainly about the time she spent away from him. From 1939 on, she would go on commissions to Puerto Rico, to interview survivors from merchant ships targeted by the Japanese; she also took a trip to the Caribbean to see what was happening there, then went off to New York and Washington (as well as St. Louis to see her mother), and then traveled to England and into Europe to cover the war. Hemingway was less keen than she was to go looking around the world for trouble, and she found his drinking parties at Finca difficult to handle with all their messy rowdiness. Perhaps the difference in their ages was telling—he seemed less able to cope with the exertions of traveling quite so much, preferring to stay home. It seems Gellhorn wasn't too troubled about being away so often though, which may have piqued him a little, too, although her letters to him are always endearing, making it clear how much she misses him. Gellhorn repeatedly reassured him that being apart was nothing—and she chose what she thought would be the irrefutable thing between them. It was their writing that held them together no matter where they were, she told him: "The book is what we have to base our lives on, the book is what lasts after us and makes all this war intelligible. Without the book our work is wasted altogether. And as I love you I love your work and as you are me your work is mine. I could not have you maul that about and mess it up."

• • • •

"*as you are me your work is mine*"—just how close as writers were Gellhorn and Hemingway? How much impact did they have on each other? From the earliest days, Martha Gellhorn's lack of self-confidence as a writer of fiction had plagued her. Even after the success of *The Trouble I've Seen*, she needed the following advice from Hemingway: "He tells me what is wrong with me now is that I've worried too much and gotten the whole thing dark in my mind, and says the thing to do is simply write it and be brave enough to cancel it out if it's no good. We agreed that anyone writing ought to have time to fail and waste effort and not howl about it."

In Spain, Hemingway would work on his submissions, and then look at hers: "she in turn copied out his material and they combined their thinking and sometimes their phrases in magazines under one byline or the other." Certainly two of her books which emerged during and after her time with Hemingway, a collection of short stories called *The Heart of Another* and then *Point of No Return* (published initially as *The Wine of Astonishment*), were considered by critics to have been too heavily influenced by Hemingway, especially the latter, which was published just three years after she left him, in 1947, and which was dedicated to her soldier lover, James Gavin.

Working on that latter novel was particularly difficult for her, as she confided first to Eleanor Roosevelt—"I've been panic-stricken about it several times, and decided to abandon it, because whereas men apparently have no nerves in writing about women (from Madame Bovary to Kitty Foyle), the reverse is rare, and I found myself launched on writing about men as if I were one"—and later to Campbell Beckett—"The novel has been abandoned for this year; I was not up to it." She found it tricky to write about a hero, instead of a heroine, and it is interesting that she chose to make the character who witnesses the horrors of the liberation of Dachau in 1945, as Gellhorn did, a man. Perhaps she needed to distance herself: not only is it a male character, Jacob Levy, who is changed by Dachau, but much of the writing is distanced. Even the opening lines recall Hemingway's *A Farewell to Arms*, with a bucolic description of "black mean-looking pine trees" and the constant rain, and her officers sound like Hemingway's officers, too ("Ah, he said to himself, you may be a hard little bitch but you feel like heaven to me"). Writing about men at war had been done already; this woman who did it, didn't, alas, do it differently, as she had with her journalism. In her fiction, she merely repeated.

Why? When Hemingway was the one who encouraged her along a trajectory of a new kind of journalism, one that she pioneered and made all her own, why couldn't he do the same for her fiction? In 1940, she revealed in a letter that, while she and Hemingway may have collaborated in their journalism, he was "like an animal with his writing; he keeps it all in one drawer, close to him, and hides it under other papers, and never willingly shows it and cannot bear to talk about it." Keeping Gellhorn away from the secrets of his fiction was perhaps Hemingway's way of holding on to power over her—he had already surrendered power, recognizing that her journalism was finer than his. He wasn't about to do that with his fiction: he wasn't about to let her in, steal his secrets.

Gellhorn knew that there was more to writing than simply good ideas and fine words: "I have been thinking about writing until I am dizzy and a little ill. And have decided that what I have is patience, care, honor, detail, endurance, and subject matter. And what I do not have is majic [sic]. But majic is all that counts." She needed to know what the magic spell was, but the magician wasn't letting her in on it. If he had, would their marriage have been fraught with quite so many difficulties, like his rage at her trips abroad, his jealousy at her success? Or would that have been a step too far for him? Would he have felt he'd surrendered everything of himself and now there was nothing left?

Whatever Hemingway's reasons for not letting her in, it's clear that all she can do is mimic him, borrow his language (she begins to use "rare" and "fine" as he does). The heartbreaking thing is how much she rejoices in his work: "But it is very fine indeed, oh my what a book [*For Whom the Bell Tolls*]. It is all alive, all exciting, all true, and with many discoveries about life and living and death and dying: which in the end is all there is to write about. I am proud of it and so is Scrooby." It is also distressing how little joy she can take in her own: "I always envied Ernest when a book came in, because it made him so happy, and when mine came in I just generally felt sick and always disappointed and sort of scared inside and sort of regretting the whole thing." This, too, is perhaps what she meant about "worshipping at his altar" all those eight years she was with him, and perhaps why she hated herself so much after they parted. She didn't get what she was looking for, after all. What did she get?

Loving Ernest Hemingway didn't solve her confidence problem about her writing—in 1943, she was still telling H. G. Wells that "I find confidence very hard to come by." But there are hints that it wasn't quite as cut-and-dried as this. Just three weeks earlier, she told friends she was progressing with her latest book and that Hemingway had told her "it is good. I hope he knows. He has often told me stuff stinks, so I do not believe he is just being a pal." He might hide his writing from her—or, to be more precise, how he produced the writing he did—but he read hers. She worries in this letter that her writing is "flat" and her vocabulary "boring," but in a letter to Hemingway himself a few weeks later, she tells him, in response to his usual charges that she is lazy and should write every day, that "I have been writing every day fiercely all day, never wrote so long or so hard, and I believe it is good." Even more, she tells him that she never thought, when she started out "with the dream of writing," that she could have "ended up here in this perfect safe beauty, finishing my fifth book." None of this sounds like the words of a woman lacking in confidence, or who has learned nothing from her experience of spending seven years with another writer. Never before has she expressed such enthusiasm for her own writing.

It's possible to see that during this period Gellhorn really did come to believe in herself and her own fiction, really did start to think that what she was doing was good. It's from this period that her novel *Liana* emerged, a work of fiction about interracial marriage and the power game that takes place within it, and which could be said to have some input from her own personal emotional experience. This novel can't be called "Hemingwayesque"; it's all Gellhorn.

It's also at this time that Hemingway, fed up with his wife's going off on journalist missions without him, decided to trump her at her own game. After another return home from Europe in the spring of 1944, with Gellhorn reporting once again for *Collier's*, they fought particularly badly, and Hemingway decided suddenly, after all Gellhorn's previous pleadings, that he would join her in Europe to cover the war, after all. He would also write, he said, for *Collier's*. He knew he would be easily able to trump her billing at that title—*For Whom the Bell Tolls* was one of the biggest bestsellers America had ever seen, making him the bigger draw and therefore the bigger name. That wasn't enough to hurt her, though he needed something more.

In some ways, it shouldn't suprise us that Hemingway wanted to do Gellhorn physical harm. Throwing things at her, shooting bullets through windows, and even slapping her show the extent of the physical violence he was capable of, which makes one wonder how Gellhorn coped with these situations. Did she cower in a corner, or run and lock herself in the bathroom? Did she flee the house they shared, or did she stand up to him? The sheer size of Hemingway, coupled with his uncontrollable and drunken rages, would have been a pretty terrifying prospect for any woman in the same room as he was. It's little wonder she felt the need to "escape" him in the end; perhaps it's surprising she didn't leave much, much earlier.

On this particular occasion, though, it seems Hemingway went a step further, and a more disturbing one at that. He didn't actually do her damage by his own hand in this instance, but there was a kind of violence in his intentions all the same. When he was ready to go to Europe, he told Gellhorn that his seaplane from New York to London was for men only. It meant that Gellhorn would have to find her own way across the Atlantic. Remarkably, she did so, but on a Norwegian freighter, which was also carrying dynamite. She was the only passenger on a twenty-day-long voyage. According to her biographer, Caroline Moorehead, there were no lifeboats on this carrier, either. It was only afterwards that she discovered the actress Gertrude Lawrence had been on Hemingway's seaplane—women had been allowed to travel on it after all.

This was a petty, mean, not to say dangerous, action by Hemingway. Had he simply been trying to prevent her from going to Europe by telling her there was no space for her on his seaplane, or was something more sinister going on? It seems unlikely, given what he knew of Gellhorn's gritty character, that he believed she would simply have given up and stayed home. He left her to fend for herself, to take risks that could have killed her, and it's not inconceivable that a part of him wanted her badly hurt. His destructive streak was not limited to himself; he was capable, it seems, of wishing such destruction on others.

This trip marked the real beginning of the end of their relationship. The spark of self-belief Hemingway had lit in her with regard to her own work had been too much for him to take— he had to find a way to stamp it out and Gellhorn was sensitive enough to realize that was what he was trying to do. Her solution was to get away, and get away fast, before he could take back what he had given. At the end of the war, Hemingway had stationed himself in a newly liberated Paris, but Gellhorn was continuing to travel round, to Brussels and Antwerp and Rome, gathering impressions. He was drinking as heavily as ever, his alcoholism pretty much out of control, and fighting her just as hard. Finally, arriving back in Paris that autumn, she agreed to go to dinner with him. She appears to have told him she was thinking about a divorce, as she already knew about his association with Mary Welsh, a married American journalist. This evening, which ended as so many others had, in drunken recriminations and abuse, was the last such evening, however. They parted for good after it.

What, we might ask, had Gellhorn given Hemingway during their time together? Would the prizewinning books *For Whom the Bell Tolls* and *The Old Man and the Sea* have happened if he hadn't met her? In 1936, when he was getting drunk in Sloppy Joe's, he was bored with life and bored with himself, depressed and devoid of inspiration. It took Martha Gellhorn to wake him up, make him want to taste the world again, if only for a short time. Gellhorn's writing talents fired his competitive spirit and got him to see the Second World War in action (although she saw so much more than he did); it was more than many women did for him before or after.

In 1944, Hemingway wrote tellingly to his son Patrick of the end of his relationship with Martha: "Going to get me somebody who wants to stick around with me and let me be the writer of the family." He was wise enough to see that Gellhorn was good enough at what she did to threaten his sense of himself, his own identity as a writer, as the best writer, the biggest writer.

Celebrity romances exist because both parties are good at what they do, and that very thing which has drawn two such people together is often what pulls them apart. The year Hemingway died, Gellhorn wrote to her second husband's son, Paul Matthews, whose marriage had recently floundered: "You wanted it and you got it; and now you are paying and that can and should and must be chalked up to experience. The harder you learn the more you learn." Harsh words perhaps, but the words of one who had survived the hardest of all possible unions. She wanted it, she got it, and she paid for it. Martha Gellhorn always knew the value of something, and in spite of her regrets many years after the event, I think she knew the value of her literary partnership with Ernest Hemingway.

Smart and Barker with one of their four children.

8. THE "CHASER": ELIZABETH SMART AND GEORGE BARKER

I want the one I want. He is the one I picked out from the world.
It was cold deliberation. But the passion was not cold.

—Elizabeth Smart,

May 10, 1941

It was a hot summer's day, and a beautiful, wealthy, young blonde woman from Ottawa stood in a dusty London bookshop, absorbed in a book of recently published poems composed by a man who was one of the England's brightest new literary stars. Three years later, and by now likely pregnant, she sat alone and agitated in New York's Grand Central Station while she waited for that very same man, her married lover-poet. But he did not appear at all that day, in spite of their appointment.

The woman was Elizabeth Smart, author of one the greatest works on love ever written, the prose poem *By Grand Central Station I Sat Down and Wept.* The poet whose work she first read in a Charing Cross Road bookshop was George Barker. Smart's road from bookshop to train station has long been characterized as a chase—with more than a hint that it wasn't the thing for a nice young woman to be doing. It was a chase that took her from Ottawa to London to New York, from innocent girl, so the story goes, to ruined woman. From searching to needy: a slippery slope from confidence down to dependence, abandonment, and, finally, victimhood. This, so the cautionary tale of Elizabeth Smart's fate has told us, is what "the chase" means for women.

After reading Barker's poems that August afternoon in 1937, Smart apparently told friends and acquaintances she was going to marry the author. And so her chase began: she searched for him at parties, befriended writers who knew him, even bought one of his original manuscripts. Then, eventually—supposedly not realizing he was married—she obtained his address and supplied him with the means to leave the teaching post in Japan that was making him miserable and to join her in the States. "He is the one," she wrote in her journal, "I picked out from the world."

Smart continued to chase her married lover-poet all through their forty-year history. She acquired many more original manuscripts and first editions of Barker's poems (most of which, according to their son, Christopher, Barker later stole from under her nose). She spent hours lovingly crafting miniature versions of his poetry books for their four children. She waited "in her best clothes" for him to show up night after night, only to write with anguish in her journal of yet another occasion when he'd failed to keep an appointment he'd arranged with her. She urged him to leave his wife for her, then fled to another country when he wouldn't, only to continue writing to him and pleading with him. Even when all trace of a sexual relationship between them was gone, he would still preoccupy her thoughts, still merit a mention in her journals. Forever being abandoned, and forever struggling to cope with her family of four children, unaided by the man who had fathered them and who couldn't stay in the same house as her for more than a couple of months at a time, she rarely refused him her help, her home, her love.

Why? What was this immense attraction that George Barker held for Elizabeth Smart, in spite of everything? What made a passionate affair, begun in the white heat of a Californian summer in 1940, last four decades? What made her put up with the uncertainty, the lack of commitment, the constant letdowns, the other

women Barker had in his life? Reading the account of their relationship in *By Grand Central Station* is painful enough, but turning to the letters and diary entries, reproduced in two volumes of
journals and two collected works, is a dizzying experience, what
with the lies and counter-lies, the constant bartering for a moment of love, the pleading and the ultimatums, the promises made
and broken. Even Smart had to ask, finally, in desperation, "Was it
ever like that? Did we lie so close like irresistible currents driven
together?" Only a month before this entry, in February 1941,
when they both wrote on the pages of her diary, she appears to
have answered that question for herself: "But if I don't believe in
love, if I don't believe I was made only for you, if I don't believe
you are a poet, if I don't believe poetry is all there is, I don't believe in anything."

Love and poetry is all: perhaps the sentiment and the words
here can be dismissed as the overwrought emotion of a woman
now pregnant by her married lover. He was, after all, a man she
couldn't be sure of, in spite of how often he declared his love for
her, and how often he promised to leave his wife for her, as he
simply kept reneging on those promises. But in her sixties, Smart
gave the world a clue to something else that went far beyond the
love, and even beyond the poetry. She wrote in her journals that
Barker "gave me the courage to break the surface bonds, to dare
the murderous act of stepping resolutely into my own life." It
seems Smart could forgive herself for chasing so relentlessly, having always understood exactly what she was chasing, and why. But
have we forgiven her? Have we understood?

• • • •

Elizabeth Smart had always written, though not everyone knew
that. She was born in Ottawa, Ontario, on December 27, 1913,
to Russel and Louie Smart, a wealthy couple, although her father

had not always had money. He had worked extremely hard to put himself through law school as a young man—apparently even living in a tent to save money on rent at one time—and was a patent lawyer by the time Elizabeth, their second child, was born. Louie herself was from a reasonably well-off family, but she had to work, too, and was employed as a clerk when Russel Smart met her. A first daughter, Helen, had been born in 1909, followed by another girl in 1912, Olive, who died at seven months in April 1913. Louie was already pregnant with Elizabeth when this tragedy occurred. Rather like Jean Rhys's mother, Louie likely would have been encouraged to view this child as a replacement for the one she had lost.

Another girl, Jane, followed in 1915, and the very young Elizabeth seems to have dealt poorly with an additional baby in the family, but by the time she was eight years old, there was a little baby brother to cope with as well, Russel Junior. This relationship she handled better: Smart seems always to have been close to him, in spite of the age difference. But at this stage he was too young for her to play with, and she relied instead on the friends she made at school. Smart made friends easily, as she always would through her life. She never showed off how clever she was, how literary. She preferred to be considered good fun and sociable. But knowing that Louie would approve of her literary abilities, even at this age, Smart did let her mother see what she could do.

Smart attended prestigious Elmwood, a school for the children of the wealthy that had snobbish and antiquated attitudes about Canada's link with Britain and the Empire. It was a school that would have suited her mother: Louie was a socially sensitive, high-strung, intelligent woman, often given to inexplicable and frightening tantrums that didn't exclude physically attacking her three daughters (the eldest, Helen, even had her dress torn from her by her mother when she dared come in late one evening; Smart herself was locked in a closet by her mother for naughtiness when she was very young, and it was only her sisters' screams that alerted Louie to the fact that she'd trapped her daughter's bleeding fingers in the door). Ever mindful of her daughters' reputations, she then sent Smart to Hatfield Hall, another highly respectable, well-connected, British-minded school that offered its female students a full education, but whose social values would not have encouraged a literary career in any of the young women attending its establishment. Smart's earliest supporter for her literary work, then, was undoubtedly, and perhaps surprisingly, her mother—only the family really knew about Smart's juvenilia, the homemade magazines, the pieces of prose and poetry.

After graduating from school, Smart benefited further from the family wealth when her talent for music, specifically the piano, persuaded Louie that her second daughter should continue her music studies in London, under the tutelage of concert pianist Katharine Goodson. This trip marked the beginning of Smart's journal-keeping, an exercise that would prove invaluable to her in later years, as many phrases and thoughts would be tried out first in her journals before being transferred, sometimes word for word, into the prose works *By Grand Central Station* and *The Assumption of the Rogues and Rascals*.

Her journal also showed something else, though—a self-creation in the figure of the "nice girl," the kind of girl her wealthy background and socially conscious mother would expect her to be (Smart herself uses the word "nice" no fewer than nine times in this very first diary entry, on March 6, 1933). Louie didn't want her bright daughters to waste any talents they had, but she didn't want them to have jobs and careers either. A good marriage to a respectable, wealthy man was still the aim in this world that owed more to the values of Jane Austen's nineteenth-century England than twentieth-century Canada. But it was while staying at the Basil Street Hotel that Smart recorded in her journal a day that betrayed in full the kind of ambivalence she was beginning to feel, both toward her mother, and toward her mother's social ambitions for her:

"I woke up so late that there was not much point in making an effort to get up. At last under the instigations of Mummy I did—and exercised in my wide pink pyjamas with little rather prickly blue flowers in them. Washed away the horrible dull dry lotion with Pond's C and Allenbury's Basil soap. Then Mummy was finishing dressing and she insisted that I have some breakfast. She got quite heated about it so to avoid unpleasantness I went downstairs. But I couldn't go into the dining room—it was 10.30 and breakfast is usually over before 10. It was too late—it wasn't fair. Besides they snicker or they hate—or something—anyway that embarrasses me so I wrote a letter to Sue and went upstairs and Mummy called me a 'good little girl' and I did *not* feel guilty."

So much is revealed in this single entry: Smart's guilt, both at the beginning (lying in bed too long) and at the end (where she pretends to her mother that she has had breakfast after all, while in fact she has been writing a letter); her resentment at being punished twice over for sleeping in late, first by her mother's "instigations" which force her to get up, then by the humiliating behavior of the hotel staff ("they snicker or they hate"). The rules of the hotel may be broken in public ("breakfast is usually over before 10") but her mother's may not ("so to avoid unpleasantness I went downstairs"), although this obedience does eventually lead to Smart's lying to her. There is plenty in this entry to show just how much Smart felt the need to hide her real self from her mother, to keep up a veneer of the kind of "nice girl" (a "good little girl") image that her mother admired.

Later in the same journal entry, Smart tells of enjoying "a sherry in the lounge" with her mother, which left her "a little tight" but she "camouflaged it," and of her mother going out to lunch, none the wiser. Smart then takes a bus to the Ritz and walks up Dover Street, feeling unfashionable and unattractive before returning to the hotel to find both her sister Jane and her mother in their rooms. A row then ensues about having dinner ("Jane came and screwed up in a ball on her bed and Mummy screwed up or rather lay in a limp mass on her bed and both declined to have any dinner"). It is up to Smart to put things right between her mother and her sister ("Finally, however, I persuaded Mummy out of her desire to go on strike because everything doesn't turn out perfectly and we two went down to dinner"), and by doing so successfully, she wins her mother's favor and affection ("Mummy turned soft and kind just before and told Jane to put on her kimono and curl up by the fire and she would send her up some supper"). Perhaps not seeing the irony, Smart records that later she sat in a comfortable armchair reading Rose Macaulay's *Keeping Up Appearances* ("a dumb immature book"). Elizabeth Smart was in fact beginning the process of obliterating the "nice girl" her mother valued so highly. But she wasn't quite sure enough of her destruction yet; she had to hide the incriminating evidence from her mother.

Yet her mother's role in the shaping of her daughter's poetic consciousness, as opposed to her social status, was crucial. The autumn that Smart was invalided at home with a suspected leaky heart valve, when she was only eleven, seems to have been when that writerly communication between mother and daughter began, for it was then that Smart wrote a story called "Mosquitos," which she showed to her mother. Louie loved the story and boasted about her daughter's literary talents to all her friends. Five years later, Smart would gather up her various literary bits and pieces in a handmade volume called *The Complete Works of Betty Smart*, a volume that contained no fewer than thirteen prose pieces. Louie saved all of this in a little trunk she marked with Smart's name.

Inevitably, though, it was not always encouragement. In another journal entry, written almost exactly three years later on yet another trip to London with Louie in March 1936, Smart complains that "Today I have hated Mummy and she has hated me" and quotes her mother shouting at her back in the hotel room: "I've hated you all day . . . You've been sneaking. You're the meanest little thing. You haven't done anything with your time. Any child could write the drivel you've written." Louie was aware enough of her daughter's abilities to hurt her by accusing her of having only an ordinary talent. When Smart took a temporary job many years later, in December 1938, with *The Ottawa Journal*, her mother considered this another "ordinary" step, and expressed her strong disapproval once again. Nice girls didn't work for a living, and they certainly didn't write for one. If they had to write at all, they had better be geniuses, and ladylike, Austenish geniuses at that.

By the time of this first real confrontation with her mother, in March 1936, Smart was an anxious, but also an ambitious, extroverted young woman, and she could only respond to Louie's hysterical criticism of her work—as well as the dismissive words of an aristocratic young man she had met, who couldn't see what she had to offer—with the desperate response: "I must marry a poet. It's the only thing. Why don't I know any?" It's certain that her demand burst out of her at this point, when she was twenty-three years old, not simply because of her mother's unkind remarks. Smart had started to realize something important, something that had emerged both from her own long struggles to write as well as from romantic interactions with men. Only a matter of days after she made this extraordinary claim on the world, she recalled her last meeting with her then boyfriend, John Pentland, the aristocratic son of Lord and Lady Aberdeen, whom she'd met in 1935. After numerous encounters between them, he had finally been unable to have sex with her—perhaps, she thought now in her reflections, because she played the "nice girl" so well: "Sex was to him a shame. *That* is a shame, a great shame.

I don't [think of it as a shame], though I pretend I do."

But even more crucially than this, he had rubbished her writing: "And he said that my poems—or whatever other name better fits them—should be written and then destroyed—either destroyed or sent as a letter to a friend—to him!" It was a devastating response from him that drew anger and disappointment from her, as well as a determination to fight: "the farther I get from England . . . the more I resent John and the cringing shape into which he was making me."

• • • •

It's hard to imagine Smart's later lover, George Barker, receiving this kind of criticism and discouragement at the beginning of his writing career. Barker was born in London on February 26, 1913, to an English soldier, also named George, and an Irish Catholic girl, Marion Frances Taaffe. There was little money in the family after George Barker Senior left the army at the end of the First World War, but education still played a large part in his son's life, and George Barker Junior showed a precocious talent for writing at an early age. He left school at fifteen, though, and it wasn't clear what he was going to do with his life. Adored by his older sisters, as well as his mother, who took turns typing up his poems for him and anything else he cared to write, he was used to female approbation, and when he met and fell for one sister's friend, Jessica Woodward, he didn't see why the four-year age difference (she was nineteen to his fifteen) should be any barrier to their being together. But first he had to establish himself.

Barker's way into the literary world came via Katherine Mansfield's widower, John Middleton Murry. Murry, at this time in 1932, was editor of the *Adelphi* review, and Barker sent some extracts from his journal to him. Murry invited him to tea and commissioned a review from him. But it was really writing poetry, not reviews, that Barker was interested in, so Murry introduced him to Michael Roberts, who had compiled a recent anthology of modern poetry. From this meeting, Barker was introduced to David Archer, who owned a radical bookshop in Bloomsbury that attracted all the rebellious young new writers of the day. Archer also published poetry, and would publish Barker's, and later, the first works of Dylan Thomas.

Barker moved out of his parents' home, rented a flat, and lived on the proceeds from reviews and poems he published. In 1933, he published his first novel, *Alanna Autumnal*, after which he was sought out by Edwin Muir, who passed on work by Barker to his friend Walter de la Mare. De la Mare advised sending it to T. S. Eliot at Faber & Faber. Such professional encouragement made Barker feel he had to hide an aspect of his personal life, should these powerful, eminently respectable men disapprove: he and Jessica had just got married because she was pregnant. Their daughter, Clare, was given up for adoption, something for which Jessica later blamed Barker. Perhaps Barker, already making assignations with other women behind his wife's back, wasn't mature enough for the responsibility of bringing up a child. He would never really be ready for that responsibility.

Barker had long self-consciously adopted the stereotypical pose of the bohemian artist, dressing in a way reminiscent of Ezra Pound, favoring dramatic clothing like capes and flared hats. He was also good-looking, charming, and full of bravado, but his taste for drink was probably fired by depressive tendencies that only really emerged in private. In another era, he probably would never have married in the first place, because he soon developed his theory of what society and culture owed to a poet, which meant that he was not bound to honor actions or declarations, support children or mistresses or wives. They were all to support him, as society was to support him, too, simply because he was a poet. He never took another job in his life, and he also deplored those who wrote for money. Poets shouldn't be paid, he felt. They should be treasured, valued. They were special people.

His belief in himself was shored up by the praise showered on him by the literary establishment. More novels, and volumes of poetry, followed over the next few years, as Barker became one of the most celebrated poets of his generation. He would also father fifteen children by four separate women over several decades, many of whom didn't find out about one another until they were almost grown up. Flitting between his different families and different lovers, he indulged himself as he saw fit. It was, he clearly felt, a poet's life and a poet's duty.

• • • •

At the time, then, that Elizabeth Smart's poetry was being castigated by John Pentland, Barker was being lauded by T. S. Eliot, who called him a "genius." No lover ever told Barker that his work would be better sent as a letter, or destroyed. No lover, one suspects, would have dared. He didn't need their advice or their encouragement. He had the faith and endorsement of the greatest poet living in Britain.

But Smart didn't have anything like that kind of endorsement, and she did need advice and encouragement from the right people. Three years earlier, when she was still only nineteen, she had confided in her diary about her writing, "Oh! I *need* something but I don't know what it is." A month after this entry she was worrying again that she was "being influenced and making phrases . . . I am cheating. I am not being myself . . . All this pretending to get at the core." Still despondent about how to get on with it, she notes four letters from Graham Spry, a family friend some ten years older, who nevertheless seems to have been in love with her and who did try to encourage her about her work, giving her writing exercises to boost her confidence: "Oh ain't it nice to know someone has great great faith in you." But he wasn't nearly enough. All through this disturbing year, she would set herself impossible goals of productivity ("I must write three things a week—a week—and no excuses. Stories, article on travel, or opinions, poems and impressions or plays. This must happen. Yes. It can. It will"); and excoriate herself over and over again for her laziness ("Why can't I work? This blur, this apathy, haze . . . I hate this spirit of self-analysis . . . GS gave it to me. He knows it. He doesn't think it's a poison. It is. Oh! Why can't I write the truth and if I do, why isn't it right?"). She felt a desperation that time was passing her by, regardless of how young she was, and that she was achieving little, especially when she compared herself to those writers she really admired like Virginia Woolf and Katherine Mansfield: "Then the desire to accomplish something written swoops down, with an even worse churning, and different yearnings all straining to begin, and remorse at beginning twenty and having done nothing."

"Different yearnings all straining to begin"—to begin what, exactly? Sexual urges were proving to be less of a helpmeet than a hindrance at this point in her life, for all her expressions of "desire to accomplish something written." Smart had met and developed a crush on the portrait painter Meredith Frampton during that very first London trip, and thinking of him, and of Pentland, at home in Ottawa in January 1934, she again tried to write but was waylaid: "This is the fight against the powerful, the irresistible, the compelling monster Sex. So now, though I have just been writing I WILL on sheets of paper, it is not wholehearted, and at the bottom I know it is only an excuse to postpone my work and sit dreaming idly, of sensuous, earthy, vain things." Smart would always have quite a liberated attitude to sex, possibly as a rebellious action against her mother's strictness and uptight behavior and a result of reading Lawrence and Mansfield. But she was romantic about it, too, learning Shakespearean sonnets as a teenager, which she would recite by heart.

Sex was getting in the way, but she could see little that she could do about it. What was worse, she had nothing to write about, she complained later, only herself, and that wasn't good enough. On November 18, 1934, she wrote a short poem, which began, "I'm going to be a poet, I said / But even as I said it I felt the round softness of my breasts / And my mind wandered and wavered." Being a woman, and being aware of her sexual attraction as a woman, as well as her sexual needs, was not helping her to become a poet.

It was only when Smart began to write a work based on her relationship with Pentland, a novella called *My Lover John*, in February 1936, that she started to merge her desire to be a poet with sexual desire in a profitable way, in art ("Where shall it turn now—this desire, this uncontrollable desire which was towards him?"). It was at this point, as she continued to explore her feelings in words carefully crafted for her novella, that she made her epiphany, realizing finally what it was that she was looking for: "I want an ecstasy—not a comfort. If I could love him and be faithful to him all my days, I would be made bigger by this compassionate step and understand all the women in the world." Love that was enlarging, huge in scope, not small and mean, was like poetry. It was what she needed: a big love. Not sex, but something much more all-encompassing than that. Pentland, threatened by Smart's literary ambitions and seemingly alarmed by her sexual energy, didn't have a hope of measuring up. Besides her need to kill the "nice girl" future her mother had in store for her, Smart also understood that, for her, creative desire and sexual desire were bound up together.

But where to find that huge, all-encompassing love that would turn her into a poet? Smart's subsequent decision to accompany a friend of her mother's, Mrs. Alfred Watt, on a trip for the Associated Country Women of the World in 1936 can almost be seen now as a worldwide search for that love, however unlikely the trip might have been to provide her with what she needed. Alas, it didn't help her find love or advance her writing ambitions as she perhaps had hoped, and she was by now beginning to worry quite seriously (as the adolescent Plath was later to do) that the two could never be compatible: "Men, careers, one excludes all others for ever. Where is an occupation that embraces all things? And where a *man*?" Smart was also becoming aware of something else lurking deep in her psyche—her need for children, what she called her "hungry passion" for them. Men, children, poetry—she desired them all that year, as she realized that poetry had to be "something alive and kicking, the essence, the important core." Neither Frampton nor Spry nor Pentland had been able to provide anything like those things, and it was toward the end of her trip that Smart announced: "I seek a mate, not a way of life." Find a mate, and you find the poetry, and the children.

It was a tall order. But one man looked briefly as though he could meet it. In the end, he wasn't to manage it, but perhaps more importantly for Smart, he was to help her sever her very last link with the nice girl of her mother's aspirations, and in the most obvious, time-honored tradition. After she made her final split from Pentland in 1937, Smart spent some of the summer with her family in Canada, before returning to London in August. This was when she picked up George Barker's poems in that Charing Cross Road bookshop, but she made no journal record of the moment. She went back to Canada, then returned to England again in January 1938. At some point between January and May of that year, she met Jean Varda, or "Yanko," as he was known. Varda had been a dancer (Stella Bowen, Ford Madox Ford's long-time mistress, records showing him round London during the First World War) but was now an artist based in Cassis. Smart had met him at a party and was invited to join him with some friends there. "They were all artists and the idea was to work."

From this time on, Smart's journal entries show what a change in her writing style this trip effected in her. The self-dramatizing, mythic, sensuous, metaphoric style of her prose poem, *By Grand Central Station*, can be first detected in these journal entries, words tortured out of her by the confusing, often sexually threatening Yanko, who had quickly made clear his interest in her ("Am I a vamp? Or how many seeds lie on the wet ground? . . . These accusations were by him to me because I refused the body"). He chased Smart relentlessly ("I will NOT be taken like Abyssinia") with a passion she half-feared, half-wanted, and which resulted in the loss of her virginity ("Varda, the first day alone, attacked me in my room. I bit and fought like a wild animal and we scuffled around on the dusty floor").

But her victory was not in succumbing to an almost-rape by this much stronger adversary who "loved women" so much; it was in flouting Louie and destroying, as much as she could, Louie's nice girl, forever. Her mother, unsurprisingly, was horrified by the affair Smart was having with Varda. She had returned to work at *The Ottawa Journal* in December 1938, but by July 1939 had left for New York where Varda joined her. But soon, she was restless again, and ready to head for Mexico to visit some artist friends, Wolfgang and Alice Paalen: "I wrote at last to Mummy and mailed it in the night box. She had phoned and was hysterical. If I were going to marry Yanko she might just as well commit suicide. I would have killed her, etc. . . . I am glad I was out. But way below I am afraid she may catch me and drill her fierce bitter will into my escaping life, and I am troubled by her and for her." The "nice girl" was dead at last, killed by sex and by Smart's burgeoning new identity as an artist. The "chaser" was about to rise out of her ashes; the chaser would be the artist Smart had worked so hard to become.

• • • •

What exactly Elizabeth Smart was chasing, how she came to chase it, and whether she ever got it is a subject that invites speculation about an artist's deepest motives, and those motives are never easy to discern. Smart may have left no journal entry of the moment she picked up Barker's poetry in Better Books that day in August 1937 and began reading, but we do know that, desperate to meet Barker in the flesh, Smart contacted him first through a mutual acquaintance, Lawrence Durrell. Barker seems to have been under the impression that she was much, much richer than she was (an impression that was never quite to leave him, even when she was living in abject poverty in drafty cottages in Ireland or in old, rented farmhouses in England), and was more than happy to write to this enthusiastic fan of his work. That much we do know, but biographers, enthusiasts, and critics can only wonder about other details of that day in the Charing Cross Road bookshop (Which volume of Barker's was it that caught her eye? Which of his poems moved her the most?) and embroider the scene further (Was it indeed hot that day? Was the bookshop dusty? Was she beautifully dressed? Perhaps she wasn't; perhaps it was raining). Perhaps the whole moment is a myth, in the manner of her waiting that long, lonely day in Grand Central Station, of which she once commented, "He [Barker] probably met me the next day . . . one needn't be too accurate about this as it's not . . . history but fiction."

But chasing is essentially desire, and the source of Smart's desire is not so muddied over as might be feared, even if it makes for a story that is not "nice" and invites all sorts of criticism and punishment. The subject matter of *By Grand Central Station I Sat Down and Wept* was all desire. It is a slim volume, barely one hundred pages long, and it charts, in language that seems more appropriate to a long-gone, more dramatic age, one woman's love affair with a married man, from the moment he arrives to meet her in

Monterey. It was the beginning of the relationship between Smart and Barker that was painted in all its pain and anguish, as well as ecstasy, in this poem, along with the lovers' brutal disregard for the betrayed wife and the mistress's shameful chasing of her married lover. It was far from "nice." The jealousy, fear, and self-loathing that sexual desire and creative desire combined to produce were all wrenched out from their hiding place deep in the soul and exposed to the world in Smart's work, which was published five years after the affair had begun. It was reviewed favorably on publication in *The Sunday Times, The Times Literary Supplement,* and by Cyril Connolly in *Horizon,* before it disappeared, a victim of immediate postwar paper rationing. It wouldn't resurface and establish its reputation until many years later when it was published in the United States, and dramatized for BBC Radio, reaching a new audience and a new generation. That it was a difficult work, full of agony, meant it would never be a crowd-pleaser. In the last ten pages of the book, waiting for a man alone in the train station, long after promises had been made and broken, Smart's nameless female narrator is left jealously to imagine her married lover at home with his wife, while she, alone and carrying his child in her womb, "speeds through Grand Central Station," chasing a ghost. Even at the end, there is still the chase.

But when she first met Barker, Smart must have believed that chasing ghosts wasn't something she had to worry about. Her stay with the Paalens at the end of 1939 had awakened other kinds of desire in her: she and Alice Paalen had had a brief lesbian affair and she had attempted to write about it in a novella she titled *Let Us Dig a Grave and Bury Our Mother.* Wolfgang Paalens was involved in a ménage à trois with his wife Alice and another woman. Both women fluttered around him, tending to his artistic, sexual, and domestic needs in a way that Smart couldn't stomach and she lost respect for Paalen, leaving her for Varda, who encouraged her to join him at an artists' commune in Monterey, Big

Sur.

But Smart was soon bored again, and more than ready for her next love: "I know I have been sealed up, silent, unrevealed and inarticulate ... If George Barker should appear now I would eat him up with eagerness. I can feel the flushed glow of minds functioning in divine understanding and communication." Barker had taken a teaching post with the British Council in Japan in 1939 for financial reasons but he found quickly that he'd made a mistake and hated it, and it was to Elizabeth Smart, whom he knew had been buying up his manuscripts and whom he only understood to be a wealthy Canadian fan of his work, that he appealed for help. After this direct appeal from him, Smart immediately wrote letters to everyone she could think of, asking for financial support to help get Barker out of Japan, and eventually Christopher Isherwood put up the money. The cash, however, was for the fares for both Barker and his wife—this was the first time, Smart always maintained, that she found out he was married. It didn't stop her from sending him the money, though. Smart suggested the Barkers join her in Big Sur. Her relationship with Varda wouldn't survive Barker's arrival.

When Barker did finally arrive (albeit with his wife), Smart was disappointed with his appearance, which was very different from what she had imagined. Photographs of him from the time show a man with a sensuous mouth and humorous eyes, but little sign of that bohemianism he professed to live by: he had receding hair and dressed conventionally, like most men in the 1930s, in plain white shirts tucked into loose-fitting trousers. Nevertheless, within a couple of weeks, their affair had begun right under Jessica Barker's nose. Smart would type up Barker's poems while Jessica tended to the domestic side. In *By Grand Central Station*, Smart writes of kisses stolen behind other people's backs; of hands being held in the dark; of Barker "surprise[ing] her bathing" under a waterfall; of the "necessary collaboration" of writing that they pretend is their real reason for spending time together, the typewriter itself "guilty with love and flowery with shame." It's clear that on the commune there were plenty of opportunities for Smart and Barker to sneak off together without Jessica noticing—no doubt this added to the excitement of their new love for each other.

By the early autumn, though, they had left Big Sur, the three of them together, for Los Angeles. At some point either on the journey or before it, it must have been made clear to Jessica Barker what was taking place between her husband and the woman who had helped them get out of Japan. Hurt and bewildered, Jessica was left behind in Los Angeles to find a place for herself, while Barker and Smart set off together, by car, incredibly enough, across the States to New York. Both of them were arrested in Arizona as an unmarried couple attempting to cross the border, though, and this experience formed the fourth part of *By Grand Central Station*, where Smart recounts her personal interrogation by police officers ("What relation is this man to you? . . . How long have you known him? . . . When did intercourse first take place?"). Barker was released before Smart was, and immediately hightailed it back to Jessica in Los Angeles, leaving Smart to sort it out for herself. This was the first warning Smart had that he would always leave her in the lurch. It was a warning she, like most lovers caught up in the first phase of passion, chose to ignore.

Once she was eventually released, though, Barker changed his mind and came back to her, and once again they headed off for New York. Barker stayed there while Smart visited her family in Ottawa, and they commuted between the two cities over the next few months. By now we can see literal evidence of Barker in her work: he was writing in Smart's journals, contributing notes, sometimes caustic, sometimes touching, often instructive about her writing ("I say to you, keep that vision . . . Make a list, write down"). It must have seemed to Smart that her simple request made four years earlier ("I must marry a poet. It's the only thing. Why don't I know any?") had finally been answered; after all, a core image of *By Grand Central Station* is of two people writing together in the same room at the same time, using their literary endeavors as a cover for their illicit love.

But by December 1940, when Barker's promise to leave his wife for her for good had failed to become reality, the chase, which seems to have begun for Smart simply as a way of hooking a poet, had become something else entirely.

• • • •

The chaser as a sexual type may be easy to understand, but the chaser as an artistic one? What kind of implications does that title have for the artist concerned, and for the art she is producing? Chasing an artistic identity, for women anyway, was long considered almost as unseemly as chasing a husband; it could be conducted covertly (the way Jane Austen would hide her writing under embroidery or some more feminine task when she heard someone approach), but not overtly. Very few artistic women struck out on their own at this time—Smart had few role models to choose from, few precedents to follow. And so, as she moved through her early twenties, it's perhaps hardly surprising that she rarely considered herself standing alone as an artist, in spite of her doubts about whether marriage was good for the artist's soul or not. Although she claimed to be a "rebel . . . I am the cat that walks by herself," and decried the "terrible problem of matrimony! I don't want to get married any more . . . How can I possibly marry and sign away my life," she still searched for some kind of cohabitation with a man of like mind, someone in whom she could realize both her artistic and her sexual ambitions.

Chasing an artistic identity as well as a sexual partner maybe partly explains just why Smart went to such extraordinary lengths to meet George Barker after reading his book of poems, and further, why she stuck with him throughout years of abandonment and struggle (one month before he arrived in Monterey, Smart received a book of his latest poems and recorded in her diary, "how ashamed I am to have thought *mine* were poetry, for he alone says *exactly* what I wanted to say . . . my excitement made me too impotent to read. My head ached with too much greed. My eyes were glazed with wanting too much at once"). She was hungry, desperate, ravenous for him; she admitted once that she was "in love with the language of the man" before she even met him.

It shouldn't be underestimated how powerful a literary kinship can be, never mind one that involves sexual or romantic passion as well. Writers meet and talk with one another all the time and often help stimulate and develop each other's work. But very rarely does one writer meet another who understands his or her own literary project, who identifies with his or her work, while also falling passionately in love with that person, in the way that Smart and Barker did. Smart says she was in love with his words before she met him, but in the circularity of passion, it's hard to know which induced love first—the words or the man.

What Smart saw in Barker's poetry was undoubtedly a mirror of her own, only stronger and more experienced—both of them liked to indulge in mythical references, the more the merrier; both poets relied heavily on metaphor and symbolism; both wrote about similar grand subjects, the great human topics of love and death. Smart wouldn't be the first artist to go chasing her reflection, especially a reflection that somehow managed to be more dangerous, to take more risks, than her own self. There are few things more appealing than an apparent reflection of one's self, with all the confirmation of soul mates and other halves that it carries. Love is supposed to be when two divided souls come together; for Smart, this was the secret of the artistic identity, too. She believed that love was borne out of two souls coming together; it's possible to argue that subconsciously, in her chasing after Barker, she believed that art was borne of two souls coming together as well. It was the soldering of the two of them that would make her an artist.

There was a very real split, though, in how men and women generally saw themselves in artistic terms at this point in time— the early twentieth century may show a host of women confident enough to take up the pen and become writers, but as Virginia Woolf pointed out in *A Room of One's Own*, not enough of them had the advantages that men had, and she didn't just mean a room and £500 a year. Confidence and self-belief were key. Smart had enough of both to keep her writing and to imagine a future for herself as a writer, but Barker had more than enough to realize that future, and to keep himself autonomous. Autonomy wasn't what Smart wanted; she resisted Barker's attempts to hold on to it, so what emerged between the two of them, especially in the early days of their passion, was what has characterized love relationships between all men and women since the dawn of time: a struggle for power.

Barker had what Smart wanted but he always gave her just enough to keep her interested, or gave too much, then withheld it when she came back for more. It was a classic power game: a game of chase and be chased. But by chasing George Barker, Smart was also, unknowingly, for many years, chasing more than just him. Up until her middle years, love was the great power for her, as *By Grand Central Station* shows. Over and over again, she writes about the struggle, dominance, surrender, and victory that desire inspires ("On her mangledness I am spreading my amorous sheets," says the unnamed narrator of that prose poem, fully conscious of the bloody battle that is about to ensue among the three characters involved, the man, his wife and his female lover. It was the reason love was so important to her: the power it wielded, the power it had to revivify and to destroy. Smart was never anything but respectful of the power of love.

But it's possible to see that there was something else all along that she was chasing, something that, in the end, might actually have been more important to her. There are no prose poems spelling it out, but the very existence of her remarkable publications (the follow-up to *By Grand Central Station* was another prose poem, *The Assumption of the Rogues and Rascals*, published in 1978, which drew comparisons with the work of James Joyce and Samuel Beckett; in 1984, poems and prose were published in *In the Meantime*, and in 1987, a mixture of journal notes and letters were published in a volume called *Autobiographies*) testifies to what Elizabeth Smart was endlessly chasing and which she achieved only in very compromised ways during her lifetime: the power, not of the lover, but of the artist.

Only when she was thirty years old, the mother of two children already, with two more still to come, could she write: "If he had the faculty of memory, could anything that has happened have happened? And if there are never any memories that can make the paper burn, how can any words of mine expect his heart to melt?" In Smart's plea there is a genuine bewilderment that the power of the artist is not working—that she cannot draw her lover to her side with her poetry, especially given how he has reacted to her words in the past. Yet she realizes there is another power due to her, if she has the strength to record it all: "And yet I must put it all down because of all the other drowning women to whom no one has ever thought it worthwhile to speak, or to whom no one would speak."

In his memoir, her son Christopher would recall his mother hosting parties for literary men, yet never being invited to read out her own work at these parties. Her other son, Sebastian, would record his youthful surprise that his mother had ever written and published poetry at all. By the time both sons were young men, Smart had been a working mother for years. She was not an artist. She did not speak and no one spoke to her; she had become one of those drowning women who worked herself to the bone to keep a roof over the heads of her four children.

But once upon a time, Smart had been an artist, when she'd chased love, chased Barker. Why did she stay with him? For a writer, it's easy to see an answer to that question. Barker had commented on *By Grand Central Station* which Smart eventually completed just two weeks before her first child by him was born in August 1941 (he also gave her the title, protesting that her own original "Images of Mica" wouldn't do. How much she took on board is a matter of dispute). But to read his critique now is to see how irresistible he might have been to a writer as hungry for, and as responsive to, the right kind of criticism as Smart was—and how irresistible he would prove to be to her for a long time to come. Ever the perceptive critic, and a lover who knows exactly what his women want, Barker begins almost dismissively of the text itself, while acknowledging Smart's needs: "I see that one of the principal reasons for which it was written was to convince yourself that you really can write. Thus I accuse it of being too flamboyant with its gifts and glories . . . I mean that this is a minor martyrdom," the last comment being something he repeats later in the same critique: "Here and also there where I spoke before of the minor martyrdom I saw the slip of your soul showing." It would seem at first that this critique was written in December 1940, as Smart responds to the notion of "minor martyrdoms" in her journal that month, while they were spending Christmas apart: "Why does he say minor martyrdoms? Didn't the crucifixion only last three days? . . . How can anything so total not be major?" Yet it's equally possible that "minor martyrdoms" was a favorite trope of his when discussing their relationship too: Smart's journal entry says nothing about his critique, which she surely would have had it been written at this time, so perhaps she is just referring to a conversation between them, not to what he said in his critique. When Barker writes "where I spoke before" may also indicate a previous conversation where the subject of "minor martyrdoms" in relation to what they were both doing in this ménage-a-trois, came up. The fact that Smart used some of his suggestions in his critique before her book was finalised suggests that she received it some time before August 1941, although not necessarily in December 1940.

Barker was warning her then, apparently more than once, not to overplay everything, in life as well as in art. Many of his jottings in her diary are witty ripostes to her pain and suffering. Smart would write, "He did the one sin love won't allow," to which Barker replied, "I did bloody well not." Given how metaphorical both writers were, it's almost impossible to know what this might have been, whether an emotional betrayal of some sort, or an actual, forbidden, sexual act. Although occasionally angry at her representation of events that have taken place, he also acknowledges what she has done with this work—"it is to my knowledge the first true native prose poem in English the thing I've waited ten years to see happen"—and, as ever, praises with one voice while deriding with the other—"indeed I do not know anyone now writing the English language with a more florid fountain of simple sensuality than you, my dear lizzie . . ."

Barker's comments, which show a sensitive, close reading and understanding of what Smart has written, are important not just because she was in love with him, but also because of his own standing as a poet, of which he reminds her: "Eliot wrote me about my Johannesburg Masque . . . that it was simply bogged in metaphor . . . And now I say that Grand Central Station is written not with the word, the phrase, the sentence, the cadence, the paragraph or the mood as unit but with the metaphor as unit" and that "this is wonderful so long as it remains clear which is which."

Not only is he taking her work seriously, but he's comparing it to his own—this, for Smart, would have been a huge compliment. Remarkably, given his behavior toward her over the years, she never really lost respect for his writing and his critical abilities.

He's not above getting personal, either. He declares that Smart is "the only poet born on the American continent since Whitman" and acknowledges that now he has some literary competition and he's not absolutely sure he likes it: "Im [sic] not in love with you because of this at all at all: I am in love with you in spite of this and would sooner sit listening and watching you play Scarlatti than have the certitude that Emily Bronte and Heloise and George Eliot and Virginia Woolf will bear the pall at your funeral. For I love you."

Barker follows this extraordinarily powerful declaration with more detailed criticism ("The syntax is crazy. What has absolutely no dam? The explosive facts? Why explosive?") and recommends brisk cutting and chopping to get it all into shape. But most importantly, he tells her that he makes such criticism in order to make her work the best it can be: "I WANT THE MOST BEAUTIFUL PROSE POEM FROM YOU NOT A SERIES OF FANDANGOES OF THE VOCABULARY BECAUSE I KNOW YOU CAN DO THAT." Then he sums up her task in words that could only have excited her: "This is merely a matter of running your hand over the body of the book and ascertaining whether or not its got feet legs genitals (my god has it got genitals!) breast head etc."

Perhaps only a writer can appreciate just how hugely affecting and enticing this statement of support for Smart was, what a seal it put on her feelings for him, how it would ensure that no one would ever match up to him. For Barker was able to understand Smart's mind, her work, her sexuality, and her desires perfectly. Possibly because his own writing was not dissimilar, as she and he had both by now recognized, and possibly because he, too, was inclined to "leap into the infinite." Smart would comment many years later, in late middle age, when she came across Barker's critique, that she had found "a tender criticism of *By Grand Central Station* by him, which I had forgotten." That remark makes one think not that she didn't value his judgment because she'd "forgotten" it, but that it was so much of a piece of their everyday talk together. For a writer, unsure of herself and longing for the kind of intellectual stimulation that would enhance her own gifts, such a regular interaction would be worth gold. In this light, Barker's appeal gets easier and easier to understand.

Both Barker and Smart responded to their needs and desires in similar ways, in that they went after what they wanted. They also both hid things if they feared disapproval—Barker would tell Jessica that he wanted to be with her, just after telling Smart he wanted to be with her instead (Smart caught him out on one occasion, by reading a letter intended for Jessica, where he told his wife, "My mind is quite made up. I want to go on living just as I have always lived—with you. It's all you, and forever"), but Smart would also lie to her parents about her first pregnancy. It's honesty between lovers that she prizes, she tells him.

Before the birth of her first child, Barker had accompanied Smart to Vancouver, where she had decided she would like to give birth and where they stayed in a series of cheap hotels (she was worried about getting the baby back into the country if she gave birth outside it). He had broken yet again with Jessica, with whom he still carried on a relationship, but he wrote to his friend John Fitch, asking him to visit and, inexplicably, to bring Jessica with him. Fitch arrived without Jessica, but his appearance was still a surprise to Smart. When the two men left one day—to get groceries, according to Smart; to drive all the way to Big Sur, according to Fitch, with Smart's permission—the pair simply never came back. Smart waited in a state of disbelief for her lover to reappear: "It is not possible he will not return . . . For to say he will not and never come is to throw myself into the whirlpool and to deliver my mind into madness."

For most women, this would have been the last straw. Barker had a homosexual fling with Fitch on this trip, which Smart was savvy enough to guess at ("I know that perhaps tonight his mouth like the center of a rose closes over John's burning mouth with apologies of love like a baby at the breast"). But still, none of it was enough to make her abandon hopes of him returning to her. Why not?

She decided on Pender Harbour at random, a quiet place where she could give birth to her daughter, and where she could mourn the loss of Barker alone: "I am only waiting and waiting for my life to begin, which it never can until he comes back." Barker had gotten in touch when his daughter was born, but Smart wouldn't answer his letters; by November, he was back living with Jessica in Nyack. Smart left Georgina behind with a friend she had made in Pender Harbour and went to meet Barker in December—incredibly, she stayed for two days with him and Jessica in their cottage in Nyack, a "horrible two days," she records in *Autobiographies*. One can only wonder at what was said during this time, what recriminations were made. She also records in the same journal that "George phoned often and said Will you marry me but that didn't help"—presumably because he was still very much married.

In February, Smart wrote to Barker, "I'm not running away from you because God knows that would be an impossibility since you are what makes my blood continue to flow," but in April, Jessica wrote to her to say that Barker had been living with her "happily and very passionately" and that he had finished with Smart for good. Strangely enough, this was just before she left him. He had met Anaïs Nin by this time, was writing some erotic fiction for her, and having sex with her. By May, Smart was sure that the relationship between her and Barker was over for good:

"No, I will not allow him to wreck my life or turn bitter and broken because, after all, he was only certain of loving me for perhaps three days or weeks." But she was wrong—in November, she met up with him again in Vancouver, where she had told him she was going to live permanently, and conceived her second child there. Jessica, desperate for children, demanded a child from him as well, and she conceived twins by Barker in December.

In February 1942, Smart left for England, hoping to get away from Barker once and for all. She had Georgina back with her, and they sailed together. She settled in the Cotswolds with a female friend, Didy Asquith: in June, Barker turned up, and in July, Smart's second child, Christopher, was born. Once again, though, Barker was not present at the birth. In August, Jessica gave birth to his twins, a boy and a girl (the girl named Clare, after the first child they gave up for adoption).

Smart didn't know it at the time, but her move to England set a pattern for her relationship with Barker forever after: Barker turned up at the Cotswold cottage then disappeared; he then came back weeks later, and they moved to London, as a family, where they lived for six months. Wartime bombing frightened Smart and sent her back to the country, where she moved to Condicote in Gloucestershire. Barker divided his time between there and London; Smart was financially dependent on the allowance she still got from her parents. Her third child was conceived, but Barker's relationship with Jessica still wasn't completely over and wouldn't be until 1944, frustrating Smart as much as ever ("he can get me but I can't get him. Do I want to record these days? These purgatorial days which I forget even before they are gone? George, you must do something. I CAN'T stay alone in this house for so many hours. I AM GOING MAD. Where are you? It is nearly 9. You said you would be here at 5. You said you loved me. You said you'd rather be at home than out and about"). Smart would bear Barker two more children, Sebastian, in April

1945, and Rose, in February 1946.

Soul mate and reflection Barker may well have been, but he could never give her, or any other woman, enough. Over the four decades of their relationship, Barker treated Smart as a mistress, a bit on the side, not a partner. He seems to have found her sexually irresistible, as his first wife, Jessica, complained, and it's likely that sex between them was good, especially in the beginning, given her descriptions of sexual ecstasy in her prose works.

But as time went on, and the babies appeared, Barker's sexual interest in Smart seems to have waned. By 1945, Smart was effectively a single mother. She had decided to move back to London after the war ended and found a flat to rent in Chelsea. Smart's biographer notes that Barker "was more or less absent" during this time, apparently still divided between his wife and his lover. Unable to afford London, Smart then moved first to Ballyrogan House in County Wicklow in Ireland, then to a cottage in Galway. There was precious little money in those days while she took care of three children—Sullivan talks of her having to walk miles for water, and picking nettles to make soup. She gave birth to her fourth child here—Barker had appeared but disappeared again and wouldn't see the new baby for over six months.

Smart then moved to Tilty Mill in Essex, a happier time and a location that allowed her to go up to London to work for magazines and newspapers. In 1949, she got a job with *House and Garden* where she stayed for two years and which gave her enough money to afford to send her children to boarding school. She sublet a flat in London and moved her children there. Barker contributed not a single penny to the family's upkeep. Instead, he turned up from time to time, just as a married man would with a mistress, never warning her in advance, expecting her full attention, wanting comfort, and drinking everything she had in the house. Whether flats in London or in one of the dilapidated houses in the country she would rent for her family, she would consistently invite Barker to join her, but he would only turn up for short periods of time.

Smart's biographer, Rosemary Sullivan, believes that Barker was threatened by her love for him, which he interpreted as possessiveness. "He wanted the women in his life to be there as adjuncts," Sullivan writes, "not as the central theme." Smart was another adjunct; she wanted to be the central theme. In spite of a later love affair with Michael Wickham, an artist, she remained wedded to the idea that Barker was the man for her—until 1957, anyway, when their relationship began to deteriorate. Barker had been abandoned for the first time by a woman: his much younger girlfriend known as "Cass" had gone off with another man. On December 15, Smart recorded that she had bitten Barker's lip, badly enough for him to have to have it sewn up at hospital. She herself was sporting a black eye. It was typical for their rows, fueled by drunkenness on both sides, and by real frustration on hers, to end with blows. But this row ended things, or at least it seems to have marked the end of any sexual relationship between them. Finally, Smart seems to have accepted he would never come and live with her or be a father to their children. For his part, Barker seems to have thought that committing himself to any woman would rob him of his identity as an artist, not confirm it ("Take me," wrote Smart in a notebook she and Barker shared in 1941. "I'll take you—for a ride," Barker warned her.)

• • • •

In April 1945, Smart had written that it was "unbearable loving George," that "he won't let me leave him, yet he won't stay with me." From a grand passion, a terrible love that had produced a great work of art, Smart was reduced to the regular complaints of a married man's mistress: "I love him desperately, but he continually ruins my hopes that we are going to lead a happy married life together. I *always* believe that this time it will really happen and there is never anything but the same disappointments and frustrations. He never comes when he says he will. He always stays away two or three times as long as he says he will. He always vanishes and lets me sit waiting for him in my best clothes, relishing the hour to come."

What had happened to the great love? What had happened to her art? Both had gotten bogged down by this time in the mundane details of daily life—mundane details that one always senses Barker was fleeing from, as much as he fled from Smart herself—amongst those normal tasks of looking after small children and trying to make a living at the same time. It's hardly surprising that Smart's journals from this time on are sparse and more trivial, preferring to note children's birthdays rather than work out grand allusions. Two whole decades produced precisely fourteen pages of journal entries, a pitiful amount, as she herself acknowledged sadly in her journal on February 13, 1976: "Love. Children. Earning a living. Friends. Drinking. Pushed too far, to do too much. Silent years . . ." None of it left space for writing, and it wasn't until this decade that she actually got back the time and the space for art once again. Chasing that moment that she had experienced with Barker in California back in 1940, chasing that moment of love and power and art, she had had it once, and briefly. And it wasn't until her children had grown up and Smart had some money (yes, Woolf was right about the room and the £500 a year, after all) that she figured out what she should, and could, be chasing now.

The power of the artist lies in the ability to speak. Smart had been silenced during the decades of bringing up her children: love had given her a voice, but it had also given her babies, and babies have to be looked after. Now the love was gone and the babies had grown up; Barker had met Elspeth Langlands in 1963, an Oxford graduate, while he was still with Dede Farrelly, who gave birth to their third son, Francis, that year. By the following year, his relationship with Farrelly was over and Langlands was pregnant with the first of her five children by him. Smart didn't record her feelings about any of this, but biographers have insisted that while she accepted the relationship with Farrelly, Barker's taking up with Langlands initially distressed her. The two women would, however, become friends.

"Love," Smart wrote in 1977, "[i.e. George) was worked out alone, resolved to the last painful echo dying away, a metamorphosis into an impersonal unpowering love. I never cry out in my sleep for *him*. Sometimes (when memory reruns) there's a regret, a piercing poignancy for what might have been. But no. That is done. With those ingredients, that was all that could have been made (I did my best when I was let). Will my daughters ever forgive *me*?"

Smart was beginning to speak again by this time ("*Speak, memory*," as she wrote in her journal, trying to inspire herself). As always, in this entry, she shows that she recognizes the connection between love and power, and that by now, her feelings for Barker are an "impersonal unpowering love." I don't believe she was being disingenuous when she wrote this: everyone has a breaking point, and Smart's had come, eventually. What's important is that once she started speaking, she found she couldn't stop: *By Grand Central Station* was republished in the UK in 1966, with a new hardback edition in Canada in 1977, and *The Assumption of the Rogues and Rascals* came out the following year. Suddenly, Smart was being invited to give readings—people wanted to hear her speak.

At a writer's conference in 1980, she actually shared a public platform with Barker where both read from their work, something he appeared to find difficult to handle. She had "begun to eclipse Barker as a public literary figure," according to Sullivan, and at one literary conference in Glasgow, he dismissed the idea that he was the man she wrote about in *By Grand Central Station* as "carfuffle, what you could read in any woman's magazine." His public dismissal of her work showed a man clearly perturbed by the possibility of her reputation exceeding his: that wasn't supposed to happen. Smart also returned to Canada, invited by a new generation of fans of her work. The chase, for Smart, had ended with a long-sought and rarely bestowed prize: literary recognition. She had been right about Barker all along—he had given her the courage "to break the surface bonds." He had helped her to do what she had to do, eventually— to step out into her own life.

It would be inaccurate to say that Elizabeth Smart would not have produced the great works she did had she not met George Barker. By the time she met him, a large part of *By Grand Central Station* had already been written. But the emotional and sexual intensity, the poetic mirroring, the sheer drive of their relationship galvanized something extraordinary in her and urged her on to greater things, in a way that few things in this world can ever do. It was a remarkable relationship in many other ways, too, partly for lasting as long as it did, when all the evidence points to it having been better suited to the white-hot blast of passion recorded in *By Grand Central Station*, and not a forty-year dalliance crowded by children and other lovers. Having chased love and gotten love, however briefly, Smart was understandably reluctant to let go and relinquish the momentousness of it; but out of that momentousness, many years down the line, she found what it was she'd really been chasing all that time. For many, it was chasing that had made her an abandoned woman with four children to feed; it was chasing that had forced her to work for many years on magazines that undervalued her talent; and it was chasing that had left her often lonely in her later years, for all the family she had around her. It was chasing that, for those interested in her story afterwards, gave her the hue of ruin and victimhood.

But it was chasing that made Elizabeth Smart a lover and a mother. And it was chasing that made her an artist. Those were the things that mattered to her most. And, however compromised and however temporary some of those things may have turned out to be, she is one of the few to be able to say that, at one time or another, she achieved them all.

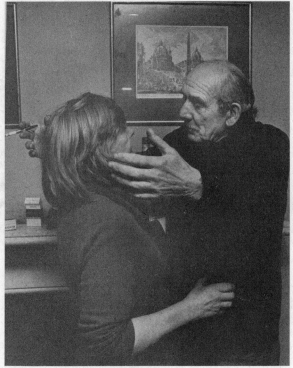

Elizabeth Smart and George Barker.

Ted Hughes and Sylvia Plath.

9. THE "WIFE": SYLVIA PLATH AND TED HUGHES

After a while I suppose I'll get used to the idea of marriage and children. If only it doesn't swallow up my desires to express myself in a smug, sensuous haze. Sure, marriage is self expression, but if only my art, my writing, isn't just a mere sublimation of my sexual desires which will run dry once I get married. If only I can find him . . .

—Sylvia Plath, 1950

Shut eyes to dirty hair, ragged nails. He is a genius. I his wife.

—Sylvia Plath, 1958

Of all the literary couples in this book, Sylvia Plath and Ted Hughes have generated the most fascination and commentary on both sides of the Atlantic about the real nature of their relationship. Never before has the ending of a literary and sexual partnership caused so much to be written about it. Literary critics find it impossible to restrict themselves solely to the work when they mean to write about Plath's poetry, speculating instead on her suicide at the age of only thirty, which took place while she was separated from Hughes. Biographers are drawn into family squabbles and separate factions when they require permission to quote from the Plath estate in their books, finding themselves part of the story, not simply the tellers of it.

What more can there be to say about this relationship? Indeed, who would want to try to say anything more? How can it help to add more speculation to a story that is already so overloaded with the thoughts and opinions of those who knew the couple directly or indirectly, or those who didn't know them at all, never mind those who have their own political, poetic, or personal agendas to pursue? And yet, with the publication of every "primary source," several secondary sources inevitably spring up, as they must do. After Ted Hughes's death in 1998, and the publication of his final volume of poems, *Birthday Letters*, which were mostly about Plath, Emma Tennant's controversial memoir of the affair she had with Hughes in the 1970s, *Burnt Diaries*, was published in 1999, and in 2001 a sympathetic biography of Hughes by the poet Elaine Feinstein, an attendee at his funeral, appeared. Ranged in the other corner were Paul Alexander's 1991 biography of Plath, *Rough Magic*, which was republished with a new introduction in 2003, and Ronald Hayman's *The Death and Life of Sylvia Plath*, also in 2003. Then, a "restored edition" of Plath's *Ariel* was published in 2004, coinciding with Diane Middlebrook's biography of the Plath-Hughes marriage, *Her Husband*. This latest biography was greatly dependent on a reading of the *Birthday Letters* poems for its interpretation of their relationship. Most recently, in 2007, a volume of selected letters by Ted Hughes was published. And this is not to mention the numerous critical studies of both poets' work

Perhaps more sadly, when a tragic family death occurs, newspapers are filled with commentary and exposition from those who knew the parties concerned, or those who have studied the work of those related family members, as happened in the spring of 2009 with the suicide of Plath and Hughes's son, Nicholas. The Plath-Hughes relationship has become an industry in itself, in a way that no other relationship in this volume has. It is also the most divisive relationship in this book: when one writes about it, one has little choice but to come down on one side or another. As Jacqueline Rose has argued, "the pull of the Plath story is that it calls up a language of victimisation and blame with such force. Pathology . . . makes her guilty—her tragedy the inevitable outcome of the troubles of her mind. Patriarchy means that man, meaning Hughes or the male sex he stands for, is to blame . . ."

Which is why it must be included here: to ignore this relationship and all that followed in the wake of its demise would be to ignore one of the most remarkable literary partnerships of the twentieth century. It is also equally open to the suggestion, as the previous partnerships have been, that it was a relationship that benefited both partners, but particularly the woman involved; indeed, moreover, that she actively sought it out, not from some self-destructive impulse, but to benefit her art.

Plath and Hughes, whose relationship began in the latter half of the twentieth century, are closer to us today than any of the other couples mentioned here in their experiences of the world around them, with greater freedom enjoyed by women (even though this was pre-second-wave feminism, Plath did at least have the vote when she began writing, unlike Rebecca West) and new technology waiting in the wings. There is a sense of working toward a new kind of literary celebrity, too, with prizes to be won and internationally broadcast programs to be recorded; of a literary establishment within easier reach than before, and with a wider base, which is also more recognizable to us now than, say, the literary milieu of H.D. and Ezra Pound. However, the sense of a male-dominated literary establishment is still very strong when we come to the Plath-Hughes story: Plath had a few female friends at Smith, but once she met Hughes, the women she befriended tended to be partners of those literary men Hughes knew.

The Plath-Hughes relationship exemplifies both the rewards of the Faustian pact that so many of the literary women in this volume made with their male partners as well as the dangers. Very much like Elizabeth Smart before her, Plath was a young woman looking for a particular kind of man; as in Smart's case, finding him was almost as important to her as the literary fame she sought. The two goals were completely intertwined for both women. The crucial difference between them is that when Smart found the man she wanted, she survived the price she had to pay for him. She managed, somehow, to find a way to deal with the personal trouble and anguish that came with the literary help, the vitally important encouragement and support. Plath, unfortunately, did not.

• • • •

Born to Aurelia and Otto Plath on October 27, 1932, in Boston, Massachusetts, the young Sylvia Plath showed an early interest in stories and storytelling. Her mother was a bright woman who taught English and met her future husband when she signed up for an Arts degree at Boston University—Otto Plath taught the course. After a courtship of two years, they were married; Aurelia Plath notes rather tersely in *Letters Home*, the volume of letters Sylvia Plath sent her mother over a period of thirteen years from 1950 to 1963, "Then I yielded to my husband's wish that I become a full-time homemaker." It seems very clear from this volume that Aurelia Plath regretted giving up her career, and that her subsequent interest in her daughter's literary abilities, as well as her promotion of a good marriage, was a way of compensating for her own disappointments on two counts: her lack of a career and her short, unsatisfactory marriage.

For by the time Sylvia Plath was eight, her father, who had ignored signs of illness, was diagnosed with lung cancer. He developed an advanced state of diabetes, which brought on gangrene in one leg: he did not survive long after the operation to remove the infected limb. Plath made her mother promise never to marry again, something she later mocked herself for in her analysis with Ruth Beuscher. Aurelia Plath then moved her young family to Wellesley, where she could be closer to her relatives.

Perhaps because of her father's absence, Sylvia Plath and her mother became very close as Aurelia encouraged her daughter both in reading and writing, buying her a diary, sharing poetry. She notes, too, that in her early teens, her precociously talented daughter "was soon to become wary of dating boys who 'wanted to write,'" aware too quickly that boys didn't appear to like clever or bookish girls. And yet, much later, it was the writerly boys to whom Plath would be drawn. Plath fulfilled her mother's ambitions for her in print, although *Letters Home*, which first appeared in 1976, was published not just to show her affection for her daughter, but to counteract other publications, specifically Plath's novel, *The Bell Jar*. Aurelia Plath had been horrified by the British publication of the novel, which came out just before her daughter's death in 1963, as it painted her in less than flattering terms, and in 1971, when *The Bell Jar* was published in the United States, it was done against Aurelia's objections. In 1975, she asked for permission from Ted Hughes, Plath's literary executor, to publish the letters Plath had written to her up until her death in 1963: "the idea was to show that Plath was not the hateful, hating ingrate, the changeling of *Ariel* and *The Bell Jar*, but a loving, obedient daughter."

It is from July 1950, just before she left for Smith College in Northampton, that Plath's journals exist in published form; her first letter to her mother in *Letters Home* is dated September 27, 1950. Plath was almost eighteen when she began writing to her mother from Smith. Most teenage girls would feel a need to keep things from their mothers; the need for privacy marks the end of childhood and the beginning of adulthood. But Plath wrote gushingly to Aurelia: "Dear Mummy . . . so far, I've gotten along

with everyone in the house. I still can't believe I'm a SMITH
GIRL! . . . The whole house is just the friendliest conglomeration
imaginable . . ."

As many readers of Plath's work have pointed out, she had
many different voices for the letters to her mother, for her journals, and for her poetry. If her mother could have read her gloomy
journal entry, she would hardly have recognized the same girl
who had written to her in such gushing prose: "Now I know
what loneliness is, I think . . . I am alone in my room, between
two worlds. Downstairs are the few girls who have come in—no
freshman, no one I really know. I could go down with letter paper
as an excuse for my presence, but I won't yet . . . not yet. I won't
try to escape myself by losing myself in artificial chatter . . . I'll
stay here and try and pin that loneliness down . . . I can't deceive
myself out of the bare stark realization that no matter how enthusiastic you are, no matter how sure that character is fate, nothing
is real, past or future, when you are alone in your room with the
clock ticking loudly into the false cheerful brilliance of the electric light. And if you have no past or future, which, after all, is all
the present is made of, why then you may as well dispose of the
empty shell of present and commit suicide."

Even allowing for the literal possibility that Plath then went
"down with letter paper" and wrote the more cheery version of
the same evening to her mother once she felt a bit better, it is hard
to reconcile these two versions of the same evening, and such po-
larity in representation suggests someone clearly having trouble
engaging with her environment, as well as a slightly disturbing
ability almost to separate into colliding, clashing selves, an ability that would show itself in much of the *Ariel* poems that Plath
wrote before she committed suicide.

This was no isolated moment either—by January, her misery
had both deepened inside her and turned outward to hatred and
envy of her fellow students, even though she had arrived at Smith

with the backing and financial support of a scholarship offered by the writer, Olive Higgins Prouty, author of bestsellers like *Stella Dallas* and *Now, Voyager*. Plath had already published a short story in *Seventeen* magazine, "And Summer Will Not Come Again," the year before, as well as poetry in *Christian Science Monitor*. There was little real reason for her to feel envious or anxious.

Needless to say, Aurelia Plath was shown nothing of this. Plath's later repudiation of her mother during her sessions with Ruth Beuscher only emphasizes the strategies she employed when she felt she could not live up to her mother's ideal for her as a bright, high-achieving, popular, respectable, bourgeois young lady. Just as Elizabeth Smart would repudiate the "nice girl" her mother valued so highly, Plath would in later years similarly rebel against that standard set for her by her own mother, writing in her journal about Hughes at the end of 1958, for instance, that "I knew what I wanted when I saw it." She implies here that she made a life-choice her mother would not only have disapproved of, but had actually been steering her away from: "I did what I felt the one thing and married the man I felt the only man I could love, and want to see do what he wanted in this world, and want to cook for and bear children for and write with. I did just what mother told me not to do: I didn't compromise. And I was, to all appearances, happy with him, mother thought."

Plath blames her mother here for encouraging her to compromise when she was younger for the sake of a "nice," respectable, bourgeois life, and certainly in her letters from Smith she kept Aurelia up-to-date on the young men she was seeing, as if to reassure her that she was doing the right thing, dating the right boys, making the right progress toward that much desired end point, marriage. But she wasn't just presenting a face to her mother: her feelings were much more complex than that. Being a writer could be dangerously unfeminine for a woman, she felt: shortly after meeting Hughes, she would write in her journal:

"Not to be bitter, save me from that, that final wry sour lemon acid in the veins of single clever lonely women." How terrified she was of anything that would "unfeminize" her! And the single woman writer's life, devoid of sex or physical intimacy, represented just such a lack of femininity.

Yet it was her mother who encouraged those unfeminine artistic ambitions in her daughter in the first place. Aurelia Plath recalls in *Letters Home* how she would invent bedtime stories to read to Plath and her brother, Warren, encouraging Plath to make up rhymes, giving her diaries for Christmas: "Sylvia was writing rhymes constantly and making sketches to accompany them, which she hid under my napkin to surprise me when I came home from teaching." Even at this time (from 1944 to 1945, when Plath would have been a mere twelve-years-old), she was thinking of becoming a writer, according to her mother. Aurelia Plath is keen to stress the part she played in her daughter's growing artistic consciousness, without seeming to see how smothering a great deal of it may look to the outside world: "we were critical of our verbal and written expression, for we shared a love of words"; "Between Sylvia and me there existed . . . a sort of psychic osmosis"; "Sylvia and I were more at ease in *writing* words of appreciation, admiration and love than in expressing these emotions verbally."

The letters her daughter wrote home in her first year at Smith confirm the importance of her mother's opinion to Plath in all her literary efforts. She sends her mother "a snatch of verse"; diligently repeats any praise or acknowledgment of her writerly abilities from her fellow students; keeps her informed of any stories or poems that she sends out to magazines and competitions; asks directly for a critique of some work ("What do you think of the following merely descriptive lines: The acid gossip of the caustic wind, The wry pucker of the lemon-colored moon, And the sour blinking of the jaundiced stars . . . Or have I degenerated horribly in my verbal expression?"). In amongst girlish gossip about boys and student life are constant references to writing, extracts from poems she was composing, and even encouragement of her mother's own efforts, as though she were the mother and not the daughter ("Do write for Dr. Christian . . . Every year you will, until you win. You have the background and technical terms. Go to it!"). It was Aurelia who forwarded the telegram from *Mademoiselle* magazine telling Plath she had won their $500 prize for her short story "Sunday at the Mintons" in June 1952 (it wasn't the first prize Plath had won, although it was the biggest; in 1950, she won third prize in a short story competition in *Seventeen* magazine for "Den of Lions"; and more stories would appear in *Christian Science Monitor* in 1951). It was in Aurelia that her daughter confided her ideas for new stories ("I've got an idea for a third story for *Seventeen* called, of all appropriate things, 'Side Hall Girl' . . .").

By contrast, in one of the few references to her mother during the same period in her journals, in June 1951, Plath worries to herself, in the second person, that "with your father dead, you leaned abnormally to the 'Humanities' personality of your mother. And you were frightened when you heard yourself stop talking and felt the echo of her voice, as if she had spoken in you, as if you weren't quite you, but were growing and continuing in her wake, and as if her expressions were growing and emanating from your face . . ." Without the evidence of *Letters Home*, one could be forgiven for thinking that Plath barely communicated with her mother or liked her, so negligible and negative is her presence in the journal entries.

But it was Aurelia who unintentionally encouraged dangerous contradictory impulses in Plath: to want to be a writer, but also want, very much, to be a wife. Perhaps unsurprisingly, then, Plath subsequently had hugely conflicting attitudes towards her mother as well. Plath worried repeatedly about how to combine these two ideals of poet and wife that she had inherited from her mother. She realized it could only be done if she found the right kind of man, one who wouldn't take away her artistic impulses and smother them in "bed and babies." Plath also needed a partner, needed not to be alone, as she said over and over again ("I need someone to pour myself into"; "I must have a passionate physical relationship with someone"; "I need a strong mate"; "I am in danger of wanting my personal absolute to be a demi-god of a man"; "Sex is never enough for you, you want a brilliant mind"). So she had to have a union with a man of like mind, another poet. These often competing aims of marriage and literary fame could be highly dangerous. Bequeathed to her by her mother, they would eventually be the death of her.

• • • •

To us now, Sylvia Plath seems to have been trapped in some kind of rigid 1950s American Mom-and-apple-pie type of domestic dream at this time in her life. Why was it so important to her to be a good wife as much as a great poet? Her attitudes to marriage were complex from the start. The quotation at the beginning of this chapter indicates certain serious reservations she had about marriage, even about marrying a writer ("I have decided I cannot marry a writer or artist—after Gordon, I see how dangerous the conflict of egos would be," she wrote in February, 1953). In other places in her journal she bemoans the possibility that she will never be married, will never find the right man. There is no hint that she ever wanted to be single: she doesn't see that as a viable alternative. But she doesn't want marriage to damage her art. Her problems were perhaps closer to the kind of problems women, in a post-feminist culture, tend to write about now: how to have both a marriage and a career. But Plath didn't know what kind of marriage she wanted: she couldn't envisage a bohemian, open marriage, nor would a conventional one suit her. Growing up in conservative 1950s Wellesley, Massachusetts, she knew that only "nice girls" could become wives, the kind of girls who "demurred at a certain point" even while they "know they're dressed to seduce." Like Elizabeth Smart, Plath was too clever not to see the mix of innocence and knowingness that underpinned the social hypocrisy demanded of young women at this time for exactly what it was. But she fell for some of it nonetheless.

That she would feel that she had failed miserably at her aims is not surprising given how confused they were. Plath displayed much later what many consider her true nature, her "not niceness," in her final poems, for all the world to see, just as her marriage to Ted Hughes was disintegrating in front of her, and this display is partly what has made her such a heroine to female poets of succeeding generations, as well as to feminist critics and scholars. For up until that point, there is something truly puzzling about a brilliantly gifted young literary woman who can confess, as Plath did in her letters to her mother as well as in her journals, that what she really wants is "to be anchored to life by laundry and lilacs, daily bread and fried eggs, and a man, the dark-eyed stranger who eats my food and my body and my love ... who will give me a child." Why lust after domesticity and convention when you want literary immortality? How can you write poems when your children are crying for you? How can you think clearly and deeply when your husband is demanding his fried eggs for breakfast? It was a dilemma that was constantly changing shape and focus for Plath, and she never quite resolved it until these final poems, when anger at Hughes's abandonment of her for another woman could erupt in a repudiation of the domestic. Now she is aiming high, not scrubbing about, picking up other people's mess from the kitchen floor. After all, what is the point in being the perfect wife if your perfect husband leaves you anyway?

And Plath did think Hughes was the perfect husband. Over

and over again, in both her diaries and her letters to her mother, she talks as if she has won a huge prize ("I have met the strongest man in the world, ex-Cambridge, brilliant poet whose work I loved before I met him, a large, hulking, healthy Adam, half French, half Irish, with a voice like the thunder of God—a singer, a storyteller, lion and world-wanderer, a vagabond who will never stop . . . ."). No one, least of all Plath, could have thought that the road to nabbing the perfect husband could have begun at a Cambridge party one late-February evening in 1956, where Plath bit Hughes on the cheek in a frenzy and let him rip the hair band from her hair. Or that it could have ended with her getting up at four in the morning during a freezing British winter six years later, writing, writing, writing, after the same perfect husband had left her for someone else. Plath's sense of failure at being the perfect wife, along with the savagery of her final poems and the tragic nature of her subsequent death, have all combined to make her the poster girl for those women writers everywhere who have also found themselves unable to function in that conventional role, who couldn't be the perfect wife either. Here, for them at last, was that truly angry female voice, a Medea for the modern age, unashamedly vengeful, scorning, repudiating, self-pitying, denouncing.

But she wasn't just a bad, failed wife who was spitting her rage at her own inadequacies and her husband's—Plath was a bad, failed daughter, too, as she showed in her semiautobiographical novel, *The Bell Jar*, published the month before her death in 1963 under an assumed name, Victoria Lucas, then published posthumously under her own. There is a link between what Plath was, as a young girl, and the woman that she became: both the confused desire to be a wife and the clear desire to be a poet existed in her from early on. Neither mother nor daughter really believed that such aims could be incompatible with each other. Why should they be? On the contrary, they were part of the same goal, and they would merge, as Plath struggled to articulate what she wanted, to become the way she finally identified herself: as a perfect wife and as a great poet. The danger with this double identification never seems to have occurred to her until it was too late: if you stop being one, can you continue to be the other? Is it possible to be a poet without being a wife?

• • • •

During her college years and beyond, Plath struggled to answer those questions, tried to establish exactly what kind of desire she felt, and what its implications would be for her if she ever realized it, writing in her journal in May 1952: "Once there is the first kiss, then the cycle becomes inevitable. Training, conditioning, make hunger burn in breasts and secret fluid in vagina, driving blindly for destruction. What is it but destruction? Some mystic desire to beat to sensual annihilation—to snuff out one's identity on the identity of the other—a mingling and mangling of identities? A death of one? Or both? A devouring and subordination? No, no. A polarization, rather—a balance of two integrities, changing, electrically, one with the other, yet with centers of coolness, like stars."

The young man she was writing about here with such violent need, a Harvard medical student named Dick Norton, could not respond to that need anywhere near adequately enough—he told her that she could not have it all, that she could not be a wife and a mother and an artist, and that she would have to choose which mattered most to her, an insipid response to one desperate for polarization, electrical changes, the heat of desire, and the coolness of achievement. Where would she find the man to respond in the right way? "Physically," she told Aurelia in February, 1953, "I want a colossus . . . mentally, I want a man who isn't jealous of my creativity in other fields than children."

At this time, three years into her time at Smith, she was seriously worrying about ending up an "old maid." After she was rejected that summer for Frank O'Connor's creative writing course at Harvard, she famously disappeared for two days. Her brother Warren discovered her in the basement of the family home, having overdosed on sleeping pills. It was her first serious suicide attempt, and in an unsent letter written while she was staying at the McLean Hospital in Belmont, where she was treated with insulin and electric shock therapy, Plath wrote: "I need more than anything right now what is, of course, most impossible, someone to love me, to be with me at night when I wake in shuddering horror and fear of the cement tunnels leading down to the shock room."

It is hard to think of greater suffering than the mental torture Plath was experiencing at this point, which seems to have come at the end of a particularly exhausting and intense period of work. She had been guest editor at *Mademoiselle* for a month in New York and was worried about her future now that the chance of attending Harvard summer school had evaporated. On July 14, a month before her disappearance, she wrote in her journal, once again in that disconnected, second-person voice: "and you felt scared, sick, lethargic, worst of all, not wanting to cope. You saw visions of yourself in a straight jacket, and a drain on the family, murdering your mother in actuality, killing the edifice of love and respect."

Plath's panic is the panic of the artist, always setting impossible goals for herself, always exhorting herself to work harder, produce more, better work. No one is harder on her own work, no one more self-critical than the artist struggling to make her way; hence, perhaps, her need for a soul mate, for support, to take away the panic, to take away the "shuddering horror and fear" that comes in the middle of the night. Male artists might long for a muse; female artists, or at least artists like Plath, long for a partner.

What was worse, though, than the absence of a sexual and creative partner was the wrong sexual and creative partner. In 1954, Plath began dating Richard Sassoon, an intellectual, artistic history graduate from Yale. Sassoon had grown up in Europe and had developed what seemed to Plath as slightly decadent and exotic ways. The fact that he was related to Siegfried Sassoon, the war poet, only added to his allure. Plath's bedazzled view of him didn't completely override her vanity—she was concerned that he was smaller than she was, which meant she couldn't wear heels when they were out together. Her journal entries of this courtship begin, however, in 1955, from the time she arrived in Cambridge, the result of winning a highly prestigious Fulbright scholarship to study there. Biographers tend to underplay the importance of this award, but Plath had to work hard to pass the entrance exams she sat for both Oxford and Cambridge, as well as study for the Woodrow Wilson scholarship. It demonstrates just how able and serious a scholar she was.

Her ambition for graduate study in England was part of her general intention to carry on studying—she also considered applying to Yale, Harvard, and Columbia, but a friend, Mary Ellen Chase, had told her that "the English universities will give me time to write, travel, and are nowhere as rigid with planning time as America's enormous grad schools." In spite of a fear of spinsterish female academic types, Plath was willing enough to take the risk that the intellectual advancement she craved, bright student that she was, wouldn't turn her into the kind of woman she dreaded becoming. But when she got to Newnham College, she found to her delight that there wasn't much chance of ending up an old spinster after all—there were ten men to every woman at the university, and as a middle-class American, she was much better dressed and far more glamorous than her dowdier English counterparts. Britain was only ten years out of the Second World

War, and in many ways still on its knees, dilapidated and shabby, struggling with debt and trying to rebuild itself, while standards of living in the States simply raced ahead. English women students record being almost horrified by Plath's glamorous appearance in Cambridge, which, while sheltered from many of the ravages of the war, would still have been a cash-strapped town. There was little that an American would call glamorous about Britain in the 1950s.

Plath's journal entries about Sassoon, though, show how preoccupied she still was with him, even in this exciting new environment where she strolled about like a queen, and they track the pain and struggle and disappointment of a relationship that is not working—from the adolescent "do you realize that the name sassoon is the most beautiful name in the world . . . in the beginning was the word and the word was sassoon," and absorption of him into her writing aspirations, "because my love for Richard is in the story," to more adult dreams of him giving her a child and wondering if he will "ever need me again?" Interestingly, Sassoon is hardly ever mentioned in her letters to her mother until November 1955, when she matter-of-factly says, "I have been constantly surprised by how much I miss Sassoon, who is now at the Sorbonne, and spent hours talking about him with Dick." The next day he is "my brilliant and sympathetic Richard," and by January 6, 1956, she is talking again about her desire to have children, but "the only man I have ever really loved . . . is Sassoon of course" and she is concerned about his physical health and ability to conceive and bring up children.

Plath hides the pain of this love affair from her mother as she hides so many things, but her journal traces its whole story, even through Plath's meeting with Ted Hughes in February 1956 and beyond ("I got a letter from Richard this afternoon which shot all to hell . . . love that damn boy with all I've ever had in me and that's a hell of a lot. Worse, I can't stop," she wrote on March

6). She has learned, from her first humiliating encounter with the boy in the barn almost six years previously ("I wish I could be smart or flip but I'm too scared. If only he hadn't kissed me. I'll have to lie and say he didn't. But they know. They all know. And what am I against so many . . . ?"), through the Princeton dates and conventional boys who would smother her creativity and deny her artistic talents, that what she wants is not easily found; she has learned to suffer. She has learned that as a poet, she must endure isolation and misunderstanding. But it has not made her a victim. Plath's suffering has simply reinforced for her what it is she needs to survive.

. . . .

"I long so for someone to blast over Richard . . . My God, I'd love to cook and make a house, and surge force into a man's dreams, and write, if he could talk and walk and work and passionately want to do his career," wrote Plath in her journal, the day before she first met Ted Hughes in February 1956 at the launch party of the *St. Botolph's Review*. She would attract his attention at this party by shouting out lines of his poetry, to which he'd respond, "You like?" In this journal entry, she coalesces domesticity, sexual passion, and writing in the one figure, the one man who can give her all of it—not, interestingly enough, the man she meets at the party, who takes her into another room where they can talk and be alone, the man who kisses her hard, so that she bites him on the cheek in retaliation and draws blood. Diane Middlebrook has written that Plath came "looking for a husband" the night of the party, and this image, together with this kind of quotation ("I'd love to cook"), has seared onto the brain of many a reader of her story the notion of Sylvia Plath as "husband-hunter."

Just a month after Plath met Ted Hughes for the first time, she wrote a poem called "Pursuit," in which a panther stalks a woman. Richard Sassoon was uppermost in her mind in this letter to her mother, which includes the poem and which refers to him: "It would be a good thing if someone from this world could overcome his image and win me, but seriously I doubt that, however I seek, I will find someone that strong. And I will settle for nothing less than a great soul." Yet the poem itself was dedicated to Hughes. And only a day after she wrote this letter to her mother, Plath also wrote in her journal, "Oh, he is here; my black marauder; oh hungry hungry. I am so hungry for a big smashing creative burgeoning burdened love." Anyone reading both the letters and the journal could be forgiven for feeling confused. Which is it to be? Sassoon or Hughes? The man who doesn't want her (Sassoon), or the man who does (Hughes)?

• • • •

Plath, of course, chose Hughes. And so began the writing partnership that lasted almost seven years. Within four months of meeting at that party, they were married. Ted Hughes had come from a small Yorkshire town called Mytholmroyd to study at Cambridge. By the time that Plath met him, he was living in London and working at Rank studios assessing potentially filmable manuscripts, but returning to Cambridge on weekends as many former students did. He was twenty-five and already considered a poet to watch. Together, though, he and Plath made an even more eye-catching pair: he was very tall, dark, and handsome, with straggly hair, and usually dressed in a great leather overcoat; she was tall, too, dark blonde with a broad smile, and fashion-conscious.

In a letter to his brother almost three months after they were married, Hughes said of Plath, "I went to Spain with an American poetess. As a result of her influence I have written continually and every day better since I met her." The feeling was mutual: Plath testified repeatedly to the beneficial effect that Hughes was having on her writing, too ("I also feel a new direct pouring of energy into my own work"), while giving accounts of "Mr. and Mrs. Ted Hughes' Writing Table" in her journal. It seems that by this time, Plath had come round to a more bohemian view of married life, with the lack of a permanent job, no mortgage, just "writing constantly" and living for the moment.

Their six and a half-year marriage would see a peripatetic lifestyle that both Plath and Hughes initially seemed to want, as they saw themselves following in the footsteps of a couple they both admired, D. H. Lawrence and his wife Frieda. Hughes and Plath honeymooned in Benidorm, Spain, in July 1956, then came back to Yorkshire to visit Hughes's parents. They returned to Cambridge to live together as husband and wife until Plath completed her exams in May 1957, after which they went to the States to visit Aurelia Plath in Wellesley. Plath got a job teaching at Smith, her alma mater, but found teaching too taxing, and they headed for Boston in November 1957, to work as freelance writers. By the end of 1959, though, they were ready to return to England—Plath was also pregnant with her first child. They found a flat in London, and their daughter, Frieda, was born there in April 1960. When Plath became pregnant a third time (a second pregnancy had resulted in miscarriage) they decided they needed to settle down, and toward the end of the summer of 1961 found Court Green, an old rectory, near Dartmoor. They would remain there until Hughes became involved with another woman and the marriage collapsed.

How entirely comfortable Plath was with this kind of lifestyle is not clear: she was long used to nice clothes and hygienic habits, and she often commented with joy on new kitchen implements when they could finally afford them. A meager income didn't suit her—as the years went on, she fantasized not only about becoming famous, but about earning lots of money, too. Intermittent grants and prizes, ego-boosting though they were, didn't pay for everything, but these constituted almost all the income they had, apart from the short stint teaching in the States.

Nevertheless, in ecstasy at the beginning over the prize of a man she had won for herself, Plath couldn't keep from congratulating herself, even if they were poor. Hughes was "the perfect male counterpart to my own self: each of giving the other an extension of the life we believe in living: never becoming slaves to routine, secure jobs, money: but writing constantly, walking the world with every pore open, & living with love and faith"—and that faith was borne out, between 1956 and 1963, when Plath wrote 224 poems, just slightly more than she'd written in her whole life until that point. In 1960, her first collection of poems, *The Colossus*, was published, and her work had begun appearing in publications she had long revered, like *The New Yorker* and *The Atlantic Monthly*, with the former actually giving her a contract for more work. She also won a substantial Saxton Fellowship grant in 1961, the year she finished writing *The Bell Jar*.

Hughes, too, would publish voraciously during his time with Plath, winning grants from the Guggenheim Foundation as well as the Somerset Maugham Award and the Hawthornden Prize. His first collection of poetry, *The Hawk in the Rain*, was published in 1957 as the result of winning a poetry competition. In a letter to his brother that year, he attributed his "luck" to marriage, and to Plath: "We work and walk about, and repair each other's writings. She is one of the best critics I ever met and understands my imagination perfectly, and I think I understand hers." It was true: Hughes helped Plath become "tough" in her writing like she wanted to be—the violent imagery in his nature poems began to seep into her writing, too, but by 1961 and the birth of her daughter, Frieda, she was starting to use his imagery and change it, as Diane Middlebrook has noted in a perceptive and convincing comparison of the Hughes's poem "Lines to a Newborn" and Plath's "Morning Song." The latter, she argues, shows Plath "seizing important images from Hughes and refashioning them to say something entirely different": where Hughes speaks of "the hand of the moment" and "some cloud touching a pond with reflection," Plath writes of "the cloud that distils a mirror" and "the wind's hand."

What we have here, as Middlebrook is at pains to stress, is not only evidence of influence between two writers, but evidence of how they responded to each other's work, and, even more importantly, how it changed their own. Hughes believed that there was some kind of telepathic communication between them, so quickly did they respond to each other's ideas, and they would suggest subjects for each other to write about. It's likely that Plath helped Hughes access his unconscious, to represent it in his poetry, given that that was exactly what she did in hers; he would encourage her to excise sentimentality from her writing, to be stronger, brasher, even.

Her strong creative link with Hughes could be a problem for her, though, as well as a boon to her writing. As early as March 1958, she wrote that "nothing matters but Ted, Ted's writing & my writing," in an echo of her early letter to her mother where she tells her "both of us work and write immeasurably better when with each other." From their earliest days together, she had been typing out his poems for him (she typed up Hughes's first book of poems, which then went on to win the prestigious New York Poetry Center's First Publication Prize), and this seemed to her to be a satisfactory way to be spending her time. She liked to see Hughes's success as her success, too, but one cannot help wondering if this role of the literary handmaiden also appealed to the conventional, bourgeois, "good wife" side of her that her mother had encouraged in her.

But she reacted against it, too. Only a couple of months later, perhaps in an attempt to try to understand why she attacked him so viciously in a jealous rage when she saw him talking to a young woman on the university campus, she confided to her journal that "my danger, partly, I think, is becoming too dependent on Ted. He is didactic, fanatic . . . I enjoy it when Ted is off for a bit. I can build up my own inner life, my own thoughts, without his continuous, 'What are you thinking? What are you going to do now?' which makes me promptly and recalcitrantly stop thinking and doing." In September she was still on the same theme: "I must be happy first in my own work and struggle to that end, so my life does not hang on Ted's." One year on, pregnant with their first child, Frieda, she still felt that it was "dangerous to be so close to Ted day in day out."

Writing in the same room together, something she first experienced with Hughes and remarked on in a letter to her mother ("Never before have I composed and worked with a man around"), which had been so productive for her in the beginning, was starting to weigh on her. By June 1960, she was telling her mother that they divide up their writing time thus: "the mornings at the study are very peaceful to my soul, and I am infinitely lucky we can work things out so I get a solid hunk of time off, or rather, time on, a day. Ted goes in the afternoons." There had been hints for some time that their close writing partnership was getting too close—in her journal on October 19, 1959, she writes of Hughes's getting "cross" with her negativity, and in November that he is "weary of my talk of astrology and tarot and wanting to learn, and then not bothering to work on my own." It sounds as though she very much does still want to work in the same room as him, but that he is not keen, and she is trying to convince herself that it would be better for her to work alone and not be too "dependent" on him. As she acknowledged herself, she was inclined to be too dependent on people in general—or was this something she had been told?

The marriage, which began with poetry, still had another three years to go after this journal entry. And their poetry sustained the marriage, even after the births of two children in quick succession. After Nicholas was born, Plath was writing to her mother of "managing to get about two and a bit more hours in my study in the mornings." There is a sense here that writing wasn't just about keeping her mind ticking—it was also the link to Hughes, a link she didn't want to lose.

. . . .

What goes wrong in a literary and sexual relationship? Which part dies first? In January 1959, Plath wrote of not showing any of her poems to Hughes ("Didn't show him the bull one: a small victory") as part of her attempt to be less dependent on him. Their writing partnership did not stop being conducive to creativity as it had been at the start, but Plath seems to have been more worried about its closeness than Hughes was. She doesn't appear to have thought Hughes was stealing ideas from her, or hampering the flow of creativity in her. What she seems to have been worried about was an emotional dependence growing in her. She was right to be worried: if her creativity was dependent on his being close, what would happen to it when he was far away?

Sylvia Plath, as we have seen from her teenage years, bound up being a poet and being a wife together. She was a poet before she became a wife, though, and not only did she carry on writing poetry throughout her marriage, but she continued to do so even after it had begun to fall apart at the seams. Yet, in spite of the remarkable genius of the *Ariel* poems she produced during the winter of 1962, after the marriage had disintegrated, she does not seem to have believed she could make it without having a writing partner wedded to her side. Even though she wrote to her mother in November that year, "I amaze myself. It is my *work* that does it, my sense of myself as a writer," she seemed to falter in her belief in this newfound identity two months later, when she wrote that

"I just haven't felt to have any *identity* under the steamroller of decisions and responsibilities of this last half year."

Indeed, it is hard to believe that in the early days of their relationship Plath could have existed without Hughes by her side, so deep was her emotional and literary tie to him, even though she had been a poet before she met him. Again and again, we see in her journal her sheer delight in being with him, to the point where "my whole being has grown and interwound so completely with Ted's that if anything were to happen to him, I do not see how I could live." The dependency on him, which she struggled against, and which she never quite overcame, imploded during the autumn and winter of 1962. She had discovered in July of that year that Hughes was seeing another woman. Assia Wevill was the extraordinarily beautiful, exotic, highly intelligent young wife of an aspiring poet, David Wevill, and the couple had rented the Hughes's London flat. They were invited down for the weekend at Court Green in May 1962, and it seems clear that it was during this weekend that Hughes became smitten with the twice-married Wevill, who had been born in Germany, which her Jewish parents had fled in 1933 for Palestine, then Canada. Some have speculated that Plath spotted the attraction between her husband and the thirty-five-year-old Assia Wevill during this stay and became huffy and rude—in the Hughes-approved biography of Plath by Anne Stevenson, Stevenson claims Wevill told Hughes's sister Olwyn that "she doubted whether the attraction between Ted and herself would ever have developed into an affair, as it later did, had Sylvia behaved differently"; yet according to a recent biography of Wevill, she told her husband on their drive home that "Ted kissed me in the kitchen and Sylvia saw it." Stevenson's biography also omits to mention the visit Hughes paid to Wevill at the advertising agency where she worked, on June 26, when he left a note for her saying, "I have come to see you, despite all marriages." Wevill apparently "showed it to all her friends."

Plath had little chance against a woman who was behaving in a fairly predatory way toward her husband, and against a husband who had clearly had enough of his wife's emotional and mental difficulties over the last few years. Plath was not, by any account, an easy woman to live with. She was jealous, needy, highstrung, easily depressed, high-achieving, possessive, ambitious. She was also an incredibly loyal wife to Hughes, an adoring mother of her two children, and a brilliant poet. She was a heady mixture, but the fascinating thing about Hughes's affair with Wevill is that he didn't fall for someone quieter, more sedate, more steady than Plath. He went for a woman who was also slightly unstable, needy, and high-strung.

Things between Plath and Hughes came to a head when Aurelia Plath came to stay: she witnessed rows between the couple, culminating in Plath throwing her husband out, after a phone call from Wevill which made her rip the phone from the wall. Hughes moved up to London, but visited Court Green regularly to see the children over the following weeks. There is no doubt that Hughes's affair and the subsequent disintegration of her marriage would have been disastrous for Plath, as emotionally dependent upon him as she was, and as wedded to the notion of being a perfect wife. And yet, she survived it all, initially. She decided to move to London as well in December 1962, with Frieda and baby Nicholas. She had by then written most of the poems that would form the *Ariel* collection. To the surprise and shock of many who were in touch with her at the time, she killed herself just two months later, on February 11, 1963, in her flat on Fitzroy Road.

It is Plath's suicide that prevents us from daring to suggest that Hughes might actually have done Plath a great deal of good during the seven years that they were together, both personally as well as professionally. Why Plath did not survive Hughes's

abandonment of her in 1963 is the single question that everyone asks instead, a question which presumes that it was Hughes's
abandonment that killed her. Nobody asks why she did not kill
herself before that, and yet, we know that she did try to. In 1953,
Plath survived her first suicide attempt, when she hid in the basement of the family home in Wellesley, Massachusetts, took some
pills, and was found by her brother two days later when he heard
her moaning. In February 1963, Plath succeeded in her second
attempt, gassing herself in the kitchen of her London flat, after she
had left milk and biscuits out for her children, who were asleep
in another room. That ten-year gap between two suicide attempts
is a vital period, as it is a space filled with precisely the kind of
experience the other women writers in this book had, too: the
encouragement, literary and personal, of one partner's talent by
another. The possibility that Hughes's presence in her life might
have prevented Plath from trying to commit suicide again, during
those ten years, is rarely discussed.

The charge that Hughes's leaving Plath for Wevill was what
tipped her over the edge into the abyss was, of course, refuted by
Hughes, and just weeks after his wife's death, almost as though
he anticipated how people would react to it. In a letter to Aurelia
Plath, Hughes wrote that in the last month before she died, he
and Plath had become friends again, and that "I had come to a
point where I'd decided we could repair our marriage now. She
had agreed to stop the divorce. I had that weekend cancelled all
my appointments for the next fortnight. I was going to ask her to
come away on the Monday, on holiday, to the coast, some place
we had not been . . . But the difficulties caused . . . all these things
delayed the workings of our reconciliation." This revelation of
Hughes's declaration that he and Plath were possibly going to be
reconciled has since been greeted variously by sympathy, as the
self-delusion of a man in shock, or by cynicism, as the attempt of
a guilty man to exonerate himself from blame.

Few, apart from Elaine Feinstein, his first biographer after his death, have considered the possibility that Hughes was telling the truth. It is clear from both Plath's letters to Aurelia and her behavior with friends that at some point in January 1963 something had happened to change her ability to cope with her situation. Hughes had left the family home in the summer of 1962 and by the end of August Plath was writing to her mother about the possibility of a legal separation from him. Over the next three months, she worked on the *Ariel* poems at Court Green, but by January she was living in London and attending occasional literary parties. From a letter on December 21, where she told her mother, "I have never been so happy in my life," to February 4's "I just haven't written anybody because I have been feeling a bit grim," all sorts of things had happened to make those exploring the context of Plath's suicide pin her early demise on a combination of the following: it was one of the coldest winters England had had for years, and Plath wasn't good in winter, which made her depressed; her novel, *The Bell Jar*, had been published to some little acclaim, which upset her, especially as new poems by Hughes had been greeted with an avalanche of praise; she was taking new antidepressants, and she may have had a bad reaction to them.

The cold weather, the lukewarm reviews, and the pills would all have been manageable (or actually unnecessary, in the case of the pills) if Hughes hadn't left her, so it is said. Something else, though, had made Plath turn in January from positivity and strength to fear and weakness; something had made her plummet, and had made the antidepressants necessary in the first place. To Hughes himself, her suicide was mystifying. Why would she kill herself just as they were talking about getting back together?

It is, of course, because Plath did kill herself just then that no one believes what he has said. That fact, and the fact that he destroyed her last journal, contributes to a general scepticism that he could have been telling the truth. With regard to the first of these facts, however, there is arguably a very great likelihood—which Hughes himself, alas, wouldn't and couldn't have been aware of— that it was precisely *because* they were talking about getting back together that Plath was pushed over the edge she had teetered on for so long. Months of struggle to keep herself together were going to go to waste, only to return, even worse a second time, if he cheated on her again. We suppose that Plath wanted more than anything to hear that Hughes wanted her back. But it might also have been a terrifying prospect. She had survived his betrayal once: could she survive if he did it again?

There is a strong argument to be made for reconciliation being more frightening than abandonment for the person who has been left behind for many months. Perhaps only those who have experienced such a situation can understand fully just how frightening it can be. Plath was not a cowardly woman, but she was depleted, physically and mentally, at this point. Did she have the strength to cope with Hughes's offer of reconciliation and all that that entailed? Is it possible that it was that offer, and not his act of abandonment, that might just, quite unwittingly on his part, have been the final straw for her? That the prospect of having to try to be the perfect wife once more was simply too much to take on board again?

And so we have another speculation to add to the endless speculations that have been made ever since that day in 1963. There is nothing in her last letters to her mother to indicate that Plath thought Hughes wanted a reconciliation, although of course, right up until the end, Plath maintained a facade of perfection with the mother who had wanted her daughter to be the best writer and the best wife and, his destruction of her last journal after her death militates against this argument, too. In an interview for *The Paris Review* in 1995, Hughes said in response to a question about that final journal: "What I actually destroyed was one journal that covered maybe two or three months, the last months. And it was just sad. I just didn't want her children to see it, no. Particularly her last days." But if they were talking about a reconciliation, would that not have been mentioned by Plath in her journal? Would it not have testified to the truth of what he was claiming? Perhaps the talk of reconciliation did take place but she made no mention of it—undoubtedly, this last journal would have made for unpleasant reading; given the controlled brutality of many of the *Ariel* poems, it is unnerving to think what might have been written for private viewing only.

It is impossible for us to know now whether Plath understood what Hughes was attempting to do, or what she thought of it, with the exception of pieces of reported conversation in some of the many biographies that have since been published. What we know is what we have of her own words, in her many voices, in front of us. And what we know, to repeat, is that Plath was not a cowardly woman. She was not a victim. She knew Hughes was dangerous, right from the beginning: this was the man, after all, who had kissed her "bang smash on the mouth" when they first met, who "ripped off" her headband and stole her earrings. He was the man who made her write, "such violence, and I can see how women lie down for artists" after that first encounter. But that danger, that violence, was exactly what she wanted, what she needed, what she had been looking for. She was not running toward a man she knew could hurt her because she was masochistic. He was the risk she was willing to take. That much we do know. The question is, was she right about him, or did she get it horribly wrong?

• • • •

More than with any other woman writer in this volume, there is the temptation to privilege one text over another: to say that the letters to her mother are less important, less truly revealing than the entries made in the journal, for instance, or to place the final poems as the most important site when digging around for clues to her mindset. But all of these texts are important. It would be untrue to say that Plath would never have become a published poet had she not met Hughes, but that her relationship with Hughes was crucial to her career as a professional writer is hardly to be denied. It is part of the reason she is read and remembered now. Not because she died by her own hand, tragic though that is. Such an act has not been enough for the equally tragic Assia Wevill—who killed herself and the child she had by Hughes, a little girl called Shura, in 1969, and which added to Hughes's notoriety as a man who was in some sense fatal for women— to be recalled by generations down the line. It is Plath's writing that has immortalized her as a great poet, and Hughes, like John Middleton Murry after the death of Katherine Mansfield, has to be credited with keeping her work in the public realm. Damned if he did, and damned if he didn't, he nevertheless made sure that as much of his wife's work was published posthumously.

For writers to be remembered, they need champions to hand them on to the next generation. It is unpalatable to those who blame Hughes for Plath's death to acknowledge him as any kind of champion, just as it is unpalatable for many to accept that the women in this volume needed, sought out, and relied upon their male literary partners to write and publish. But unpalatability doesn't make it any less true.

Notes

INTRODUCTION

Page 13, Christopher Barker's remarkable memoir Barker, *Arms of the Infinite.* (See Bibliography, Chapter 8.)

Page 14, desire and writing As Lynette Felber points out on page 156 in *Literary Liaisons,* "As with other women in literary liaisons (West and Nin in particular), writing embodies desire and is the catalyst that brings the lovers together." (See Bibliography, Chapter 3.

Page 14, Louise DeSalvo See Louise DeSalvo, *Conceived with Malice: Literature as Revenge in the Lives and Works of Virginia and Leonard Woolf, D. H. Lawrence, Djuna Barnes, and Henry Miller* (New York and London: Penguin, 1995).

Page 15, "If H.D. had not met Pound" Benstock, *Women of the Left Bank,* 331. (See Bibliography, Chapter 2.)

CHAPTER 1: KATHERINE MANSFIELD
AND JOHN MIDDLETON MURRY

Page 29, "I have tried through my illness" Mansfield, *Notebooks,* Column 2, 286.

Page 29, "For you and I are not of this world" Murry, *Letters Between Katherine Mansfield and John Middleton Murry* (New York: Virago, 1988, 66).

Page 31, "in some abstruse way" Quoted in Tomalin, *Katherine Mansfield,* 181.

Page 32, According to Tomalin Tomalin, *Katherine Mansfield,* 137, 95.

Page 32, "controlling, dominant" Lea, *Life of John Middleton Murry,* 30–32.

Page 32, "no doubt whatever" Scott, ed., introduction to *Katherine Mansfield Notebooks Vol. 1* by Katherine Mansfield, xiv.

Page 33, as Tomalin hints "Katherine was, of course, already chronically ill long before tuberculosis was established, and it is possible that, if her health had been good, she might have been able to make the break with Murry that half of her being desired" (Tomalin, *Katherine Mansfield,* 141).

Page 35, Tomalin reports her kissing Tomalin, *Katherine Mansfield,* 26.

Page 35, "She enthrals me" Quoted in Tomalin, *Katherine Mansfield,* 35.

Page 36, "Lying in my bed at night" Mansfield, *Collected Letters, Vol. 1,* 59.

Page 36, "put an end to" Ibid., 89.

Page 37, Pension Muller in Turkheimer Strasse This residence would provide Mansfield with the setting for her collection of short stories, *In a German Pension*, which was published two years later.

Page 38, she met her next lover See Tomalin, *Katherine Mansfield*, 71.

Page 38, "a fat Polish dictionary" Mansfield, *Collected Letters, Vol. 1*, 93.

Page 40, West knew of Mansfield Tomalin writes, "Both Vera Brittain and Rebecca West spoke of Katherine's appearance at a reputedly lesbian night club, The Cave of the Golden Calf, in 1913, where she is said to have either performed or introduced the acts" (Tomalin, *Katherine Mansfield*, 60).

Page 40, "make me your mistress" Quoted in Tomalin, *Katherine Mansfield*, 104.

Page 41, "I'm very happy, darling." Mansfield, *Collected Letters, Vol. 1*, 119.

Page 41, Claire Tomalin writes that Tomalin, *Katherine Mansfield*, 104.

Page 42, "I was a terribly 'innocent' lover" Quoted in Lea, *Life of John Middleton Murry*, 31.

Page 42, "in Murry she [Mansfield] found" Lea, *Life of John Middleton Murry*, 32.

Page 42, removal of a fallopian tube Tomalin, *Katherine Mansfield*, 75.

Page 43, "And do you know" John Middleton Murry, May 1913, *Letters between Katherine Mansfield and John Middleton Murry*, 13.

Page 43, "must have suspected something" Tomalin, *Katherine Mansfield*, 77.

Page 45, "We talked in whispers" Mansfield, *Notebooks, Vol. 2*, 12.

Page 46, Tomalin argues that lesbianism Tomalin writes: "Later in the year Katherine wrote a story called 'Leves Amores' which is undisguisedly lesbian . . . [she] had learned that there was something in her nature that would not quite fit in with the accepted pattern of behaviour required by society; at the same time, she never wanted to reject that pattern entirely. She wanted marriage and children and the outward manifestations of a conventional arrangement" (Tomalin, *Katherine Mansfield*, 37).

Page 47, "A misty, misty evening" Mansfield, *Journal*, 35–36.

Page 48. "the night before" Ibid., 44.

Page 48, making more of her brother's death Tomalin only makes a one-sentence reference to Leslie Beauchamp's death but attempts to defend her by saying that Mansfield "reacted in bursts of bitter grief, alternating, naturally enough, with fits of frenetic gaiety " (Tomalin, *Katherine Mansfield*, 139).

Page 49, "Wig, do you just treat me" Mansfield and Murry, *Letters Between*, 71.

Page 50, "By the way, I wrote to Lawrence" Mansfield, *Collected Letters, Vol. 1*, 219–220.

Page 51, "F[rancis] C[arco] as you know" Ibid., 180.

Page 51, "Don't think about the people" Mansfield and Murry, *Letters Between*, 32.

Page 52, "in many ways happy" Tomalin, *Katherine Mansfield*, 142.

Page 52, "Now—now I want to write" Mansfield, *Journal*, 42.

Page 53, "of course I am frightened" Ibid., 75.

Page 53, "Your ms came this morning" Mansfield and Murry, *Letters Between*, 112–13.

Page 53, "I have now not the slightest doubt" Ibid., 129. This inflating of his own far lesser talents has, unsurprisingly, hardly endeared Murry to biographers of Mansfield and may be part of the reason so many view his influence over her in a harsh light.

Page 54, "You gave twice to your work" Mansfield and Murry, *Letters Between*, 322.

Page 56, "Honesty (why?)" Mansfield, *Journal*, 130–33.

Page 56, "You hang on thinking" Mansfield, *Katherine Mansfield Notebooks*, Volume 2, 335.

CHAPTER 2: H.D. AND EZRA POUND

Page 61, He drags me out of the shadows H.D., *End to Torment*, 4.

Page 61, "How funny, I remember" Ibid., 30.

Page 61, her "initiators" Guest, *Herself Defined*, 47.

Page 62, she should have become a nun Ibid., 305.

Page 62, Imagist movement Imagism was the movement in poetry that, while not begun by Pound but by T. E. Hulme, was defined by Pound according to the following three rules: "1. Direct treatment of the 'thing,' whether subjective or objective; 2. To use absolutely no word that does not contribute to the presentation; 3. As regarding rhythm: to compose in sequence of the musical phrase, not in sequence of a metronome." It was a break from the excesses of the past, eschewing decoration for economy, concentration, and energy.

Page 62, recent feminist scholarship See, for example, *H.D.: Woman and Poet*, edited by Michael King (Maine: National Poetry Foundation, 1986); Shari Benstock, *Women of the Left Bank: Paris 1900–1940* (London: Virago, 1987); and Cassandra Laity, *H.D. and the Victorian*

Fin de Siècle: Gender, Modernism, Decadence (Cambridge: Cambridge University Press, 1996).

Page 63, "He is so eccentric." H.D., *End to Torment*, 14.

Page 65, Rossetti's "Bohemian masculinity" See Carr, *Verse Revolutionaries*, 98.

Page 68, "Immensely sophisticated" H.D., *End to Torment*, 3.

Page 68, "O Ezra Pound's crazy" Ibid., 20.

Page 68, "electric, magnetic" Ibid., 4.

Page 68, We know little In a new study, *Verse Revolutionaries*, author Helen Carr is forced to rely mainly on the reflections of William Carlos Williams, who knew both H.D. and Pound at the time.

Page 70, "Did Pound learn from H.D.?" Carr, *Verse Revolutionaries*, 77.

Page 70, He let a stranger stay H.D., *End to Torment*, 14.

Page 71, "The engagement" Ibid., 15 [ADD PERIOD]

Page 73, Helen Carr argues Carr, *Verse Revolutionaries*, 447–48.

Page 73, a conversation with her doctor H.D., *End to Torment*, 15–16.

Page 74, "The questions concerning Pound's role" Benstock, *Women of the Left Bank*, 331.

Page 75, "The fact that she became" Robinson, *H.D.*, 34.

Page 75, her "initiator" See Guest, *Herself Defined*.

Page 75, "Ezra would have destroyed me" H.D., *End to Torment*, 35.

Page 75, direction of Vorticism Vorticism, described once as "aggressively masculine," developed out of visual art, with "the visual image of a vortex, bound up as it is with the curvilinear and gyrating rings of whirlpool." Spiral forms had been employed by Wyndham Lewis, Vorticism's major proponent, and, as Helen Carr notes, its appeal for poets like Pound was its suggestions of "the turbulent energies of the metropolis" (Carr, *Verse Revolutionaries*, 658). In other words, it was modern, and appealed to Pound with its even more concentrated form of energy than Imagism.

Page 76, "mad old poet Ezra Pound" H.D., *End to Torment*, 55–56.

Page 76, photograph taken in London Published in Tytell, *Ezra Pound*.

Page 77, "bluff, powerful" Quoted in Benstock, *Women of the Left Bank*, 318.

Page 78, kisses she also found "pressurized" Guest, *Herself Defined*, 30.

Page 78, "electric" first kisses H.D., *End to Torment*, 4.

Page 78, "forcing" and "smudge her out." H.D., *Her*, 73.

Page 79, "Why is it I can't love" Ibid., 65.

Page 79, "Kisses forced her" Ibid., 73.

Page 79, "The face of George" Ibid., 174.

Page 79, "writing had somehow" Ibid., 71.

Page 79, "She wanted George to say" Ibid., 63.

Page 79, "George Lowndes is teaching you" Ibid., 95.

Page 79, "Curled lips" Ibid., 163.

Page 80, "She was in love" MF, 218.

Page 80, "glowering and savage" H.D., *End to Torment*, 9.

Page 81, "Ezra, at one time" Ibid., 52.

Page 82, this kind of intimacy Guest argues that H.D.'s time in London was the best of her life because she was regarded as a kind of goddess figure by all who got to know her through Pound, and that this was possibly what she'd been searching for all her life (see Guest, *Herself Defined*).

Page 82, Pound may have been dismissive I think Carr tries to argue both ways, when she says that Pound made her a poet, but it was Aldington who first encouraged her. That would make Aldington the one who really "discovered" her, and H.D. herself credits Pound with that.

Page 82, "But Dryad" H.D., *End to Torment*, 18.

Page 82, "Ezra who really introduced me" Ibid., 23.

Page 83, When she did break away Although Pound went his own way when he abandoned Imagism for Vorticism, he still expected his protégés to follow his lead, and was angry when H.D. and others agreed to contribute to a book edited by Amy Lowell on Imagism. He saw this as betrayal, but H.D. saw his move away from Imagism as the initial betrayal.

Page 83, "Run around, children" H.D., *End to Torment*, 4.

Page 83, "I was clothed with confusion" Ibid., 12.

Page 83, in Asphodel, Hermione says H.D., *Asphodel*, 13, 62.

Page 84, "I was hiding myself" H.D., *End to Torment*, 19.

Page 85, "O Fay" H.D., *Asphodel*, 91.

Page 85, "The MacPhersons are almost MYSELF" H.D., *Analyzing Freud: Letters of H.D., Bryher, and their Circle*, ed. Susan Stanford Friedman (New York: New Directions, 2002), xxxii.

Page 85, "it was characteristic of H.D" Guest, *Herself Defined*, 24.

Page 86, misadvice of a nurse See Introduction to H.D., *Bid Me to Live*, 11.

Page 86, H.D. felt left out when See Guest, *Herself Defined*.

Page 89, "The Professor said" H.D., *Tribute to Freud*, 21.

Page 89, "hoping to find my mother" Ibid., 23.

Page 89, "My brain staggers" Ibid., 85.

Page 89, "I felt like a child" Ibid., 130.

Page 90, an incident from childhood Ibid., 40–41.

Page 91, "I have a sort of split-infinitive" Analyzing Freud: Letters of HD, Bryand and Their Circle, edited by Susan Stanford Freidman, 518.

CHAPTER 3: THE "MOTHER": REBECCA WEST AND H. G. WELLS

Page 96, West is credited with inventing This is according to both Gordon N. Ray, *H. G. Wells and Rebecca West*, and Carl Rollyson, *Rebecca West*.

Page 97, as husband and wife Ray, *Wells and West*, 45–46

Page 97, Wells wrote to West Ibid., 80.

Page 98, "her need to handle" "She made such a palimpsest not only in her work but also out of the story of her life. The need to make a pattern out of random happenings led her to interpret her experience as if it were a dream, and to restructure her past as if it were, as she said, a 'bad book' which had to be improved" (Glendinning, *Rebecca West*, 24).

Page 100, "wanted to meet men" Rollyson implies that Jane Wells actually discussed with her husband the advantages and disadvantages of him taking on West as his mistress (Rollyson, *Rebecca West*, 25).

Page 100, He also presents West See Rollyson, *Rebecca West*, 24.

Page 100, "saturated with literary ambition" Wells, *H. G. Wells in Love*, 95.

Page 101, "Our drawing room was hallowed" West, *Selected Letters*, ed. Bonnie Kime Scott, 17.

Page 101, "old maid among novelists" West, *Young Rebecca*, 64.

Page 102, "did me no harm with her" Wells, *H. G. Wells in Love*, 95–96.

Page 103, Elizabeth von Arnim According to Rollyson, he was now growing tired of von Arnim: "his affair . . . had soured" (Rollyson, *Rebecca West*, 30).

Page 103, Wells's wife, Jane, apparently consented Rollyson asserts, along with Glendinning and Ray, that Jane knew about his affairs and "tolerated" them "because it did not disturb her family life" (Rollyson, *Rebecca West*, 25). Certainly she knew about West's pregnancy by her husband.

Page 104, "maidenly reserve" Wells himself claimed in later life that West "was under that urgency to get to grips with life that stirs in youthful blood, and she was too critical for commonplace lovemaking with her contemporaries. She demanded to be my lover . . ." (Wells, *H. G. Wells in Love*, 96).

Page 105, "I had never met anything" Wells, *H. G. Wells in Love*, 95.

Page 106, young woman who had canvassed Glendinning, *Rebecca West*, 31.

Page 107, "I thought of doing all those things." Quoted in Glendinning, *Rebecca West*, 48.

Page 108, This outpouring of West's feelings Bonnie Kime Scott suggests that a "similar letter" might have been sent instead (West, *Selected Letters*, 22).

Page 109, "feminine wiles" This was a young woman who had written in *The Freewoman* on July 25, 1912, in a review of J. M. Kennedy's book *English Literature 1880–1905*, "I must confess that the passage in Mr. Kennedy's book which gives me the most tranquil pleasure is an entry in the index: 'Sex, The unimportance of, p. 224' This is Napoleonic. One yearns to grovel, just a little" (West, *Young Rebecca*, 52).

Page 110, "Rebecca . . . did not respond." Ray, *Wells and West*, 25.

Page 110, "It was our second encounter" Wells, *H. G. Wells in Love*, 96. (I am assuming by "second encounter" he means a sexual one, as it wasn't the second time they'd met.)

Page 111, Weldon imagines how West See Weldon, *Rebecca West*, 53.

Page 111, West as having been an "ingénue" See Glendinning, *Rebecca West*, 38.

Page 111, "stinging jab of a style" Rollyson, *Rebecca West*, 30.

Page 112, "If young women lie down" Weldon, *Rebecca West*, 50

Page 112, "we did harm to each other" Wells, *H. G. Wells in Love*, 102.

Page 113, "the best of our relationship" Ibid., 103.

Page 113, West viewed Jane as a "hypocrite" Ray, *Wells and West*, 85–86.

Page 114, "a union of equals" Ibid., 35.

Page 114, "You have got to take care of me" Quoted in Ray, *Wells and West*, 46.

Page 115, "forced upon her idiotic lies" Wells, *H. G. Wells in Love*, 97–98.

Page 115, "under the conditions" Ray, *Wells and West*, xxii.

Page 117, "It would . . . take a psychoanalytic critic" West, *Family Memories*, 10.

Page 117, "When H. G. foundered" Rollyson, *Rebecca West*, 41.

Page 118, "I want dear Panfer" Quoted in Ray, *Wells and West*, 113.

Page 120, "I hate domesticity" West, *Selected Letters*, 26.

Page 120, "H. G. says he is coming" Ibid., 44.

Page 121, "the real reason I separated" Ibid., 420.

Page 122, "His lies" Glendinning, *Rebecca West*, 86.

Page 122, "my life with H. G" West, *Selected Letters*, 309.

Page 122, "They didn't give parties" West, *Sunflower*, 15.

Page 123, "satirizes the patriarchal values" Felber, *Literary Liaisons*, 69.

Page 123, "Everywhere they went" Ray, *Wells and West*, 117.

Page 124, "an ill conceived sprawl" Quoted in Ray, *Wells and West*, 123.

Page 124, "I have told him definitely" West, *Selected Letters*, 54.

Page 124, "I said I thought he was rooted" Quoted in Ray, *Wells and West*, 129.

Page 124, "I have stuck to him partly" West, *Selected Letters*, 55–56.

Page 125, "Dear H.G., he was a devil" Ibid., 214.

CHAPTER 4: JEAN RHYS AND FORD MADOX FORD

Page 129, "She regularly acts like" Davidson, *Jean Rhys*, 69.

Page 130, "marked by a fundamental passivity" Benstock, *Women of the Left Bank*, 449–50.

Page 131, One very painful, pitiful example See David Plante, *Difficult Women: A Memoir of Three: Jean Rhys, Sonia Orwell, Germaine Greer* (London: Futura, 1984).

Page 131, promise herself a drink Rhys, *Jean Rhys: Letters*, 103.

Page 131, "I realised perfectly that my talk" Ibid., 35.

Page 132, "the best living English novelist" Al Alvarez's *New York Times Sunday Book Review,* March 17, 1974.

Page 133, "stout, gangling, albino-ish" Glendinning, *Rebecca West*, 38.

Page 133, helpless young girl For example, writing to Evelyn Scott in 1934, she described her efforts in *Voyage in the Dark* thus: "Perhaps I was simply trying to describe a girl going potty" (*Jean Rhys: Letters 1931–66*, 25). This is only one of many examples of Rhys calling her female characters "girls."

Page 134, Ford was a fantasist West wrote: "Liars see facts as they are and transform them into fantasies, but in Ford's case facts changed to fantasies in the very instant of their impact on his senses" (Quoted in Glendinning, *Rebecca West*, 25).

Page 135, Jean Rhys was born There is some dispute about her actual age, with some recording her date of birth as late as 1894.

Page 136, "Finally, without speaking" Rhys, *Smile Please*, 49.

Page 136, "Even after the new baby" Ibid., 42.

Page 136, "they surged past the window" Ibid., 47.

Page 136, "writing poetry took away sadness" Quoted in Angier, *Jean Rhys*, 23.

Page 136, "I found when I was a child" Interview with Jean Rhys, Gourevitch, *Paris Review Interviews, vol. III*, 201.

Page 136, "I never wanted to write" Rhys, *Jean Rhys: Letters*, 65.

Page 137, "My aunt then explained" Rhys, *Smile Please*, 99.

Page 138, "when she took the first step" Angier, *Jean Rhys*, 52.

Page 138, "When my first love affair" Rhys, *Smile Please*, 114.

Page 140, "I think the death of her first child" Angier, *Jean Rhys*, 113.

Page 142, Ford was at a more desperate point Saunders argues that Ford was "feeling vulnerable" (Saunders, *Ford Madox Ford*, 281).

Page 142, As Rhys tells it Angier disputes Rhys's account of events here, finding various aspects of it "implausible." Nevertheless, she has no alternative story to tell of how Mrs. Adam got her hands on Rhys's writing (Angier, *Jean Rhys*, 130).

Page 143, However, it's tricky to know exactly Paul Delany's 1983 article, "Jean Rhys and Ford Madox Ford: What 'Really' Happened" (*Mosaic*, 16: 4, 15–24), doesn't attempt to explain the biographical facts, preferring instead to make a textual comparison of Rhys's novelistic treatment of the affair and Ford's much earlier novel, *The Good Soldier*. Judith Kegan Gardiner also compares the two texts directly in her essay, "Rhys Recalls Ford: *Quartet* and *The Good Soldier*" in *Tulsa Studies in Women's Literature I*, Spring 1982, 67–81.

Page 144, "I think it is angry" Letter from Rhys to Francis Wyndham (Rhys, *Jean Rhys: Letters*, 171). Both novels have been considered artistic failures because of the undisguised anger and hurt that they contain, and Rhys's biographer Carole Angier describes *Quartet* as Rhys's "most self-centred, vengeful book" (Angier, *Jean Rhys*, 50).

Page 144, Critics have tended An exception is biographer Max Saunders, who offers a slight reading in his consideration of the affair (Saunders, *Ford Madox Ford*, 281–99).

Page 146, "I was singularly slow" Bowen, *Drawn from Life*, 166.

Page 148, Yet her anger was the catalyst See Davidson, *Jean Rhys*, 61.

Page 148, "Ford helped me more" Interview with Jean Rhys, Gourevitch, *Paris Review Interviews, vol. III*, 202.

Page 148, her "marriage" with Ford Ford was still married to his first wife at this time, but he called the other women with whom he subsequently set up home his "wives," regardless.

Page 148, something exciting about her Shari Benstock describes Rhys's time in Paris as being "on the furthest fringes of intellectual and literary activity," making her an "outsider." This aspect of Rhys being always on the fringes is, I think, one of the things people found appealing about her (Benstock, *Women of the Left Bank*, 448–50).

Page 148, "needle-quick intelligence" Bowen, *Drawn from Life*, 166.

Page 149, Rhys was an outsider Benstock writes: "She discovered there no island havens, no communities of writers, no women friends who might support her talent" (Benstock, *Women of the Left Bank*, 448).

Page 149, such "unpublishable" things Bowen, *Drawn from Life*, 166.

Page 149, reviewers were completely divided See Angier, *Jean Rhys*, 177.

Page 150, "It is doubtful if one ought" Published in the *Daily Telegraph*, 30 January 1931; see Angier, *Jean Rhys*, 280.

Page 150, Postures When it was first published in England, though not in the United States, *Quartet* was titled "Postures."

Page 150, "I learnt what a powerful weapon" Bowen, *Drawn from Life*, 167.

Page 151, "exercise his sentimental talents" Ibid., 80.

Page 151, Rhys's later claim Diana Athill quotes a letter Rhys had written to her: "'Ford wasn't in the least in love with me—God knows what he felt, he was a mystery to me, but I think he hated being alone when Stella went into the country—and I wasn't in love with him. It's just that I was stuck and there was no-one to help me' . . . Knowing Jean, that last sentence rings very true" (see Judd, *Ford Madox Ford*, 362).

Page 151, *"In the end, of course, she lost Ford."* Angier, *Jean Rhys: Lives of Modern Women*, 49.

Page 153, *"an unsustainable reality"* Saunders writes of this double aspect: "Ford split his feelings about Rhys between the two female characters (in *When the Wicked Man*), painting 'a cruel, but not an inaccurate portrait' of her as the witch-seductress Lola Porter, and romanticizing her on the other hand as Henrietta Felise, 'that recurring ideal of his own imagination, the fragile, mournful, mysterious girl' which Jean Rhys had been to him in 1924" (Saunders, *Ford Madox Ford*, 296).

Page 155, *"the sexually charged atmosphere"* Saunders, *Ford Madox Ford*, 294.

Page 156, *apocalyptic as some have suggested* Saunders writes that both David Plante and Francis Wyndham believed "she was very much in love with Ford" (Saunders, *Ford Madox Ford*, 288).

Page 156, *a mood of anger and despair* Saunders argues that "Rhys's rage was fed by her feeling that Ford had not only been insincere about his feelings for her, but that 'all Ford had said about her writing, his concern for it, was false. That was what hurt the most.'" Saunders then goes on to argue, "But he continued trying to help her career" (Saunders, *Ford Madox Ford*, 298).

Page 157, *"It was Covici"* Rhys, *Jean Rhys: Letters*, 294–95.

CHAPTER 5: ANAÏS NIN AND HENRY MILLER

Page 163, *"Henry and June change"* Nin, *The Journals of Anais Nin Vol. 1*, 29.

Page 165, *Maruca Rodriguez* Bair, *Anaïs Nin*, 22.

Page 165, *"unbridled" sexual activity* Ibid., 177.

Page 165, *"heavy-breathing prose"* Ibid., 174.

Page 166, *It was a long courtship* See Bair's *Anaïs Nin* for a fuller account of their courtship.

Page 168, *wouldn't be much interested in her* Nin, *Journals, Vol. 1*, 11.

Page 168, *"suspicious of poetry"* Ibid., 14.

Page 168, *"what makes them necessary"* Ibid., 18–19.

Page 169, *"act of self-invention"* Podnieks, *Daily Modernism*, 284–86.

Page 169, *"generic innovation of Nin's tactic"* Felber, *Literary Liaisons*, 40.

Page 170, *who knew she lied* "Lying is the only way I have found to be true to myself, to do what I want, to be what I want with the least possible pain to others" (Nin, *Fire*, 58).

Page 170, *her fascination with Miller's wife* In a letter to Miller dated February 13, 1932, Nin writes, "I have a fear of being like June exactly—I have a fear of utter chaos . . ." (Nin, *Literate Passion*, 8).

Page 171, *June's "face and body"* Nin, *Journals Vol. 1*, 20.

Page 172, *"cultivate the wealthy Nin"* Robert Ferguson, *Henry Miller: A Life* (London: Hutchinson, 1991), 191.

Page 172, "literary fuck fest" letter by Miller dated July 30, 1932 *Literate Passion*, 82.

Page 173, "It hurts me to know" letter by Miller dated February 13, 1932, *Literate Passion*, 8.

Page 173, "to each one I can write" Nin, *Fire*, journal entry dated April 17, 1935.

Page 175, "escape from Louveciennes" Nin, *Journals Vol. 1*, 5.

Page 175, "Certain passages are" Letter by Miller, February 4, 1932 *Literate Passion*, 3.

Page 176, "I have learned from Henry" Nin, *Journals Vol. 1*, 50.

Page 176, "Henry gives me a world" Ibid., 54.

Page 176, "I want to be a strong poet" Ibid., 55.

Page 177, "I would never have asked" Quoted in Bair, *Anaïs Nin*, 219

Page 178, "black or bilious green lipstick" Ibid., 127.

Page 178, "I gave you gold and bread" Letter by Nin October 30, 1932, *Literate Passion*, 124.

Page 178, "two fragile ties" Bair, *Anaïs Nin*, 162.

Page 179, "You have gotten ingrown" Letter by Miller, April 20, 1933, *Literate Passion*, 147.

Page 179, "I insist on your showing" Ibid., 217–19.

Page 180, "Let me know when" Ibid., 219–21.

Page 182, "I love this strange" Ibid., 21

Page 183, "make her read Magic Mountain*"* Ibid., 108.

Page 184, "I owe all this to you" Nin, *Journals Vol. 1*, 185.

Page 185, "I feel empty-handed" Ibid., 128.

Page 185, "Have I permission" Letter by Miller, May 15, 1932, *Literary Passion*, 56.

Page 185, "one of the most beautiful" Ibid., 55.

Page 185, "As each page" Nin, *Journals Vol. 1*, 128–29

Page 185, a new way of writing Lynette Felber writes: "Nin's deliberate cultivation of a feminine aesthetic as a means to distinguish herself from Miller's characteristic literary production represents both a personal and a professional step toward autonomy" (Felber, *Literary Liaisons*, 48).

Page 186, "we have much influence" Nin, *Journals Vol. 1*, 166.

Page 186, "were certainly not complementary" Felber, *Literary Liaisons*, 38–39.

Page 186, "I feel the greatest peace" Letter by Miller, August 14, 1932, *Literate Passion*, 96.

Page 186, "Your pages on my journal" Ibid., 77.

Page 187, "sex, self and psychoanalysis" Podnieks, *Daily Modernism*, 284.

Page 188, "Dropped the diary" Nin, *Journals Vol. 1*, 26.

Page 188, "Otto Rank, who also advised" Ibid., 281.

Page 188, "deprived of my opium." Ibid., 285.

Page 188, "I still have something to say" Ibid., 289.

Page 188, "we talked about how Henry" Ibid., 291.

Page 188, "withdrawing from the world." Ibid., 307.

Page 189, "My faith in Henry" Nin, Fire, 50.

Page 189, "You are an artist" Letter by Miller, March 1935 Literate Passion, 297.

Page 190, "a whore by nature" Nin, Fire, 146.

Page 190, "Is it possible" Ibid., 196.

Page 191, "I want to know the inner self" Quoted in Podneiks, Daily Modernism, 306.

CHAPTER 6: SIMONE DE BEAUVOIR AND JEAN-PAUL SARTRE

Page 195, they stopped having sex According to Carole Seymour- Jones, "Simone's body had become a stumbling block between her and Sartre. As the months passed, their sexual differences grew" (Seymour-Jones, Dangerous Liaison, 96).

Page 196, "Sartre corresponded exactly" Simone de Beauvoir, Memoirs, 345.

Page 197, "Why is a nice girl" Carter, "Colette," The London Review of Books Anthology One, ed. Michael Mason, 129–39.

Page 197, "To explain fully why Beauvoir" Moi, Simone de Beauvoir, 253.

Page 197, "Why on earth" Rowley, Tête-à-Tête, xi.

Page 197, this sexually arid relationship Edward and Kate Fullbrook write: "It is ironic that the system of ethics whose origins are here in dispute grew out of a fundamental philosophical divergence between Beauvoir and Sartre. This seems to have occurred as early as April 1940 . . ." (Fullbrook, Sex and Philosophy, 133).

Page 197, "dangerous potential for evil." Seymour-Jones, Dangerous Liaison, xiii.

Page 198, "She moved me" Beauvoir, Letters to Sartre, 389.

Page 199, "compulsion to repeat her cycles" Moi, Simone de Beauvoir, 254.

Page 200, "nymph, whose childish ways" Seymour-Jones, Dangerous Liaison, 216.

Page 200, "If I'm to tell you everything" Beauvoir, Letters to Sartre, 252.

Page 200, any kind of victim Beauvoir's relationship with Sorokine would eventually result in complaints by Sorokine's mother and Beauvoir losing her teaching job.

Page 201, "Yet at the age of fifteen" Beauvoir, Memoirs, 141.

Page 202, "Whether in Paris, Rouen" Beauvoir, Prime of Life, 124.

Page 203, "Didn't we all want" Rowley, Tête-à-Tête, xii.

Page 204, "What I appreciated most" Beauvoir, Memoirs, 44.

Page 205, "the scholar, the artist, the writer" Ibid., 141.

Page 206, "By writing a work based" Ibid., 142.

Page 206, "someone more accomplished" Ibid., 145.

Page 207, "BEAUVOIR = BEAVER" See Seymour-Jones, Dangerous Liaison, 63–64.

Page 208, top prize to a woman Both Seymour-Jones's A Dangerous Liaison and Edward and Kate Fullbrook's Sex and Philosophy elaborate on this.

Page 209, "Day after day" Beauvoir, Memoirs, 344.

Page 210, "Sartre was bewildered" Seymour-Jones, Dangerous Liaison, 97.

Page 210, "We made another pact" Beauvoir, Prime of Life, 23

Page 211, "My God!" Beauvoir, Letters to Sartre, 262.

Page 212, "jettisoned all past attachments" Beauvoir, *Prime of Life*, 14.

Page 212, "For you must understand" Beauvoir, *Letters to Sartre*, 4.

Page 213, "space which the admiration" Seymour-Jones, *Dangerous Liaison*, 119.

Page 213, "Simone, nine years older" Ibid., 120.

Page 214, "She was overcome" Beauvoir, *Letters to Sartre*, 8.

Page 215, "she had the painful impression" Beauvoir, *She Came to Stay*, 114.

Page 216, "vexed with Sartre" Beauvoir, *Prime of Life*, 255.

Page 217, "It was the first time" Ibid., 226.

Page 217, "I worked away assiduously" Beauvoir, *Letters to Sartre*, 156.

Page 217, "What you say about Bienenfeld" Sartre, *Witness to My Life*, 339–40.

Page 218, "it went straight to essentials" Beauvoir, *Memoirs*, 158.

Page 218, "fiddling detail" Possibly, of course, this was deliberate. Edward and Kate Fullbrook posit the notion in their book that, from 1939 to 1940, Beauvoir kept back the philosophical ideas she was developing from Sartre—did she think he would steal them? (Fullbrook, *Sex and Philosophy*, 91).

Page 218, "fits of disquiet" Beauvoir, *Memoirs*, 50.

Page 218, "ugly little spinster" Ibid., 288.

Page 218, "the mechanism that explains" Fullbrook, *Sex and Philosophy*, 62.

Page 219, objective or subjective way Ibid., 63.

Page 219, "devoted to Katherine Mansfield" Beauvoir, *Prime of Life*, 100.

Page 222, "you didn't yet love me" Beauvoir, *Letters to Sartre*, 10.

Page 222, "first time I've slept with a brunette" Sartre, *Witness to My Life*, 155.

Page 223, "you are on the horizon" Ibid., 318.

Page 223, "you haven't left me" Beauvoir, *Letters to Sartre*, 146

Page 226, "with a possible KGB agent" As Seymour-Jones asserts in *A Dangerous Liaison*.

CHAPTER 7: MARTHA GELLHORN AND ERNEST HEMINGWAY

Page 231, newspapers and magazines In the 1987 biography, *Hemingway*, Kenneth S. Lynn cites several glossy magazines from the late 1940s that focused on Hemingway's personal life and showed pictures of his ex-wives.

Page 232, "I weep for the eight years" Gellhorn, *The Letters*, 204.

Page 234, "Hell hath no fury" Ibid., 488.

Page 234, "trip to China" A newly published book claims that Hemingway had been recruited by the KGB just before this trip, with the code name "Argo." It claims he never passed on any political information and that contact had ceased by the end of the decade (John Earl Haynes, Harvey Klehr, and Alexander Vassiliev, *Spies: The Rise and Fall of the KGB in America*; New Haven: Yale University Press, 2009).

Page 234, "feels like a strait jacket" Gellhorn, *The Letters*, 164.

Page 234, "short and sharp" Rollyson, *Beautiful Exile*, 141.

Page 234, Furious rows would rage Ibid., 129.

Page 234, On one occasion he slapped her Moorehead, *Martha Gellhorn*, 235.

Page 235, dressed him as a girl See Lynn, *Hemingway*.

Page 235, The diaries that she kept Caroline Moorehead, who had access to the diaries for her biography, *Martha Gellhorn: A Life*, quotes only occasionally from them and in small chunks.

Page 235, "I left him because" Gellhorn, *The Letters*, 206–13.

Page 235, "You said E. was a king" Ibid., 211.

Page 237, "Who is this Martha Gellhorn?" Lewis Gannett, quoted in Lynn, *Hemingway*, 466.

Page 238, "She implied to me" Quoted in Rollyson, *Beautiful Exile*, 138.

Page 238, "she was more excited" Ibid., 141.

Page 239, "was the most 'traumatic'" Rollyson, *Beautiful Exile*, 176.

Page 240, (she did) Gellhorn wrote, "This is the first and last book about him I'll ever read" (*The Letters*, 456), she wrote, in spite of earlier saying that "I avoid knowing about the apocrypha and read none of the Papa books" (442).

Page 240, "talked about him at length" Bill Buford's foreword to Gellhorn, *Travels with Myself*, xvi.

Page 240, "we are all his debtors" Gellhorn, *The Letters*, 436.

Page 240, It was Hemingway's writing It is interesting that Rollyson makes the same case, but for him the implication is a negative one: "[Gellhorn] never profited from the Hemingway name, she insisted, and never allowed him to support her. She had a well-established career before she met him. *Yet she sought him out, believing that she had much to learn from Hemingway,* and she received attention from the press and from reviewers because of her marriage to him" (Rollyson, *Beautiful Exile*, 139; my italics). What was wrong with her "seeking him out" when she had always praised his writing before? And it is not true to say she received attention from critics because of him: her novels had already received attention before she met him.

Page 241, "stodgy and genteel" Rollyson, *Beautiful Exile*, 18.

Page 242, "read Ernest Hemingway and tried" Ibid., 23.

Page 242, "borrowed the money" Ibid., 28.

Page 242, "Edna lent her the money" Moorehead, *Martha Gellhorn*, 34.

Page 242, shipping line apparently offered Ibid.

Page 243, she also had an abortion Moorehead writes: "From remarks made at various times by both of them, it seems probable that Martha had an abortion at about this time. The moment for them to have the daughter Hemingway had wanted had clearly passed, though whether it had ever really existed for Martha is impossible to say. Restless, feeling herself isolated from events in Europe she longed to be part of, and now frequently quarrelling with Hemingway, Martha was not in a mood for children" (Moorehead, *Martha Gellhorn*, 235).

Page 244, "I think Hemingway is pretty bum" Gellhorn, *The Letters*, 8 (1930).

Page 245, "Meantime, I take my code" Ibid., 11 (May 8–9, 1931).

Page 246, "Why the hell would I" Ibid., 469 (September 30, 1987).

Page 247, "A man is no use to me" Ibid., 38–39 (August 6, 1936).

Page 247, "the bar that Ernest Hemingway" Rollyson, *Beautiful Exile,* 61.

Page 248, Her later insistence Ibid.

Page 248, "not the only young writer" Moorehead, *Martha Gellhorn,* 123.

Page 249, "a think-book" Gellhorn, *The Letters,* 45 (January 8, 1937).

Page 249, made her the chaser "[Hemingway] would become the willing object of [Gellhorn's] pursuit, even as Pauline had chased him while he was still married to Hadley . . ." (Lynn, *Hemingway,* 442) is the standard version of the beginning of accounts of their relationship.

Page 251, "odd and glamorous" Moorehead, *Martha Gellhorn,* 128. According to Rollyson, they missed each other, as he had already headed off for Spain (Rollyson, *Beautiful Exile,* 66). Which is the correct version? Rollyson's version turns Gellhorn into a chaser, as it's Hemingway's absence that makes her book her journey to Spain, to catch up with him. Moorehead's version, meanwhile, stresses the career-driven Gellhorn.

Page 252, Both Gellhorn and Hemingway predicted "The war in Spain was one kind of war, the next world war will be the stupidest, lyingest, cruellest sell-out in our time" (Gellhorn, *The Letters,* 58; March 1938).

Page 252, "Funny how it should take" Hemingway, *Selected Letters 1917–1961,* 574.

Page 253, "he thought nothing of" Rollyson, *Beautiful Exile,* 125.

Page 253, "he considered it manly" Ibid.

Page 253, "talked about her freely" Moorehead, *Martha Gellhorn,* 254.

Page 254, "The book is what we have" Gellhorn, *The Letters,* 78 (December 4, 1939).

Page 255, "He tells me what is wrong" Ibid., 46 (January 13, 1937).

Page 255, "she in turn copied" Rollyson quoting Leicester Hemingway, *Beautiful Exile,* 77–78.

Page 255, "I've been panic-stricken" Gellhorn, *The Letters,* 184 (May 1946).

Page 255, "The novel has been abandoned" Ibid., 185 (September 12, 1946).

Page 256, "like an animal" Ibid., 90 (May 17, 1940).

Page 256, "I have been thinking" Ibid., 92 (June 8, 1940).

Page 256, "But it is very fine" Ibid., 99 (August 25, 1940).

Page 257, "I always envied Ernest" Ibid., 117 (October 17, 1941).

Page 257, "I find confidence" Ibid., 143 (June 9, 1943).

Page 257, "I have been writing every day" Ibid., 145 (June 26, 1943).

Page 260, "Going to get me somebody" Hemingway, *Selected Letters,* 576.

Page 261, "You wanted it" Gellhorn, *The Letters,* 282 (January 17, 1961).

CHAPTER 8: ELIZABETH SMART AND GEORGE BARKER

Page 264, "stole from under her nose" Barker, *Arms of the Infinite,* 273–74.

Page 264, the other women Barker had Barker was married when he met Smart, but by 1945 his marriage to his wife, Jessica, was virtually over. In 1947 he began a relationship with Betty Cass while still seeing Smart.

Page 265, "Was it ever like that?" Smart, *Necessary Secrets*, 279.

Page 265, "But if I don't believe" Ibid., 278.

Page 265, "gave me the courage" Smart, *On the Side of the Angels*, 92.

Page 268, "I woke up so late" Smart, *Necessary Secrets*, 21.

Page 270, "Today I have hated Mummy" Ibid., 85–86.

Page 270, "I must marry a poet" Ibid., 86.

Page 270, "Sex was to him a shame" Ibid., 87.

Page 271, "And he said that my poems" Ibid., 88.

Page 273, lauded by T. S. Eliot Fraser, *Chameleon Poet*, 64.

Page 273, "Oh! I need something" Smart, *Necessary Secrets*, 35.

Page 273, "being influenced and making phrases" Ibid., 43.

Page 273, "Oh ain't it nice" Ibid., 45.

Page 274, "I must write three things" Ibid., 52.

Page 274, "Why can't I work?" Ibid., 35.

Page 274, "Then the desire to accomplish" Ibid., 59.

Page 274, "This is the fight" Ibid., 62.

Page 275, "I'm going to be a poet" Ibid., 70.

Page 275, "Where shall it turn now" Ibid., 82.

Page 275, "I want an ecstasy" Smart, *Necessary Secrets*, 84.

Page 275, Mrs. Alfred Watt She had already been on one trip with Mrs. Watt in 1933 and found it tricky enough then. This trip was longer and went farther, to New Zealand, Australia, Egypt, and Palestine.

Page 276, "Men, careers" Smart, *Necessary Secrets*, 123.

Page 276, "hungry passion" Ibid., 133.

Page 276, "I seek a mate" Ibid., 153.

Page 276, "They were all artists" Sullivan, *By Heart*, 107.

Page 277, often sexually threatening Yanko Sullivan notes that Henry Miller had also met Varda and had said of him that he was a "lusty and joyous man, a poet but a real man, very youthful, and his love of women is a relief after so much disparaging I see around me. He turns them into myths, poems, collages, delights of all kinds" (Sullivan, *By Heart*, 109).

Page 277, "Am I a vamp?" Smart, *Necessary Secrets*, 183–84.

Page 277, "I will NOT be taken" Ibid., 202.

Page 277, "Varda, the first day alone" Ibid., 205.

Page 277, "I wrote at last to Mummy" Ibid., 197.

Page 278, Barker's poetry in Better Books Smart writes, "So of course I found out the bookshops that specialized in it [poetry], particularly in Better Books, in the Charing Cross Road. So about the middle of the 1930s I discovered George Barker . . ." as a chronology of the events in *By Grand Central Station* (Smart, *Autobiographies*, 45).

Page 278, "He [Barker] probably met me" Quoted in Sullivan, *By Heart*, 182.

Page 279, the mistress's shameful chasing Jessica Barker was to acknowledge Smart's "chasing" mentality when she wrote to Barker in 1944, admitting defeat: "You haven't the strength to break with her [Smart] forever and if you attempt it she will track you down again . . . There will be another child and so on and so on" (Sullivan, *By Heart*, 220).

Page 280, *"I know I have been sealed up"* Smart, *Necessary Secrets*, 257.

Page 280, *Barker had taken a teaching post* He wrote to Antonia White that it was also to avoid being called up, now that war looked inevitable.

Page 281, *"I say to you, keep that vision"* Smart, *Necessary Secrets*, 270.

Page 282, *"rebel . . . I am the cat"* Ibid., 138.

Page 282, *"terrible problem of matrimony"* Ibid., 123.

Page 283, *"how ashamed I am"* Ibid., 262.

Page 285, *"If he had the faculty"* Smart, *On the Side of the Angels*, 17.

Page 285, *"And yet I must put it"* Ibid., 17.

Page 286, *he also gave her the title* Smart's biographer, Rosemary Sullivan, says that "Although Elizabeth resisted most of his other editorial suggestions, happily she took his advice on this one [re: the title change]" (Sullivan, *By Heart*, 227), while in *Autobiographies*, editor Christina Burridge writes that "Smart certainly incorporated many of Barker's suggestions, working over passages again and again to tighten up their metaphorical structure" (Smart, *Autobiographies*, 71).

Page 286, *"I see that one of the principal"* See Smart, *Autobiographies*, 71–76, for the full critique.

Page 287, *"He did the one sin"* Smart, *Necessary Secrets*, 272.

Page 289, *"a tender criticism"* Smart, *On the Side of the Angels*, 82.

Page 289, *"My mind is quite made up"* Quoted in Smart, *Necessary Secrets*, 277.

Page 289, *"It is not possible"* Smart, *Necessary Secrets*, 280–81.

Page 290, *"I know that perhaps tonight"* Ibid., 281.

Page 290, *"I am only waiting"* Ibid., 282.

Page 290, *"I'm not running away"* Smart, *Autobiographies*, 33.

Page 290, *"No, I will not allow"* Ibid., 284.

Page 291, *"he can get me"* Smart, *On the Side of the Angels*, 16.

Page 292, *"was more or less absent"* Sullivan, *By Heart*, 229

Page 293, *"He wanted the women"* Ibid., 204.

Page 293, *"Take me"* Smart, *Autobiographies*, 35.

Page 293, *"I love him desperately"* Ibid., 29.

Page 294, *"Love. Children."* Smart, *On the Side of the Angels*, 77.

Page 295, *"Love,"* Smart *wrote in 1977* Ibid., 91.

Page 295, *"Speak, memory"* Ibid., 71.

Page 296, *"that wasn't supposed to happen"* See Sullivan, *By Heart*, 340–41

CHAPTER 9: SYLVIA PLATH AND TED HUGHES

Page 299, *Biographers are drawn into* In the introduction to her study of Plath's work, *The Haunting of Sylvia Plath*, Jacqueline Rose describes her dealings with the Plath estate, held by Ted Hughes before his death in 1998 and administered until then by his sister, Olwyn. In *The Silent Woman*, Janet

Malcolm also details the effect that being drawn in, in this way, had on Anne Stevenson, author a biography of Plath, *Bitter Fame: A Life of Sylvia Plath*, in 1989, which had the approval of the Hughes family, specifically Olwyn Hughes, to the extent that Stevenson felt obliged to call it "almost a work of dual authorship" (see Malcolm, 10-12).

Page 300, poet Elaine Feinstein Feinstein, author of *Ted Hughes: The Life of a Poet*, claims her publisher contacted her just days after Hughes's death about a biography.

Page 300, suicide of Plath and Hughes's son The tragic suicide of Nicholas Hughes resulted in inevitable comparisons to his mother's death more than forty years earlier, as well as numerous articles on the links between depression and suicide.

Page 301, "the pull of the Plath story" Rose, *Haunting of Sylvia Plath*, 6.

Page 302, "Then I yielded" Plath, *Letters Home*, 10.

Page 303, analysis with Ruth Beuscher See Plath, *Journals*, 433.

Page 303, "the idea was to show" Malcolm, *Silent Woman*, 33.

Page 304, "Dear Mummy" Plath, *Letters Home*, 46.

Page 304, "Now I know what loneliness is" Plath, *Journals*, 30.

Page 305, "I did what I felt" Ibid., 435.

Page 306, "Not to be bitter" Ibid., 224.

Page 306, "Sylvia was writing rhymes" Aurelia Plath, ed., *Letters Home*, 30.

Page 306, "we were critical" Ibid., 31–32.

Page 306, "a snatch of verse" Plath, *Letters Home*, 51 (October 5, 1950).

Page 306, diligently repeats any praise See Plath, *Letters Home*, 65–75 (February–March 1951).

Page 306, keeps her informed Ibid., 71 (July 7, 1951).

Page 306, "What do you think of" Plath, *Letters Home*, 74 (August 24, 1952).

Page 307, "Do write for Dr. Christian" Ibid., 83 (February 7, 1952).

Page 307, "I've got an idea for" Ibid., 89 (June 21, 1952).

Page 307, "with your father dead" Plath, *Journals*, 64.

Page 308, "I need someone to pour myself" Ibid., 21.

Page 308, "I must have a passionate" Ibid., 100.

Page 308, "I need a strong mate" Ibid., 173.

Page 308, "I am in danger of wanting" Ibid., 182.

Page 308, "Sex is never enough" Ibid., 163.

Page 308, "I cannot marry a writer" Ibid., 173 (Feb 12, 1953).

Page 309, "nice girls" "This is I, I thought, the American virgin, dressed to seduce. I know I'm in for an evening of sexual pleasure. We go on dates, we play around, and if we're nice girls, we demure at a certain point . . ." (Plath, *Journals*, 13).

Page 309, her "not niceness" "In 1971, in *The New York Review of Books*, Elizabeth Hardwick wrote of Plath that 'she has the rarity of being, in her work at least, never a 'nice person' . . . Plath's not-niceness is the outstanding characteristic of the *Ariel* poems . . ." (Malcolm, *Silent Woman*, 31).

Page 309, "to be anchored to life" Plath, *Journals*, 201.

Page 310, "I have met the strongest man" Plath, *Letters Home*, 233.

Page 311, "Once there is the first kiss" Plath, *Journals*, 105.

Page 311, "I want a colossus" Plath, *Letters Home*, 104.

Page 312, "I need more than anything" Ibid., 132.

Page 312, "and you felt scared" Plath, *Journals*, 187.

Page 313, "the English universities" Plath, *Letters Home*, 146.

Page 314, "the name Sassoon" Plath, *Journals*, 192–93.

Page 314, "because my love for Richard" Ibid., 201.

Page 314, "ever need me again?" Ibid., 202.

Page 314, "my brilliant and sympathetic Richard" Plath, *Letters Home*, 208.

Page 314, "I got a letter from Richard" Ibid., 217.

Page 315, "I wish I could be smart" Plath, *Journals*, 12.

Page 315, "You like?" See Plath, *Journals*, 209.

Page 316, "It would be a good thing" Plath, *Journals*, 223.

Page 316, "my black marauder" Ibid., 233.

Page 316, "I went to Spain" Hughes, *Letters*, 46–47.

Page 317, "I also feel a new direct pouring" Plath, *Journals*, 249.

Page 317, "Mr. and Mrs. Ted Hughes'" Ibid., 271.

Page 318, "the perfect male counterpart" Ibid., 271.

Page 318, "We work and walk about" Hughes, *Letters*, 97 (May 1957).

Page 319, "seizing important images" Middlebrook, *Her Husband*, 153.

Page 319, "nothing matters but Ted" Plath, *Letters Home*, 279.

Page 320, "my danger, partly" Plath, *Journals*, 401.

Page 320, "I must be happy first" Ibid., 421.

Page 320, "dangerous to be so close" Ibid., 524.

Page 320, "Never before have I" Plath, *Letters Home*, 250.

Page 320, "the mornings at the study" Ibid., 386.

Page 320, "weary of my talk of astrology" Plath, *Journals*, 525.

Page 321, "managing to get about two" Plath, *Letters Home*, 448.

Page 321, "I amaze myself" Ibid., 478.

Page 322, "I just haven't felt" Ibid., 495.

Page 322, "my whole being has grown" Plath, *Journals*, 274.

Page 322, "she doubted whether the attraction" Stevenson, *Bitter Fame*, 244.

Page 322, "Ted kissed me" Quoted in Koren and Negev, *Lover of Unreason*, 90.

Page 322, "I have come to see you" Ibid., 95.

Page 323, It is Plath's suicide that prevents Diane Middlebrook's biography, *Her Husband*, published six years after Hughes's death and the publication of his final volume of poems, *Birthday Letters*, takes a rare sympathetic view of the relationship without carrying the "taint" of being "endorsed" by Hughes's family the way that Anne Stevenson's 1989 biography of Plath, *Bitter Fame*, did. For an excellent account of Stevenson's experience writing this book, see Janet Malcolm's *The Silent Woman*.

Page 324, "I had come to a point" Hughes, *Letters*, 215.

Page 325, This revelation of Hughes's Both Diane Middlebrook and the authors of the first biography of Assia Wevill, Yehuda Koren and Eilat Negev, cast doubt on Hughes's claims here, the latter quoting Aurelia Plath's "cynical note" which she wrote on the letter she received from Hughes informing her of Plath's death and his reconciliation attempt: "through adultery with Acia [sic] Wevill" (Koren and Negev, *Lover of Unreason*, 119). Ronald Hayman, however, does say that Plath made mention of a reconciliation to Jillian Becker on the Friday before she died, though she dismissed it (Hayman, *Death and Life of Sylvia Plath*, 6).

Page 325, she was taking new antidepressants Prescribed by Dr. John Horder; see Hayman, *Death and Life of Sylvia Plath*, 6–7).

Page 326, a terrifying prospect Elaine Feinstein does suggest that for Plath, looking happy on the Friday evening before her suicide "as if something had been settled," this may have been "the occasion on which she recognized for the first time that Ted was prepared to come back to her" (Feinstein, *Ted Hughes*, 162), and wonders if that possibility became too much for her ("even if Ted had intimated that he very much wanted to be reunited with her, Sylvia might still have wondered whether any happy ending was possible for them . . . may have decided that she could not bear the uncertainty, and that only death offered any guarantee of release from pain") (Feinstein, *Ted Hughes*, 163), but she allies this interpretation more with the belief that Plath's suicide bid was meant to be a failed one.

Page 326, Plath maintained a facade In fact, on January 16, she wrote: "It is the starting from scratch that is so hard—this first year . . . How I would like to be self-supporting on my writing!" which would suggest that she still believed she would be on her own for the time being (Plath, *Letters Home*, 495).

Page 326, "What I actually destroyed" Interview with Ted Hughes, Gourevitch, *Paris Review Interviews, vol. III*, 290. It has been claimed there was another journal that went missing. Emma Tennant based her 2001 novel *Sylvia and Ted* on what she imagined those missing journals might contain.

Page 327, pieces of reported conversation Elaine Feinstein notes that Hughes's friend Lucas Myers also claimed that "Ted said they would probably have been back together within a week if she had not killed herself " (Feinstein, *Ted Hughes*, 164).

Page 328, the equally tragic Assia Wevill Some can't even get her name right when they do remember her—John Tytell repeatedly calls her Assia Weevil in his book, *Passionate Lives*.

BIBLIOGRAPHY

CHAPTER 1: KATHERINE MANSFIELD AND JOHN MIDDLETON MURRY

Lea, F. A. *The Life of John Middleton Murry*. London: Methuen, 1959.

Mansfield, Katherine. *Journal*. London: Persephone Press, 2006. First published 1927 by Constable.

———. *Selected Stories*. Oxford: Oxford University Press, 1983.

Mansfield, Katherine, John Middleton Murry, and Hankin, Cherry A., ed. *Letters Between Katherine Mansfield and John Middleton Murry*. London: Virago Press, 1988.

Mansfield, Katherine, and Margaret Scott, ed. *The Katherine Mansfield Notebooks: Complete Edition*. Minneapolis: University of Minnesota Press, 2002.

Mansfield, Katherine, and Vincent O'Sullivan with Margaret Scott, eds. *The Collected Letters of Katherine Mansfield, Volume 1: 1903–1917*. Oxford: Oxford University Press, 1984.

———. *The Collected Letters of Katherine Mansfield, Volume 2: 1918–19*. Oxford: Oxford University Press, 1987.

———. *The Collected Letters of Katherine Mansfield, Volume 3: 1919–20*. Oxford: Oxford University Press, 1993.

———. *The Collected Letters of Katherine Mansfield, Volume 4: 1920–21*. Oxford: Oxford University Press, 1996.

Tomalin, Claire. *Katherine Mansfield: A Secret Life*. London: Penguin, 1988.

CHAPTER 2: H.D. AND EZRA POUND

Adams, Bronte, and Trudi Tate, ed. *That Kind of Woman: Stories from the Left Bank and Beyond*. London: Virago, 1991.

Benstock, Shari. *Women of the Left Bank: Paris 1900–1940*. London: Virago, 1987.

Carr, Helen. *The Verse Revolutionaries: Ezra Pound, H.D. and the Imagists*. London: Jonathan Cape, 2009.

Collecott, Diana. *H.D. and Sapphic Modernism*. Cambridge: Cambridge University Press, 1999.

Friedman, Susan Stanford. *Analyzing Freud: The Letters of H.D., Bryher and Their Circle*. New York: New Directions, 2002.

Guest, Barbara. *Herself Defined: The Poet H.D. and Her World*. London: Collins, 1985.

H.D. *Asphodel*. North Carolina: Duke University Press, 1992.

———. *Bid Me to Live*. London: Virago, 1984. First published 1960 by New York: Grove Press.

———. *End to Torment: A Memoir of Ezra Pound*. New York: New Directions, 1979.

———. *Her*. London: Virago, 1984. First published 1981 by New York: New Directions.

———. *Tribute to Freud: With Unpublished Letters by Freud*. Pantheon: New York, 1956.

Robinson, Janice S. *H.D.: The Life and Work of an American Poet*. Boston: Houghton Mifflin, 1982.

Tytell, John. *Ezra Pound: The Solitary Volcano*. Chicago: Ivan R. Dee, 1987.

CHAPTER 3: REBECCA WEST AND H. G. WELLS

Felber, Lynette. *Literary Liaisons: Auto/biographical Appropriations in Modernist Women's Fiction*. De Kalb: Northern Illinois University Press, 2002.

Glendinning, Victoria. *Rebecca West: A Life*. London: Phoenix, 1998.

Ray, Gordon N. *H.G. Wells and Rebecca West*. London: Macmillan, 1974.

Rollyson, Carl. *Rebecca West: A Saga of the Century*. London: Sceptre, 1995.

Smith, David C. *H.G. Wells: Desperately Mortal*. New Haven and London: Yale University Press, 1986.

Weldon, Fay. *Rebecca West*. Lives of Modern Women. London: Penguin, 1985.

Wells, H. G., and G. P. Wells, ed. *H.G. Wells in Love: Postscript to an Experiment in Autobiography*. London: Faber & Faber, 1984.

West, Rebecca. *The Return of the Soldier*. London: Virago, 1993. First published 1918 by London: Nisbet.

———. *Sunflower*. London: Virago, 1990.

———. *The Fountain Overflows*. London: Virago, 1994. First published 1957 by London: Macmillan.

———. *The Strange Necessity: Essays and Reviews*. London: Virago, 1987. First published 1928 by London: Jonathan Cape.

———, and Faith Evans, ed. *Family Memories*. London and Toronto: Lime Tree, 1992.

———, and Bonnie Kime Scott, ed. *Selected Letters*. New Haven and London: Yale University Press, 2000.

———, selected and introduced by Jane Marcus. *The Young Rebecca: Writings of Rebecca West 1911–17*. Bloomington: Indiana University Press, 1982.

CHAPTER 4: JEAN RHYS AND FORD MADOX FORD

Angier, Carole. *Jean Rhys*. Lives of Modern Women. London: Penguin, 1985.

————. *Jean Rhys: Life and Work*. London: Penguin, 1992.

Bowen, Stella. *Drawn from Life*. London: Virago, 1984. First published 1941 by London: Collins.

Carr, Helen. *Jean Rhys*. Plymouth: Northcote, 1996.

Davidson, Arnold E. *Jean Rhys*. New York: Frederick Ungar, 1985.

Delany, Paul. "Jean Rhys and Ford Madox Ford: What 'Really' Happened." *Mosaic* 16:4 (Fall 1983): 15–24.

Ford, Ford Madox. *The Good Soldier*. Oxford World's Classics. Oxford: Oxford University Press, 1990. First published London: Bodley Head, 1915.

Gourevitch, Philip. *The Paris Review Interviews*, vol. III. Edinburgh: Canongate, 2008.

Judd, Alan. *Ford Madox Ford*. London: Collins, 1990.

Pizzichini, Lillian. *The Blue Hour: A Portrait of Jean Rhys*. London: Bloomsbury, 2009.

Rhys, Jean. *After Leaving Mr. Mackenzie*. London: Andre Deutsch, 1969. First published 1931 by London: Jonathan Cape.

————. *The Left Bank and Other Stories*. London: Andre Deutsch, 1968. First published 1927 by London: Jonathan Cape.

————. *Quartet*. London: Penguin, 2000. First published as *Postures,* 1928 by London: Chatto and Windus.

————. *Smile Please: An Unfinished Autobiography*. London: Penguin, 1981.

————. *Wide Sargasso Sea*. London: Penguin, 1968. First published 1966 by London: Andre Deutsch.

————, Diana Melly, ed., and Francis Wyndham, contributor. *Jean Rhys: Letters 1931–66*. London: Penguin, 1985.

Saunders, Max. *Ford Madox Ford: A Dual Life*, vols. I and II. Oxford: Oxford University Press, 1996.

CHAPTER 5: ANAÏS NIN AND HENRY MILLER

Bair, Dierdre. *Anaïs Nin: A Biography*. London: Bloomsbury, 1996.

Fergusin, Robert. *Henry Miller: A Life*. London: Hutcvhinson, 1991.

Nin, Anaïs. *Fire: From 'A Journal of Love': The Unexpurgated Diaries of Anaïs Nin, 1934–1937*. London: Harvest Harcourt, 1995.

————. *The Journals of Anaïs Nin Volume I: 1931–1934*. London: Peter Owen, 1966. Reprinted 1970.

————. *A Spy in the House of Love*. London: Peter Owen, 1971.

————. *Winter of Artifice*. London: Peter Owen, 1974.

————, Henry Miller, and Gunther Stuhlmann, ed. *A Literate Passion: Letters of Anaïs Nin and Henry Miller, 1932–1953*. London: Allison & Busby, 1988.

Podnieks, Elizabeth. *Daily Modernism: The Literary Diaries of Virginia Woolf, Antonia White, Elizabeth Smart, and Anaïs Nin*. London: McGill-Queen's University Press, 2000.

CHAPTER 6: SIMONE DE BEAUVOIR AND JEAN-PAUL SARTRE

Bair, Deirdre. *Simone de Beauvoir*. London: Jonathan Cape, 1990.

Beauvoir, Simone de. *Memoirs of a Dutiful Daughter*. London: Penguin, 1984. First published 1958 by Paris: Gallimard.

————. *She Came to Stay*. London: Harper Perennial, 2006. First published 1943 by Paris: Gallimard.

————. *The Prime of Life*. London: Penguin, 1975. First published 1962 by Paris: Gallimard.

————. *The Second Sex*. London: Vintage, 1997. First published 1949 by Paris: Gallimard. First English translation 1953 London: Jonathan Cape

————, and Quintin Hoare, trans.. ed. *Letters to Sartre*. New York: Arcade, 1991.

Carter, Angela. "Colette." *The London Review of Books, Anthology One,* ed. Michael Mason. London: Junction Books, 1981.

Fullbrook, Edward and Kate. *Sex and Philosophy: Rethinking de Beauvoir and Sartre*. London: Continuum Press, 2008.

Moi, Toril. *Simone de Beauvoir: The Making of an Intellectual Woman*. Oxford: Blackwell, 1994.

Rowley, Hazel. *Tête-à-Tête: The Lives and Loves of Simone de Beauvoir and Jean-Paul Sartre*. London: Vintage, 2007.

Sartre, Jean-Paul. *Witness to My Life: The Letters of Jean-Paul Sartre to Simone de Beauvoir, 1926–1939*. London: Penguin, 1994. First published 1983 by Paris: Gallimard.

Seymour-Jones, Carole. *A Dangerous Liaison: Simone de Beauvoir and Jean-Paul Sartre*. London: Century, 2008.

CHAPTER 7: MARTHA GELLHORN
AND ERNEST HEMINGWAY

Gellhorn, Martha. *Liana*. London: Virago, 1987. First published 1944 by New York: Scribner.

————. *The Novellas of Martha Gellhorn*. New York: Vintage, 1991.

————. *Point of No Return*. Lincoln: University of Nebraska Press, 1989. First published as *The Wine of Astonishment* 1948 by New York: Scribner.

————. *Travels with Myself and Another: A Memoir*. New York: Putnam, 2001. First published London: Allan Lane, 1978.

————, and Caroline Moorehead, ed. *The Letters of Martha Gellhorn*. London: Chatto & Windus, 2006.

Hemingway, Ernest. *A Farewell to Arms*. London: Jonathan Cape, 1978. First published 1929 by New York: Scribner.

————. *The Fifth Column*. New York: Scribner, 1969.

————, and Carlos Baker, ed. *Selected Letters 1917–1961*. London: Granada, 1981.

Lynn, Kenneth S. *Hemingway*. New York: Simon & Schuster, 1987.

Moorehead, Caroline. *Martha Gellhorn: A Life*. London: Chatto & Windus, 2003.

Rollyson, Carl. *Beautiful Exile: The Life of Martha Gellhorn*. London: Aurum, 2002.

CHAPTER 8: ELIZABETH SMART AND GEORGE BARKER

Barker, Christopher. *The Arms of the Infinite*. Hebden Bridge: Pomona, 2006.

Echlin, Kim. *Elizabeth Smart: A Fugue Essay on Women and Creativity*. Toronto: Women's Press, 2004.

Fraser, Robert. *The Chameleon Poet: A Life of George Barker*. London: Pimlico, 2002.

Smart, Elizabeth. *The Assumption of the Rogues and Rascals*. London: Paladin, 1991. First published 1978 by London: Jonathan Cape.

———. *By Grand Central Station I Sat Down and Wept*. London: Flamingo, 1992. First published 1945 by London: Editions Poetry.

———. *In the Meantime*. Ottawa: Deneau, 1984.

———. *On the Side of the Angels: The Second Volume of the Journals of Elizabeth Smart*. London: Flamingo, 1995.

———, and Christina Burridge, ed. *Autobiographies*. Vancouver: William Hoffer, 1987.

———, and Alice Van Wart, ed. *Necessary Secrets: The Journals of Elizabeth Smart*. London: Grafton, 1991.

Sullivan, Rosemary. *By Heart: Elizabeth Smart, A Life*. London: Lime Tree, 1991.

CHAPTER 9: SYLVIA PLATH AND TED HUGHES

Alexander, Paul. *Rough Magic: A Biography of Sylvia Plath*. New York: Da Capo, 1999.

Feinstein, Elaine. *Ted Hughes: The Life of a Poet*. London: Weidenfeld & Nicolson, 2001.

Hayman, Ronald. *The Death and Life of Sylvia Plath*. London: Sutton, 2003..

Hughes, Ted. *Birthday Letters*. London: Faber & Faber, 1998.

———, and Christopher Reid, ed. *Letters of Ted Hughes*. London: Faber & Faber, 2007.

Koren, Yehuda, and Eilat Negev. *A Lover of Unreason: The Life and Tragic Death of Assia Wevill*. London: Robson, 2006.

Malcolm, Janet. *The Silent Woman: Sylvia Plath and Ted Hughes*. London: Granta, 1994.

Middlebrook, Diane. *Her Husband: Hughes and Plath: A Marriage*. London: Little Brown, 2004.

Plath, Sylvia. *Ariel: The Restored Edition*. London: Faber & Faber, 2004.

———. *Collected Poems*. London: Faber & Faber, 1981.

———, and Karen V. Kukil, ed. *The Journals of Sylvia Plath: 1950–1962*. London: Faber & Faber, 2000.

———, and Aurelia Schober Plath, ed. *Letters Home: Correspondence 1950–1963*. London: Faber & Faber, 1976.

Rose, Jacqueline. *The Haunting of Sylvia Plath*. London: Virago, 1991.

Stevenson, Anne. *Bitter Fame: A Life of Sylvia Plath*. London: Viking, 1989.

Tennant, Emma. *Burnt Diaries*. Edinburgh: Canongate, 1999.

Tytell, John. *Passionate Lives*. New York: St. Martin's Press, 1991.

Wagner-Martin, Linda. *Sylvia Plath: A Biography*. London: Chatto and Windus, 1988.

INDEX

About the Author

Lesley McDowell is an author and critic living in Scotland. She earned a Ph.D. for her work on James Joyce before turning to literary journalism. She has written for the *Times Literary Supplement* and the *Independent on Sunday*. Her first novel, *The Picnic*, was published in 2007, and she currently holds a Scottish Arts Council award for her second novel.